The Spaces of Latin American Literature

THE SPACES OF LATIN AMERICAN LITERATURE

TRADITION, GLOBALIZATION, AND CULTURAL PRODUCTION

Juan E. De Castro

THE SPACES OF LATIN AMERICAN LITERATURE
Copyright © Juan E. De Castro, 2008.
All rights reserved. No part of this book may be used or reproduced in any manner whatsoever without written permission except in the case of brief quotations embodied in critical articles or reviews.

First published in 2008 by
PALGRAVE MACMILLAN™
175 Fifth Avenue, New York, N.Y. 10010 and
Houndmills, Basingstoke, Hampshire, England RG21 6XS
Companies and representatives throughout the world.

PALGRAVE MACMILLAN is the global academic imprint of the Palgrave Macmillan division of St. Martin's Press, LLC and of Palgrave Macmillan Ltd. Macmillan® is a registered trademark in the United States, United Kingdom and other countries. Palgrave is a registered trademark in the European Union and other countries.

ISBN-10: 0-230-60625-3
ISBN-13: 978-0-230-60625-8

Library of Congress Cataloging-in-Publication Data

Castro, Juan E. De, 1959–
 The spaces of Latin American literature : tradition, globalization, and cultural production / by Juan E. de Castro.
  p. cm.
 Includes bibliographical references and index.
 ISBN 0-230-60625-3
 1. Latin American literature—History and criticism. 2. Literature and society—Latin America. I. Title.
 PQ7081.C349 2009
 860.9'98—dc22   2007039536

A catalogue record for this book is available from the British Library.

Design by Westchester Book Group.

First Edition: May 2008

10 9 8 7 6 5 4 3 2 1

Printed in the United States of America.

For my mother, Dahlia Oritz

Contents

Acknowledgments		ix
Introduction: The Criollo Location of Culture and the Spaces of Latin American Literature		xi
1	Sor Juana, Lunarejo, and the Colonial Literary Space and Its Limits	1
2	Rubén Darío Visits Ricardo Palma: Tradition, Cosmopolitanism, and the Development of an Independent Latin American Literature	17
3	The Intellectual Meridian Debate and Colonialist Nostalgia	33
4	Jorge Luis Borges and (Western) Tradition	49
5	Caetano Veloso: *Tropical Truth* and Tropical Questions	65
6	Reading, Publishing, and Writing Networks: The Hispanophone and Latin American Literary Spaces in the Twenty-first Century	91
7	*The Movies of My Life;* or, A Bridge to North America	105
Epilogue: Latin America beyond Latin America?		129
Notes		141
Works Cited		191
Index		205

Acknowledgments

THIS BOOK HAS BENEFITED FROM COMMENTS MADE BY friends and colleagues in various stages of its composition. Among them I must single out Nicholas Birns, Elaine Savory, and Ignacio López-Calvo. The book is infinitely better thanks to them. Obviously, all remaining flaws are my responsibility.

An earlier draft of chapter 2 was published in *Chasqui* 36.1 (May 2007); parts of chapter 4 appeared in *MLN* 199.2 (March 2004), *Iberoamericana* 26 (2007), and *The International Reception of T. S. Eliot* (Continuum, 2007).

I also want to thank my wife, Magdalena, for her personal support during the writing of this book.

Introduction: The Criollo Location of Culture and the Spaces of Latin American Literature

THIS IS A BOOK ABOUT THE CRIOLLO TRADITION IN Latin American literature. It studies how the region's mainstream writers, artists, and intellectuals have negotiated their relationship with an evolving Western culture, which due to colonial and neocolonial cultural and economic structures has relegated them to marginal positions.

The Criollo Location of Culture

The term *criollo* may merit a few words. After all, it is not frequently used in the English language. *Merriam-Webster Online* provides two relevant definitions of the word: "1a: a person of pure Spanish descent born in Spanish America" and "b: a person born and usually raised in a Spanish-American country."[1]

The contradictions implicit in the term *criollo* raised by *Webster's*—does it refer to the descendants of Spaniards or to all people born and raised in the region regardless of racial, ethnic, or national background?—are not a result of mistranslating a coherently defined and used Spanish word. In fact, one can find in the dictionary of the Real Academia de la Lengua, the generally accepted source of meaning in the Spanish-speaking world, a similar tension.[2] In addition to providing a definition of *criollo* as creole, in its linguistic meaning (definition 6) as a hybrid language "formed by elements proceeding from both languages," it provides five contradictory definitions of the word. In its first definition, a criollo is "a descendant of European parents: Born in the ancient Spanish territories in America and in some European colonies from said continent." This entry defines *criollo* as Euro-American and even vaguely includes descendants of Europeans born in some of the non-Hispanic areas of the Americas, without specifying which former colonial areas are included.

At least one major theorist has described the so-called North American founding fathers as criollos. Benedict Anderson, in his classic *Imagined Communities*, writes about "Creole Pioneers," noting that the new American states of the late eighteenth and early nineteenth centuries were "formed and led by people who shared a common language and a common descent with those against whom they fought" (47). Anderson also provides his own definition of the term: "Creole (*Criollo*): a person of (at least theoretically) pure European descent but born in the Americas (and, by later extension, anywhere outside Europe" (47n). For Anderson, not only are southerners like George Washington and Thomas Jefferson criollos—or creoles, which he presents as synonymous—but even the Puritans qualify as such. Moreover, Anderson's implicit acknowledgment of a criollo who is in practice impure, though theoretically of pure European descent, is another expression of the contradictions implicit in the term.

The confusion becomes even greater when one looks at the third, fourth, and fifth definitions provided by the Real Academia: "Said of a person: born in a Spanish American country to emphasize that he or she possesses the qualities considered to be characteristic of that country"; "autochthonous, proper, distinctive of a Spanish American country"; and "peculiar, proper to Spanish America." While as in all definitions there is a strong element of ambiguity, one cannot be anything but surprised at the enormous contrast between these definitions and the first and supposedly principal meaning of the word. Rather than being a possible sign of foreignness by its partial identification not only with Spain but, according to the Academia, also with Europe as a whole, criollo is now presented as that which defines national or regional difference and, by extension, identity. In fact, based on the third definition one could make the case that the Amerindian population and cultures of the region are criollo. After all, can any other group in the region claim to be autochthonous? Moreover, since many of the characteristic traits and cultural products—from food to music to clothes—of the region are of hybrid nature, the mestizo can also be described as criollo. Finally, the Academia's second definition, presented as obsolete, describes criollo as "a person of the black race born in those territories" (Spanish America or the "some colonies" of the first definition). Given all six definitions, one cannot avoid concluding that all ethnicities and cultures can qualify as criollo depending on the context.

Carlos Altamirano's and Beatriz Sarlo's analysis of the changing meaning of criollo in the Argentine cultural field during the *Centenario,* the one-hundred-year celebration of the independence of Argentina (1910), may serve to clarify some of these questions. According to Altamirano and Sarlo, the term, which had a series of negative connotations "as primitive, elemental," acquired at the time "a meaning that evoked positive values and virtues and which was counterpoised to the term 'gringo' or 'immigrant'" (183, 184).[3] Given the fact that the Buenos Aires of 1910 was characterized by the presence of numerous immigrants from Europe, the ambiguities implicit in the term disappeared as the older native-born population laid claim to the word. Criollo was that which was neither gringo—that is, British or North American—nor immigrant, and which was associated with Argentina before mass immigration. The opposition between what was considered local and foreign is, however, far from static. Thus, what was seen as foreign in one generation could easily be seen as part of a local tradition at a later date. Today it is not unusual to hear or read the term "criollo rock" or "criollo rap" used to describe originally foreign cultural products that have acquired cultural and historical roots throughout Argentina and Latin America.[4]

The situation was somewhat different in those countries in which indigenous cultures had managed to survive brutal exploitation, violence, and discrimination. In the case of Peru, for instance, more than a decade after the resemantization of criollo in Argentina, José Carlos Mariátegui, the brilliant Marxist critic, writes about the origins of Peruvian literature:

> The Inca civilization destroyed by Spain, the new government constituted without the Indian and against the Indian, the aboriginal race subjected to serfdom, Peruvian literature had to be criollo, coastal, to the degree that it no longer was Spanish. That is why in Peru a vigorous literature could not arise. The mixing of the invader with the indigene had not produced in Peru a more or less homogeneous type. To the Iberian and Quechua blood had been added a copious flow of African blood. Later the importation of coolies added some Asian blood. Therefore, there were not one but rather diverse types of criollos and mestizos. (243)[5]

Despite being marred by the biologistic obsession of the time, Mariátegui's text is characteristically illuminating. In fact, all of the defining traits, as well as the ambiguities, present in the word and concept criollo are found in this passage from *Siete ensayos de interpretación de la realidad peruana*.[6]

For Mariátegui, the concept of criollo is clearly linked to Spanish culture and population. But, rather than an exclusively Iberian offshoot, the real-life criollos present indigenous, African, and even Asian influence. As the last sentence of the passage indicates, for Mariátegui, mestizo and criollo are closely linked, if not synonymous. Nevertheless, the true opposition here is between criollos, presented as inheritors of the Spaniards, if not necessarily descendants, and the indigenous cultures and population in the Andes. Given that throughout both the colonial and republican periods, and even before the massive migration from the countryside to the cities in the second half of the twentieth century, individuals of indigenous heritage have lived along the coast, it is possible to interpret this text as implying principally a cultural opposition without denying that it has an important racial component. A criollo is a person who accepts the Spanish inheritance or benefits from it, regardless of racial makeup.

In a repositioning of Mariátegui's ideas, I argue that his thought may help us decouple the frequent automatic pairing of hybridity with multicultural empowerment. Mariátegui's implicit linkage of mestizo and criollo can serve as a reminder that the criollo position, which is hegemonic at least in the national sphere, is compatible with hybridity. In fact, the discourse of *mestizaje,* so important in the development of Latin American nationalisms, attempts to reconcile the cultural heterogeneity of the region by means of a celebration of cultural and/or racial mixture as the founding trait of national identity.[7] However, rather than subverting homogeneity, mestizaje imagines a new, unified culture capable of integrating indigenous and other subaltern populations into national projects established and led by criollo elites. One could argue that mestizaje and, therefore, hybridity have been the preferred ideological justification for the criollo elites' domination. The frequent association of hybridity with resistance or subversion of systems of domination is thus not automatically applicable to the Latin American literary and cultural tradition.

Nevertheless, despite this link between power and hybridity, there is frequently an artistic and epistemological subversiveness to the criollo intellectual production. In her analysis of the colonial "criollo difference," Mabel Moraña has described this group explicitly as subverting the basic premises of Western culture from within:

> Without the hegemonic positionality of the peninsular but also without the definitive subalternity of Indians, blacks, and castes, the criollo elaborates during the colony the place of mediation and hybridity in a process of complex real and symbolic negotiations, which inscribes in the Western category of civilization the principles of another rationality, that challenges, contaminates and destabilizes the dominant epistemology. ("La diferencia criolla" 55)[8]

Given the unfortunate structural permanence of colonial racial and social relations in Latin America, this criollo "place of mediation" long survived the disappearance of the actual colony. It is also significant that Moraña includes as exemplars of criollo writers figures long considered mestizos with close ties to indigenous traditions, such as the Inca Garcilaso de la Vega, the son of a conquistador and an Inca princess, and Juan de Espinoza y Medrano, the seventeenth-century polyglot cleric from Cuzco (58).

From the analyses provided by Altamirano and Sarlo, Mariátegui, and Moraña, it is possible to reach some conclusions regarding the criollo. The criollo is opposed positionally, though not necessarily personally, to both the foreign and the indigenous; in other words, to the colonizer and the colonized. Frantz Fanon, in his influential analysis and defense of anticolonial agitation *The Wretched of the Earth,* claims that "the colonial world is world cut in two" (38). For Fanon, a colonial society is one in which the European colonizer faces the colonized local subject.[9] But the criollo presents a third position that puts into question much of what is generally understood outside Latin America about the colonial and postcolonial conditions. If the criollo is the inheritor of Hispanic culture, this does not imply racial or cultural purity. In fact, there is often a strong mingling of indigenous, Afro-Latino, and, in Cuba, Panama, Brazil, and Peru, Asian populations. But the criollo is necessarily differentiated from subaltern ethnic groups, especially Amerindians.[10]

The criollo position has frequently led to the creation of "difference" within the Western tradition rather than outside it. If one wants to see in criollos a source of resistance, it is an unusual one, in which participation and collusion are as constitutive as opposition to unequal world economic and cultural systems. Moreover, after the independence achieved by the "Creole Pioneers in the early nineteenth century, the criollos became the hegemonic group within national societies while unable to free themselves from a subaltern position in the international sphere.

Mainstream intellectuals and writers from Latin America thus differ from those belonging to other postcolonial societies. Unlike Latin America, which, as the name implies, sees itself as participant in European culture, other postcolonial societies often trace their history to a pre-European past as justification for claims of cultural independence from their metropolis. Needless to say, the separation from, even opposition to, subaltern ethnic groups that is constitutive of the criollo has made it difficult for Latin American intellectuals to go beyond the rhetorical claims of cultural and racial communality of mestizaje. Moreover, mestizaje has often been used to justify national and regional rather than civilizational difference from the West. After noting that both Latin American and Asian countries are "semi-colonial," Mariátegui argues, "The noble or bourgeois from China feels profoundly Chinese . . . In Indo-America [Latin America], the circumstances are not the same. The criollo aristocracy and bourgeoisie do not feel solidarity with the people by means of a common history and culture" ("Punto de vista anti-imperialista" 88).[11] Mariátegui's description of China implies the clear-cut opposition between the colonizer and the colonized that is characteristic of exploitation colonies and nominally independent societies under similar neocolonial conditions. One may add that the supposed existence of a solid non-Western culture and identity was one of the main propellants of the anticolonial and anti-imperialist revolutions of the twentieth century.

Mariátegui's point of reference remains Peru even when he is writing about "Indo-America. Therefore, the cultural distance between the elites and the "people" he so eloquently describes correlates with that between the Hispanophone coast and the Quechua-speaking and culturally indigenous Andean rural populations. This radical separation described by the Peruvian critic does not take place to the same degree in those countries in the region where large, culturally and linguistically distinct, indigenous populations no longer exist. Moreover, later in the same essay, Mariátegui qualifies his optimism about Asian anticolonialism by noting the "betrayal of the Chinese bourgeoisie," to that country's anti-imperialist struggle, which "showed how little one could trust, even in countries like China, in the nationalist revolutionary sentiment of the bourgeoisie" (89).[12] In other words, the existence of class divisions in postcolonial countries contradicted and overwhelmed any apparent commonality that existed when bourgeois and/or aristocratic interests were not in play.

The fact remains that the position of the criollo writer or intellectual, at least in its imaginary aspects, differs substantially from that occupied by intellectuals in other postcolonial areas. Like English-speaking "criollos" from the United States, Canada, and Australia, those from Latin America share a common language and, to a degree, intellectual traditions with the former colonizers. But unlike writers and intellectuals from the Anglophone postcolonial world, in particular those from the United States, they have not been able to unproblematically take on the mantle of inheritors of Western culture. Like writers from Asia and Africa, they live in semi-colonial countries. Thus the criollo is firmly located in Western culture, but at its margins. And while the West's cultural or literary "meridian," to use Pascale Casanova's term, has migrated from Madrid (or Lisbon), to Paris, and today to New York, the criollo cultural location has remained central to the literary and intellectual production of Latin America.

I do not intend in this book to deny the existence of other traditions within Latin America. As many critics have noted, there are several significant continuous indigenous, as well as regional, cultures that cannot be assimilated into the culture of the criollo. Having experienced the persistence of the colonial opposition between colonizer and colonized, in addition to contemporary capitalist modes of exploitation, indigenous and other subaltern groups have in response frequently created cultures of resistance. Because the criollo also represents a location at which the majority of literary production—that is, the act of writing and publishing—takes place, it is difficult for a Latin American author to find an alternative location without jeopardizing a work's potential readership. Literature—both oral and written—in indigenous languages, testimonial narratives, folk performances, and even popular media permit the Latin American subaltern to speak. But given the neocolonial cultural, political, and economic structures in the region, one is tempted to paraphrase Gayatri Spivak's famous question about the subaltern: In Latin America, can the subaltern write without becoming criollo?[13]

While singularity of the Hispanic criollo position within colonial experiences deserves emphasis, one must also be aware that the colonial and postcolonial worlds have their origin precisely in the Spanish and Portuguese conquest. Iberian colonialism signaled a turning point in world history. Not only did European power and culture begin its process of expansion and imposition throughout lands and populations unknown to the West, but also new, unequal flows of resources favoring colonial powers were for the first time established on a planetary scale. As Enrique Dussel notes, Spain "inaugurates . . . the first world hegemony" and, with it, "the world-system" and "modernity" (9).[14] British and French colonialism, even contemporary international trade relations, are subsequent developments within this unequal planetary system. Furthermore, the pivotal role played by Spain and Portugal is evidenced by the fact that they developed two of the central institutions characteristic of eighteenth- and nineteenth-century colonialism and beyond—slavery and the plantation system—as well as the ultimate ideological basis on which colonialism would be built: racism. The arguments of the Spanish philosopher Juan Ginés de Sepúlveda in the sixteenth century exemplify the proto-racist rhetoric that for many in Spain justified the colonization of the Americas and the exploitation of the Amerindians. According to Sepúlveda, "Those barbarians of the New World and nearby islands . . . are as inferior to Spaniards as children are to adults and women to men . . . and there being between them [Amerindians and Spaniards] as much difference as there is between . . . monkeys and men" (33).[15] Although mixing of races was more frequent in Iberian colonies than in

French or English ones, it was not incompatible with the development of intricate racial hierarchies that also became legacies of the Spanish and Portuguese empires. Indeed, the scientific racialism of the nineteenth century would ground discriminatory discourse not on philosophical and religious reasons, as Sepúlveda did, but on pseudoscientific ones. Thus despite the obvious differences between colonial and postcolonial situations in Latin America and elsewhere, there is an underlying structural commonality. But the condition of the criollo, neither colonizer nor colonized, both exploiter and exploited, establishes a significant cultural and objective regional difference.

Globalization is, among other things, the complete incorporation of the postcolonial areas, already part of the world economy, into an international cultural system. Thus one can raise the question as to whether the criollo cultural location—one of full though, paradoxically, at the same time marginal and frequently resistant belonging—is not becoming the norm. Without denying the existence of groups and individuals that reject this cultural expansion of the world system and the preservative evolution of the neocolonial structures within it, it is possible to see much contemporary postcolonial culture as written from a quasi-criollo position. In fact, the role played by Latin American literature in the development of postcolonial literature—as well as, to a lesser degree, the development of literature of other semi-peripheric areas—can be seen as a de facto indication of the similarity between the cultural locations occupied by these postcolonial elites and those occupied by Latin American criollos.[16]

Furthermore, the postcolonial cultural homogeneity that, according to Mariátegui, was the central divergence between the "semi-colonial" nations of Asia and Latin America may belong to the past. As we have seen, economic and class differences that are constitutive of the world economic system contradict any putative commonality among classes and groups in former colonies. Even more relevant given the incorporation of postcolonial elites into a global culture, the existence of a linguistic difference between the elites and the subaltern, a situation characteristic of the Andean region, has become the norm throughout much of the postcolonial world. For instance, the participation of writers from the Indian subcontinent in what Casanova calls the "world republic of letters" is almost always predicated on their publishing in English.[17]

In other words, today, at the beginning of the twenty-first century, a quasi-criollo subject position has become characteristic of postcolonial writers. At the same time, as we will see, the notion of Latin America, as well as the existence of a distinct Latin American identity, has been problematized by economic and cultural globalization.

LATIN AMERICA AND WORLD/WESTERN LITERATURE

While in *The Spaces of Latin American Literature* I make no attempt at a thorough diachronic analysis of the region's literary and cultural production, I have consciously chosen moments, cultural polemics, and writers that strike me as exemplifying key stages in its evolution. But these specific moments must be viewed in relation to Latin America's economic role within the world system. The authors, texts, and polemics described in each chapter overlap chronologically with periods when changes were happening in the manner in which Latin America participated in the world economy. The poetry of Sor Juana Inés de la Cruz in New Spain and the essays of Espinoza y Medrano in Peru coincided with the seventeenth-century consolidation of the Spanish colony. The encounter between the Nicaraguan poet Rubén Darío and Ricardo Palma, the author of *Tradiciones peruanas,* took place during Latin America's commercial expansion of the second half of the nineteenth century. The backdrop to the polemic of the intellectual meridian and the writings of Jorge Luis Borges was the progressive rise of the United States as the center of the world economic and cultural systems. The music and writings of the Brazilian pop star Caetano Veloso responded to the crisis of the world system in the late 1960s and to the rise of an international youth movement firmly centered on U.S. and British popular culture. The last two chapters and the epilogue deal with globalization as experienced in Latin America. Since the 1980s, there has been a resurgence of Spanish capital in the region's culture and economy. At the same time, the cultural, political, and economic influence of the United States has become even more prevalent, a fact reflected in Alberto Fuguet's 2003 *Las películas de mi vida* (*The Movies of My Life*).

The correlation between social, economic, and literary changes described above should not be taken as implying a vulgar Marxist perspective in which modifications in the economic infrastructure—the full establishment of colonial economic relations, capitalist modernization, globalization, and so on—directly determine the evolution of literary styles—American baroque, *modernismo,* and post-boom. Nor does the fact that Latin America has been economically subordinated to European and North American capital necessarily imply that the region's literary and cultural production is unoriginal, backward, or merely reactive.

Some of the key questions raised by the subordinated insertion of Latin America in world economic and cultural systems were discussed in an important exchange published in *New Left Review* during 2002 and 2003. As the first salvo in the debate, Franco Moretti argued in "Conjectures on World Literature" that "in cultures that belong to the periphery of the literary system (which means: almost all cultures, inside and outside Europe), the modern novel first arises not as an autonomous development but as a compromise between a Western formal influence (usually French or English) and local materials" (58). In fact, for Moretti, the novel, and, one assumes, other Western literary forms, can be seen as "a wave that runs into the branches of local traditions" (67). Literary production in Latin America and all other peripheric areas would thus be the result of the interaction of the Western tsunami and the local trees.

From a different critical perspective, Casanova, in her contribution to the debate, emphasizes the fact that Latin American and other writers from the periphery have had to "search for a literary present" ("Literature as a World" 75). Basing her analysis on Octavio Paz's Nobel Prize acceptance speech, titled "In Search of the Present," Casanova sees modernity as defined by a "literary Greenwich meridian," which she identifies with Paris. In *The World Republic of Letters,* Casanova writes that "the literary Greenwich meridian makes it possible to evaluate and recognize the quality of a work or, to the contrary, dismiss a work as an anachronism or to label it as 'provincial'" (90). She also states, "anachronism is characteristic of areas distant from the literary Greenwich meridian" (100). However, in what is one of the most appealing aspects of Casanova's theories, Latin American writers—and other writers from what she calls "dominated" areas of the "World Space"—are neither condemned to eternal obsolescence nor necessarily denied agency ("Literature as a World" 80n14). Writers from dominated areas can appropriate modernity and bring themselves and their literary traditions up to date: "Forms, innovations, movements, revolutions in narrative order may be diverted, captured, appropriated or annexed, in attempts to overturn existing literary power relations" (88). In "Literature as a World," the prime example of this "appropriation of literary capital" is Darío (88). Despite her emphasis on the importance of the innovations achieved by the dominated as they search for and appropriate modernity, this agency is only reactive. Even though Casanova describes this second-degree literature as a source of formal invention—she claims "many of the great literary revolutions have taken place on the margins and in subordinated regions" (89)—the ever-changing outline of modernity has already been determined in the center.

Although, as we will see, there are problems with both Moretti's and Casanova's theorizations, at least when it comes to their application in the field of Latin American literature, they foreground in a systematic manner questions that have long been central to the region's cultural production.[18] In fact, tropes and ideas proposed much earlier in Latin

America are frequently raised anew by both authors. For instance, in his famous essay "Nuestra América" (originally published in 1891), José Martí uses the image of the branch, so dear to Moretti, but gives it a much more radical bent by demanding that "the world be grafted into our republic; but the trunk must be that of our republics" (89).[19] In this manner, Martí emphasizes the centrality of Latin America and the region's agency in promoting cultural contact. Also, Casanova's idea of a literary "greenwich meridian" is clearly predicted by the Spanish critic Guillermo de Torre's notion of an "intellectual meridian," which was hotly debated in the region in the late 1920s. The idea that peripheric literatures are in principle anachronistic, a notion central to Casanova, had been already proposed by the Mexican Alfonso Reyes. In his 1936 "Notas sobre la inteligencia americana," Reyes complains about Latin America having "arrived late to the banquet of European civilization" (89).[20] But he believed that the lag was in the process of disappearing (90).[21] Moreover, much of the region's critical production—from Fernando Ortiz's and Angel Rama's theories of transculturation to Oswald de Andrade's *antropofagia* to Néstor García Canclini's notion of hybridity or to Roberto Schwarz's analysis of "misplaced ideas"—has attempted to come to grips precisely with Latin America's subordinate belonging in Western culture. The emphasis, however, has frequently been placed on the transformations made on European and North American culture rather than on its imitativeness. Martí's reference to grafting or de Andrade's to cannibalism makes clear this emphasis on Latin American agency. Many Latin American critics, without denying the inequality inherent in world cultural and economic systems, have found in the region's marginality a source for artistic and intellectual innovation.

Efraín Kristal, the one Latin American who participated in the *New Left Review* debate, describes a completely different relation between the region's literature and that of the West than the relation presented by Moretti and Casanova (Although Kristal's essay was written before Casanova's, many of his arguments contradict those later proposed by the French critic.). As Kristal writes:

> I am arguing . . . in favor of a view of world literature in which the novel is not necessarily the privileged genre for understanding literary development of social importance in the periphery; in which the West does not have a monopoly over the creation of forms that count; in which themes and forms can move in several directions—from the centre to the periphery, from the periphery to the center, from one periphery to another, while some original forms of consequence may not move much at all. (73–74)

As evidence for this statement, Kristal provides a powerful and surprising example: Samuel Beckett in his best-known play *Waiting for Godot* borrowed images and even phrases from the Peruvian César Vallejo's poems "Considerando en frío, imparcialmente" ("Considering Coldly") and "Los heraldos negros" ("Black Heralds") (71–72). Moreover, he correctly notes that there are other examples of forms moving from the periphery to the center, such as Jorge Luis Borges's influence on Umberto Eco, or Julio Cortázar's on Michelangelo Antonioni (70).

Furthermore, not only forms are created in the periphery, but also there is an internal dynamic to literary creation in Latin America. In fact, Kristal notes that "in the writings of Palma and Darío, the basis for many of the developments of the new Spanish American novel were already in place" (69). Rather than representing the appropriation of European cultural capital as a reaction to the wave of the modernist novel, García Márquez's Magical Realism would be a development internal to Latin American literature. After all, as Kristal notes, in Palma's writings "the fantastic and the magical are narrated with the conventions of realism" and "several of García Márquez's conceits . . . are episodes from Rubén Darío's autobiography" (69).

It is possible to provide additional examples that put into question Moretti's explicit or Casanova's implicit Eurocentrism. For instance, the development of the novel in Spanish America contradicts Moretti's image of a wave originating in France and England. The text generally considered to be the first novel published in Spanish America is José Joaquín Fernández de Lizardi's *El periquillo sarniento* (*The Mangy Parrot*) (1816). However, rather than arising exclusively "as a compromise between a western formal influence (usually French or English) and local materials" (Moretti 58), Lizardi taps directly into the Hispanic novelistic tradition of *Don Quixote* and the picaresque. Responding to criticisms that *El periquillo* dealt with local everyday life rather than more noble topics, Lizardi argued, "I look at *Don Quixote,* the masterpiece of romances and I don't see in its action anything unusual, anything extraordinary, anything prodigious. All the events are in extreme common and usual" (xiv).[22] Moretti's model is further problematized when one takes into account that this Hispanic tradition was a major influence on the French and British novel of the eighteenth century—and indirectly on the novels of later writers. In fact, it could be argued that Lizardi's "Mexicanization" of Cervantes places him in a position similar to Henry Fielding or Tobias Smollett, to mention two of the founders of the novel in English, who about seventy years earlier had also "grafted" Cervantes into English culture. Thus the appropriation of the novel by Latin American writers implies a very different process from that experienced by writers from other regions of the periphery. Writers had been aware of the Peninsular novelistic tradition, even if, for bizarre political reasons, Spain forbade the publication of novels in the region.[23]

One can add the name of Palma as another instance of a narrator tapping into the Hispanic literary tradition in order to create Latin American narrative. Although not a novelist, but rather the inventor of a sui generis brief narrative genre, the *tradición,* Palma's writing had as one of its sources Cervantes and the whole Spanish Golden Age prose tradition.[24] In a late tradición, "Sobre el *Quijote* en América," Palma informs the reader that he read the novel for the first time in a copy autographed by Cervantes to his friend Juan de Avendaño, a Spanish functionary in Lima (311). The transplantation of the modern novel and, more generally, narrative to Latin America, therefore, implies the adoption of genres separated by only one degree from the Hispanic narrative tradition. The examples of Lizardi and Palma also put into question what strikes me as a problematic aspect of Kristal's article: the separation of Latin America from the West. Being part of the economic periphery cannot annul a history of cultural participation.[25]

One can also add that Casanova's emphasis on the time lag between the periphery and the putative Parisian Greenwich literary meridian is partially contradicted by the history of Latin American literature.[26] As we have seen, Alfonso Reyes acknowledged a constitutive Latin American anachronism, but he also believed that by 1936, when he wrote "Nota sobre la inteligencia americana," it was in the process of disappearing:

> For some time there has existed between Spain and us a sense of a leveling process and of equality. And now I say before the tribunal of international thinkers that is listening: recognize the right to universal citizenship which we have won. We have attained our majority. Very soon you will get accustomed to having us with you. (95)[27]

The history of Latin American poetry gives justification to Reyes's hopes. In 1922, the annus mirabilis of international modernism, when Joyce's *Ulysses* and Eliot's *The Wasteland* were published, Vallejo released *Trilce,* a poetic experiment that equals in aesthetic radicalism these two canonical works. Moreover, if one expands one's survey to Brazil, that same year the "Semana de Arte Moderna" ("Week of Modern Art"), in which Oswald de Andrade participated, introduced modernist and avant-garde art and literature to the general public of São Paulo. Therefore, in my opinion, by 1922, writers in Latin America had achieved near contemporaneity with those of Europe. The fact that "obsolete" forms, such as naturalism in the novel, continued existing supposedly past their expiration date ought to be seen as responding to the particular local dynamics of Latin American culture and society, rather than as a sign of intrinsic cultural backwardness.

There is a certain utopian aspect to Kristal's description of the cultural exchanges between Latin America, Europe, and North America. Kristal is correct in noting what should be obvious: Forms, that is, innovation, not to mention literary works of the highest caliber, can be created just as well in the periphery as in the center. He also proves convincingly the presence of sometimes explicit and sometimes hidden transference of forms from the periphery to the center. But the existence of innovative work in the periphery does not necessarily imply a full equality of exchange. Thus it took Kristal's unusually perspicacious analysis to notice the presence of Vallejo's influence in Beckett's work. One assumes that if Vallejo, or any other Latin American writer, exhibited the direct influence of Beckett, it would be a central topic in criticism of that author's work.

Moreover as Moretti retorts, "Movement from one periphery to another (without passing through the centre) is almost unheard of" ("More Conjectures" 75). Magical Realism is a case in point. After all, Toni Morrison or Salman Rushdie became aware of García Márquez through Gregory Rabassa's celebrated English translation. One must also note that the role played by New York and English in the dissemination of *Cien años de soledad* (*One Hundred Years of Solitude*) contradicts Casanova's Franco-centrism.

The critical response to Darío is another example of the asymmetry present in world literature. Despite being mentioned in the *New Left Review* debate as an example of cultural appropriation by the dominated (Casanova), and as a key moment in the emancipation of Spanish American literature from the literature of Spain (Kristal), the fact is that from the viewpoint of the literature of the center, Darío is at best a marginal figure. (And one can add that Palma is an unknown name.)[28]

Kristal's emphasis on the systemic independence of Latin American literature, while understandable as a corrective to Moretti's and Casanova's implicit Eurocentrism, is not fully convincing. Of course, it is possible to see Darío's modernismo as responding to the dynamic of Latin American literature as a whole rather than as the mere imitation of European trends. As Kristal reminds us, Darío "addressed local imperatives, and produced native solutions whose international impact transformed the repertoire of literary possibilities in Spanish" (70). Undoubtedly, he is correct in emphasizing the creativity of Latin American literature, as well as in foregrounding the links between literary innovation and social evolution. But one must still take into account the fact that modernity—which can be rejected, copied, or transculturated—is still determined and defined in Europe and North America. Darío's appropriation of French and, to a lesser degree, U.S. and British literary innovations (Poe, Whitman, and Swinburne) responded to needs internal to the Latin American literary field. However, the Nicaraguan poet felt the need to turn to French literature in order to modernize Latin American literature. In fact it is impossible to understand the region's literature without taking account of European and, more recently, North American developments.

One must remember that in addition to the world or pan–Latin American literary systems, there are supranational, national, and intranational literatures that have divergent and, on occasion, alternative logics to the larger fields. Kristal did not deal with these smaller regional, national, and local literary fields due to the fact that the explicit topic of the *New Left Review* debate was world literature.[29] However, even a cursory look at local literary problematics raises questions about aspects of world analyses such as Moretti's and Casanova's. The case of *indigenismo*—a literature that attempted to represent the lives of Andean Indians—can serve as an example of how the internal logic of specific national and regional literatures helps explain phenomena that from a world perspective can only seem to exemplify aesthetic backwardness. The heyday of indigenismo is roughly synchronous with that of international modernism—1930s and 1940s. In fact, even Vallejo wrote an *indigenista* novel, *El tungsteno* (*Tungsten*) (1931), despite the profoundly avant-garde nature of his poetry. Indigenismo was a reaction to the fact that Peru was an agrarian country with a rigid division between urban and rural regions, where the exploitation of the indigenous peasants was the most blatant example of class and racial oppression. Rather than a mere case of "anachronism," the supposed "persistence" of "naturalism" through indigenismo responds to the internal logic of Peruvian and Andean literature. This logic is related to a specific national and (sub) regional cultural, social, and economic reality.[30] Moretti's model of world literature would, one assumes, see indigenismo as simply the interaction between a local indigenous or mestizo cultural tradition and the wave of the realist or naturalist novel. But such an approach would be able to explain neither the persistence of the genre even after naturalism had become passé nor the interest it generated among writers knowledgeable of the avant-garde. From Casanova's perspective, indigenismo would simply appear as an anachronism, but its evolution would remain unexplained. The case of indigenismo underscores the need to supplement theories of world literature with careful analyses of local cultural and social realities.

I thus propose a reading of Latin American literature that is sensitive both to Euro-North American influences—which are not necessarily seen as alien, but frequently as part of the region's inheritance—and to the transformation exerted on Western forms in response to local realities and needs. Latin American literature, therefore, exhibits an uncanny sense of similarity and difference from that of the central countries. In other words, Latin American writers are both part of the Western tradition and, at the same time, alien to it. In fact, this simultaneous participation and distance from the Western cultural mainstream has frequently been seen by writers themselves as being at the core of Latin American creativity. Jorge Luis Borges in "El escritor argentino y la tradición" ("The Argentine Writer and Tradition") describes this mainstream Latin American position in clear terms: "I believe that our tradition is the totality of Western culture, and I also believe that we have a right to this tradition, a greater right than that which the inhabitants of one Western nation or another may have"; and "I believe that the Argentines, the South Americans in general, we can take on all European topics . . . without superstition and with . . . irreverence" (161).[31] Unlike the hypothetical European author—famously described by Eliot as surrendering before tradition—the Latin American writer is seen implicitly as a creator of forms through irreverence in the handling of those provided by the West. Moreover, the Latin American writer has been free to draw from local indigenous, African, and Asian traditions in order to create new hybrid forms.

From Palma and Darío, through Borges, to the Brazilian pop music master Caetano Veloso—who describes Brazil in neo-Borgesian terms as "a West to the west of the West" (*Tropical Truth* 323)[32]—Latin American cultural products, including those from Brazil, can be seen as textually representing the ambiguous criollo location. Latin American literature is a literature that inherits the West but also betrays it. This Western inheritance is composed of the Western canon as well as popular culture. It is centered not only in Paris but also in Madrid, London, New York, and why not Los Angeles, the Mecca of film? Latin Americans have used and abused, acculturated, and transculturated this cultural tradition. And as a globalized culture becomes both the raw material used and the environment in which all artists work, cultural criollos proliferate throughout what was once known as the Third World.

ORGANIZATION OF THE TEXT

In chapter 1, "Sor Juana, Lunarejo, and the Colonial Literary Space and Its Limits," I study two seventeenth-century Spanish American writers, the Mexican poet Sor Juana Inés de la Cruz, and the Peruvian philosopher and playwright Juan Espinoza y Medrano, known as Lunarejo, who wrote during a period of consolidation and economic expansion of the Spanish colonies in the Americas. Rather than attempting an in-depth reading of the works of these two authors, this chapter maps the intellectual, ideological, linguistic, and geographical boundaries of what I call the colonial cultural space, as reflected in Sor Juana's celebrated "Respuesta a Sor Filotea de la Cruz" ("Response to Sor Filotea de la Cruz") and Espinoza y Medrano's *Apologético en favor de don Luis de Góngora* (*Apologetic on Behalf of Don Luis de Góngora*) and his preface to his *Philosophia Thomistica*, better known as "Prefacio al lector de la lógica."

In chapter 2, "Rubén Darío Visits Ricardo Palma: Tradition, Cosmopolitanism, and the Development of an Independent Latin American Literature," I analyze the encounter between the Nicaraguan poet and the author of the *Tradiciones peruanas* (*Peruvian Traditions*) in 1888. The importance of this meeting resides in that both writers represent divergent approaches to the creation of a postcolonial literature. On the one hand, Darío favored the direct assimilation of the most up-to-date European literary trends as a way of overcoming and replacing the Spanish colonial legacy. On the other, Palma believed that a critical reassessment of local literary and cultural traditions, including colonial traditions, would permit the construction of truly independent national and regional literatures.

Chapter 3, "The Intellectual Meridian Debate and Colonialist Nostalgia," is a study of the polemic originated by the publication of the article "Madrid, Meridiano Intellectual de Hispanoamérica" by the Spanish poet and critic Guillermo de Torre in 1927. In this article, de Torre proposed that Madrid be the center of Hispanic culture in both the Peninsula and Spanish America. The importance of this debate resides in that it showed the degree to which the new generation of writers who had come of age in the 1920s saw themselves as fully incorporated into world letters, free of any residual postcolonial subordination to Spanish culture. Among the Latin American participants are Mariátegui, the Argentine writers Leopoldo Lugones and Borges, the Cuban novelist Alejo Carpentier, and the Spaniards Miguel de Unamuno and, of course, Guillermo de Torre.

In chapter 4, "Jorge Luis Borges and (Western) Tradition," I study the Argentine writer's interpretation of how Latin American literature should relate to that of the West as presented in two of his best-known essays: "Kafka y sus precursores" ("Kafka and his Precursors") and "El escritor argentino y la tradición" ("The Argentine Writer and Tradition"). In particular, I analyze how Borges uses some of the concepts proposed by

T. S. Eliot in "Tradition and the Individual Talent" in order to justify the agency of the Argentine and South American writer.

In chapter 5, "Caetano Veloso: *Tropical Truth* and Tropical Questions," I study the songs and essays produced by the Brazilian *tropicalista* singer and songwriter. What makes the musicians identified with *tropicalismo* of particular interest is that they explicitly attempted to create what they called a "global sound" participant in the 1960s rock that would, at the same time, continue the Brazilian innovations of João Gilberto's bossa nova. Therefore, in a manner parallel to the other writers and essayists also examined in *The Spaces of Latin American Literature*, Veloso is concerned with the relation of Brazilian and, by implication, Latin American culture with that of the center. But now modernity is represented by North American and, to a lesser degree, British pop and rock, rather than by the literary coteries of Madrid, Paris, or New York.

In chapter 6, "Reading, Publishing, and Writing Networks: The Hispanophone and Latin American Literary Spaces in the Twenty-first Century," I look at the impact on the region's literary production of the increasing hegemony of Spanish capital and presses in Spanish America. In particular, I study what has been called the "liberal pan-Hispanist discourse" developed by Spanish elites during the Columbus Quincentennial and adopted by many in Latin America. This discourse celebrates a presumed Hispanic or Ibero-American identity shared equally by the Iberian Peninsula, including Portugal, and Latin America, including Brazil. I also study the relation between the Latin American book market and literary creation, both during the 1960s Latin American literary boom and today.

In chapter 7, "*The Movies of My Life;* or, a Bridge to North America," I analyze Chilean Alberto Fuguet's novel. As the title suggests, Fuguet's novel incorporates references to North American films throughout the narrative. The description of fluid locations and identities, frequently caught in between Chile and the United States, can also seen as subverting traditional definitions of Latin America as necessarily opposed to the United States. One of the traits that makes *The Movies of My Life* significant is that opposition to the United States is precisely what led to the adoption of the term *Latin America*.

The book concludes with a brief epilogue titled "Latin America beyond Latin America?" In it, I analyze some of the theoretical discussions about the concept of Latin America by, among others, Walter Mignolo in *The Idea of Latin America* and Mario Vargas Llosa in several of his recent essays. In this epilogue, I argue that Latin America as an agglutinating concept has been weakened by globalization, the implementation of neoliberal free-market reforms that have undermined national and regional institutions, and the rise of alternative ethnic and gender identities. But if one understands Latin America as linked to particular subject and writerly locations, it could be argued that it has not completely disappeared even if what is meant by it is in flux.

In conclusion, *The Spaces of Latin American Literature* attempts to understand the region's literature within a changing and evolving world literature. *The Spaces of Latin American Literature* aspires, therefore, to be a contribution to the development of a postcolonial analysis of the region's literature rooted in its specific history and cultural location.

CHAPTER 1

SOR JUANA, LUNAREJO, AND THE COLONIAL LITERARY SPACE AND ITS LIMITS

INTRODUCTION

In 1690, Sor Juana Inés de la Cruz, nee Juana de Asbaje, the most famous of all Spanish American colonial poets, published a theological essay with the unwieldy title "Athenagoric Letter of Sister Juana Inés de la Cruz, a Professed Nun in the Most Spiritual Convent of San Jerónimo . . . Printed and Dedicated to That Same Sister by Sister Filotea de la Cruz, Her Studious Follower in the Convent of the Most Holy Trinity in Puebla de los Ángeles."[1] Called by Octavio Paz "an ill-fated letter" (389),[2] the official reaction to its publication by Mexican ecclesiastical authorities led to Sor Juana's being forbidden to write and, indeed, practice any intellectual activity in 1694. The persecution of Sor Juana by the Church was a manifestation of its entrenched misogyny, which made her incursion into the field of theology unacceptable. But before her imposed silence in 1694 and death the following year, she would compose an intellectual defense, her 1691 "Respuesta a Sor Filotea de la Cruz" ("Response to Sor Filotea de la Cruz"), a true *apologia pro vita sua.*

It is not my intention to examine Sor Juana's theological arguments or to comment on her tragic life in any significant depth. What I am interested in are the inferences about the Spanish American colonial literary and cultural fields that can be derived from her writings. This chapter analyzes the characteristics of the cultural, ideological, and even geographical space implicit in Sor Juana's "Response."

In addition to Sor Juana's "Response", I examine the writings by an older contemporary, the theologian, philosopher, and playwright Juan Espinoza y Medrano. While Sor Juana wrote in Mexico City, the capital of the Viceroyalty of New Spain and the richest city in the New World, and belonged to the viceregal court, Espinoza y Medrano wrote in Cuzco, the former capital of the Inca Empire. Despite its illustrious past and the enormous symbolic status it still held in the Andean imagination, Cuzco had been displaced as the center of the Andean world by the capital of the Viceroyalty of Peru, the newly founded coastal city of Lima. By the mid-seventeenth century, Cuzco was a relatively small city on the geographical, cultural, and even linguistic outskirts of the Spanish Empire. Better known as Lunarejo, from *lunar,* meaning "mole," Espinoza y Medrano, like many in the Andes, was fluent in Spanish and Quechua and, as a cleric and philosopher, also wrote in Latin.[3] By analyzing together Sor Juana and Espinoza y Medrano, I attempt to create, no matter how superficially, a map of the colonial literary space that independent Spanish American literature will attempt to leave behind.

The Colonial Criollo Location of Culture

In fact, both writers exhibited a profound awareness of their precise position in the colonial Hispanophone literary field. As Jean Franco reminds us, in *Los empeños de una casa,* her best-known play, Sor Juana

> referring to the *Celestina* answered ironically to the supposed superiority of the center, writing "always the [plays] of Spain are better," to then compare them with the Mexican *Celestina* that was "mestiza/ finished with rags/ and if it lacked style had pieces/ with diverse genius/ was formed in a sugar mill and a machine." Even though Sor Juana admits the sophistication of imported works—"never are boring/ things that cross the waters"—she defends local production. The combination of sugar mill and machine produce something that has value: sugar. (187)[4]

An even greater awareness of American literary marginalization can be found in the writings of Lunarejo. The Andean writer complained about the temporal lag experienced by himself and other criollo intellectuals in their access to European and Spanish culture. Admitting that his defense of the poetics of long-dead Luis de Góngora, the topic of his best-known work, the *Apologético en favor de don Luis de Góngora* (*Apologetic on Behalf of Don Luis de Góngora*) (1662), could be seen as anachronistic, Lunarejo argues, "It seems I come late to this task, but we criollos live very far and if interest is not involved, things from Spain take long to visit us" (17).⁵ And with even greater anger, he says, "What can there be that satisfies the Europeans, who doubt [our intellectual activities] in this manner? They judge us satyrs; they assume us tritons, [and] brutes of soul, they attempt to denounce our masks of humanity" (17).⁶

However, as the literary production of both Sor Juana and Lunarejo proves, they did not limit themselves to denouncing European and Spanish prejudice, but, rather, insisted on their right to cultural production and created important literary and critical works. Both were rewarded by the ultimate success an American author could achieve at that time: publication in Europe.

Sor Juana: The Margins (Almost) at the Center

As stated above, Sor Juana lived in the richest and the most cosmopolitan location of the imperial periphery. The historian E. Bradford Burns writes about Mexico City, the capital of New Spain, the colonial name for what later became Mexico, Central America, and the U.S. Southwest:

> In 1600, Mexico City boasted a population exceeding 100,000, making it a major world metropolis. It was the seat of the viceroy, *audiencia,* and Inquisitor General, as well as the episcopal seat. Its university dominated the educational and cultural life of Middle America. Printing presses flourished. An impressive cathedral and imposing governmental buildings surrounded the ample central plaza. (59)

But as Burns also notes, "Grandeur, comfort and elegance mixed with poverty, squalor and disease" (59). Thus Mexico City also exposed the profound inequalities of the colony, in which much of the wealth flowed to Spain (and then to Europe), while a minority of Peninsulars and criollos benefited from social structures based on the brutal exploitation of the majority of Amerindians, blacks, and mestizos.

The ambiguities of Sor Juana's personal and writerly location are thus linked to those of her society. As a (white) *criolla,* she belonged to one of its privileged groups. Before becoming a nun, she was a member of the viceregal court. Moreover, even after ordination, she remained a close friend of two vicereines.⁷ Given her personal background and location, one can see in her writings the colonial cultural field at its most expansive.

But at the same time, as a criolla, and even more so as one born poor and out of wedlock, Sor Juana was in a clearly hierarchically underprivileged position when compared to Peninsular and most criollo members of the court. Moreover, the fact that she was a woman, together with Indians, blacks, and mestizos, the *other* in the intensively patriarchal colonial society, marked her writings. (However, the obvious social difference between Sor Juana's position and the positions of the frequently, completely marginalized and exploited Indians and blacks must also be kept in mind.) Therefore, it is possible to see in her texts not only a paradoxically central expression of the colonial literature of the time, but also an expression of a marginal, even to a degree, antisystemic attitude to the mainstream of the Hispanophone cultural field. As Mabel Moraña points out, "The 'Response' remains the most direct testimony of the limitations and challenges posed to her by her subaltern condition regarding Peninsular powers and the patriarchal authoritarianism that directed the spaces of the court and the convent" ("Barroco y transculturación" 36).[8]

Religion as the Central Value

One of the central traits of the culture of seventeenth-century New Spain unavoidably reflected in Sor Juana's writings is the centrality of religion. Paz writes:

> The medieval dichotomy of pagan vs. Christian assumed greater force and immediacy in New Spain than in the mother country: Catholicism vs. all others . . . Orthodoxy created a dualism, a definitive line of demarcation. Its authority relied on both the law and the sword, the Church and the state. Spain was, at the dawn of the modern age . . . different from other European states. In them central power was strengthened, and in them, in one way or another, state and nation—two separate entities until then—became one. But no other nation-state identified as totally as Spain with a single religion. (29)[9]

If in other European countries the slow process of the separation of church and state had already begun, seventeenth-century Spain and, to an even greater degree, its colonial possessions were characterized by the omnipresence of religion. However, this should not necessarily be seen as a subordination of the state to religion, but rather as the intertwining of state and religion, in which the latter became a central tool for the eradication of dissidence, both political and religious. For unlike medieval Christianity, in which the Church had autonomous political power and, in fact, constituted the only true organized institution throughout Europe, colonial Catholicism was never fully independent from the state.

For instance, the Inquisition, while in appearance an exclusively religious institution, also fulfilled political and even economic functions.[10] This linkage between politics and religion, however, did not imply that there was no friction between secular and ecclesiastical authorities and spheres of influence, as exemplified by the case of Sor Juana, celebrated in the viceregal court and by readers throughout Spain, but persecuted by Mexico City's religious establishment.

Moreover, precisely because religion was more than an individual spiritual concern in the Spanish colony, Sor Juana's decision to become a nun should not necessarily be seen as implying an ecclesiastic vocation. In fact, in the "Response," she even insinuates that she lacked any personal interest in religion: "And so I entered the religious order, knowing that life there entailed certain conditions (I refer to superficial, and not fundamental, regards) most repugnant to my nature" (15–17).[11] However, becoming a nun was arguably the only option available in the patriarchal society of New Spain that would have granted her the necessary time and space to study and write. As Electa Arenal points out:

> Her choice to stay in the world or to enter the convent she saw as fraught with difficulties for her main purpose in life, "*de querer vivir sola; de no querer tener ocupación obligatoria que embarazase la libertad de mi estudio . . . el sosegado silencio de mis libros*" . . . (to live alone, to avoid any obligation which might disturb my freedom to study, the tranquil silence of my books). She chose religious life not because it was her true vocation but because it seemed the only way of attaining that purpose. (169)

The fact that religious life was the only door open to women who wanted to dedicate themselves to letters is another sign of the centrality of the Catholic Church in colonial life, as well as of the manner in which the patriarchal structure of society and that of the Church were intertwined.

The hegemonic position of the Church in colonial society and the totalitarian aspects generated by its intersection with political authority help explain the presence of theological and religious arguments not only in Sor Juana's "Athenagoric Letter," which after all is a theological essay, but also in her "Response." The "Response" is an attempt at justifying her participation not only in theological debate but also in the cultural field as a whole. In fact, all intellectual endeavors that claimed to be such had to be ultimately justified by theological arguments, if the former were to be seen as having any value. The central position of theology made an incursion into the field a temptation that the great poet, who was also a true polymath, could not resist. It also helps explain why Sor Juana, who had been celebrated as a poet throughout the Hispanophone world, would run afoul of the ecclesiastical authorities over the "Athenagoric Letter." But it is also the reason why her "Response," which attempts to answer the criticisms leveled against her earlier text and more specifically the attacks made on the possibility of women participating in the field of culture, would need to marshal theological arguments. If Sor Juana's entry into theological discussion was intolerable for the extremely misogynistic Mexican Church, she had to respond in kind. Theological arguments were the ones that held ultimate validity in the colonial world of letters.

"The Response"
In the "Response," Sor Juana argues that her intellectual activities were not only compatible with the Catholic religion, but they were also actually conducive to a better understanding of what she, in a term that reflects the colonial disciplinary hierarchy, calls "the queen of sciences," that is, theology: "it seeming necessary to me, in order to scale those heights, to climb the steps of the human sciences and arts; for how could one undertake the study of the Queen of Sciences if first one had not come to know her servants?" (19).[12]

What makes Sor Juana's emphasis on the centrality of theology particularly significant is that the obvious purpose of her "Response" is to undermine the intellectual basis on which her right to write was being challenged. Moreover, one must remember that patriarchy was frequently justified by biblical and theological argumentation. In the "Response," she contradicts the misogyny of the New Spanish Catholic Church and, therefore, of the colonial cultural field as a whole. In order to create a space for her intellectual activity, she discovers, maybe invents would be a more appropriate description, a genealogy of Catholic, Greek, and Roman women intellectuals—she mentions Nicostrata, Aspasia, Saint Teresa, and Christina of Sweden, among others. Sor Juana, therefore, points out the existence, within the Christian and the classical past, which Christianity had annexed, of an alternative tradition of women writers and intellectuals that the misogynistic Church authorities were purposefully ignoring. Moreover, she also analyzes Saint Paul's notorious dictum in 1 Corinthians 34, the biblical justification for the criticisms she received for the "Athenagoric Letter": "Let your women keep silence in the churches." Sor Juana, in the "Response" asked:

I would want these interpreters and expositors of Saint Paul to explain to me how they interpret that scripture, *Let the women keep silence in the church*. For either they must understand it to refer to the material church, that is the church of pulpits and cathedras, or to the spiritual, the community of the faithful, which is the Church. If they understand it to be the former, which in my opinion is its true interpretation, then we see that if in fact it is not permitted of women to read publicly in church, nor preach, why do they censure those who study privately? And if they understand the latter, and wish . . . that not even in private are women to be permitted to write or study—how are we to view the fact that the Church permitted a Gertrude, a Santa Teresa, a Saint Birgitta, the Nun of Agreda, and so many others, to write? (59)[13]

Sor Juana justifies her activity as a woman writer not by undermining the role of religion, biblical exegesis, and theology in the colonial cultural field, but rather by using these hegemonic discourses to justify her own intellectual activity. Furthermore, as Paz has pointed out, "Scholasticism was crucial in shaping her. What could be called the structure of her thought—that is, not only the ideas but the manner of ordering them—derives from that philosophy" (253).[14] Her arguments, therefore, frequently apply in a creative manner the syllogistic structure characteristic of scholasticism, which, it must be pointed out, was at the core of colonial theology.

Due to the centrality of Catholicism in the Hispanophone cultural field of the seventeenth century, even a discourse, such as Sor Juana's, that in its proto-feminism can be seen as contradicting central colonial values must do so by acknowledging and implicitly reinforcing what arguably was the principal trait of this cultural field: the primacy of Catholic orthodoxy and, therefore, of theology. The question of Sor Juana's sincerity, whether she privately agreed on the "truth" of all or part of the dogmas of Catholicism, is beside the point. (However, given the environment in which she lived, full dissidence, even if private, with Catholicism is almost impossible to imagine.) The fact is that in the New Spain of the time, intellectual and even public discourse had at least to be compatible with the doctrines of the Catholic Church and, at its most sophisticated, with the accepted logical and rhetorical format of scholasticism for it to be even intelligible as discourse. Given the rigid colonial censorship, orthodoxy was also required for any text to be published. Furthermore, any public deviance from Catholic dogmas and orthodox positions could very well lead to the intervention of the Inquisition, a fact of which Sor Juana was fully aware.[15]

Espinoza y Medrano: The Margins of the Hispanophone Cultural Field

The successful expansion of the Spanish colonial cultural field and the imposition of its central traits—among them, the hegemony of those discourses associated with the Catholic Church—throughout the whole of the Empire is exemplified in the life and works of Juan Espinoza y Medrano, Lunarejo. As previously mentioned, unlike Sor Juana, Espinoza lived and wrote in Cuzco, a city located in the hinterlands of the Empire. Nevertheless, Espinoza's writings, as well as his career, share many of the basic traits previously examined with regard to the New Spanish poet.

The religious and intellectual orthodoxy of Lunarejo is already evidenced in the title of his philosophic text, *Philosophia Thomistica* (1688), and in the text itself where he proclaims, "I belong to the Thomist school ['Yo profeso la escuela tomista']" ("Prefacio al lector de la lógica" 328). However, Lunarejo adds, in a manner that makes clear how the Catholic Church controlled education helped perpetuate the centrality of its discourses in colonial society: "But could I profess another [philosophical doctrine], having been raised since childhood and instructed until I took charge of the principal chair at the celebrated Principal Seminary of San Antonio for clerics? It is true that, thanks to the grace of God, we have drunk with passion only the pure, authentic, and genuine doctrine of the Angelic Doctor" (328).[16] Moreover, Espinoza, as a priest and university professor, belonged to the two institutions that had as their main function the twin defense of Catholic orthodoxy and of the colonial political and religious structures. They did this by means of their monopoly of education and by their emphasis on the "apologetic" nature of intellectual activity.[17]

As mentioned above, the dominance of the Catholic Church in the cultural field in Spain and the Spanish Empire as a whole contradicted a central historical tendency present in the rest of Western Europe: the slow but ineradicable breaking free of the humanities, as well as other intellectual fields, from religion and, in particular, the Catholic Church. In fact, the creation of an independent literary space was predicated on the separation of literary creation from the religious or theological fields and from ecclesiastical control. As Pascale Casanova notes about the rise of Renaissance humanism, "The humanist enterprise is therefore to be understood at least in part as an attempt by the laity, in its battle against Latinist clerics and the scholastic tradition, to achieve intellectual autonomy reappropriating a secularized Latin heritage" (*The World Republic of Letters* 48). On the other hand, in the Spanish colonies in the seventeenth century, the Catholic Church and the scholastic tradition, including theology, though significantly not Latin, were returned to the central position in the colonial cultural field. Another name for this return is, of course, the Counter-Reformation. In its efforts at containing the expansion of Protestantism throughout Europe, the Counter-Reformation attempted to reinstall what was felt to be the orthodox intellectual root of Catholic theology: scholasticism. But in its search to reestablish orthodoxy both within and without the Catholic world, it gave the Spanish monarchs, officially designated as defenders of the faith, the political and ideological tools to further pursue their attempt at eliminating dissidence and difference from Spain and the Empire. The fact that there was no significant attempt at reestablishing Latin as a literary language—Espinoza wrote his philosophical, but not his literary, works in Latin, while Sor Juana wrote almost exclusively in Spanish—exemplifies the limits that the Catholic Spanish monarchs placed on ecclesiastical control.

The success of the Counter-Reformation in seventeenth-century Spain and its Empire helps explain one of the lacunae in Casanova's *The World Republic of Letters:* the mysterious "delinking" of Spain and its literature from the "international literary space." According to Casanova:

> To this initial Tuscan-French core [of the international literary space] were gradually added Spain and then England, which together formed the first group of major literary powers, each endowed with a "great language" as well as a sizable literary patrimony. The highpoint of the Golden Age had passed by the mid-seventeenth century, however, by which point Spain entered upon a period of slow decline that was inseparably literary and political. This "vast collapse, this very slow sinking" created a growing gap between Spanish literary space and that of the French and English, now posed to assume their place as the leading literary powers in Europe. (55)

While one cannot separate Spain's political—and, one can add, economic—collapse from its progressive abandonment of/exclusion from the "international republic of letters," Spain's turn to dogmatic Catholicism, one of the key achievements of the Counter-Reformation, is, I believe, of paramount importance to understanding this presumed "sinking" of Hispanic letters. However, the aesthetic triumph that is Sor Juana's poetry or, for that matter, the quasi-modern formalism that Lunarejo exhibits in his *Apologético* serves to problematize the frequent blanket dismissal of Hispanic letters after the mid-seventeenth century.[18]

The World and the Colony: The Chronological and Geographical Boundaries of the Colonial Cultural Field

The separation of Hispanic cultures from those of the rest of Europe also helps explain one of the peculiarities shared by Sor Juana's "Athenagoric Letter" and Espinoza's *Apologético:* the fact that both writers participate in what could be called anachronistic polemics, in that they are respondents to long-dead antagonists. In his 1662 *Apologético*, Espinoza acknowledges that the Portuguese critic Manuel Faría y Souza, against whom he defended Góngora, had written his attack when "Góngora was dead and I had not been born" (17).[19] Sor Juana's "Athenagoric Letter" also answers a dead opponent, the Portuguese Jesuit Antonio de Vieyra, whose "Sermon of the Mandate," to which the Mexican nun responded, had originally been given in 1650, forty years earlier.[20] This disregard for temporality can be seen as a characteristic of the antimodern ideology of the Counter-Reformation. After all, matters of the spirit, unlike secular matters, are of permanent and, in principle, unchanging nature.

These polemics are anachronistic only when seen from our vantage point. For us it is clear that colonial culture turned its back on a nascent modernity that, it must be remembered, had a specific geographic location, the rest of Western Europe. Colonial culture was thus, by definition, always already obsolete, willfully closing its eyes on the philosophical, literary, and, more generally, intellectual questions that would begin the genealogy of modernity. Again, it is only when seen from outside the Hispanophone world of the time that baroque poetics, the subject of Espinoza's text, or the question of which of all of Jesus' acts was the most superior, the topic dealt in Sor Juana's "Athenagoric Letter," could be seen as no longer relevant to the intellectual life of its time. However, as the examples of Sor Juana's proto-feminism and Lunarejo's anticipation of contemporary literary criticism prove, this voluntary obsolescence did not preclude true intellectual achievement or make impossible social and cultural innovation.

The delinking of Spain from the world republic of letters also led to the exclusion of Spanish language writers from the international literary and cultural fields. In the early seventeenth century, some of the central early modern Spanish writers, such as Cervantes, Quevedo, and Lope de Vega, had been translated into English, and major libraries routinely acquired key Spanish language literary texts, but after the 1640s Hispanic writers were little known outside the Peninsula.[21] Thus Sor Juana, writing in the second half of the century, was unknown outside the Hispanic world, even if she was a celebrity within it: "Her books were found in the libraries of the cultivated men of her time" (Rivers 309);[22] and five successive editions of the second and third volumes of her complete poetry—first published in Seville in 1692 and Madrid in 1700 respectively—came out before the three volumes were reissued for the last time in the eighteenth century in 1725 (Paz 510). As Paz notes, "Few modern poets have had so many editions of their work published in so short a time" (510).[23]

Octavio Paz's reconstruction of Sor Juana's library gives a clear image of the intellectual isolation of the Spanish colonial world. Sor Juana had a large personal library—between 1,500, the number estimated by Paz, and 4,000 books, the number given by her original biographer Diego Calleja in 1700 (Paz 248). Yet, according to Paz, who reconstructed Sor Juana's library by analyzing the references found in her writings and inquisitorial records, among other sources, "the mainstay of the library—alongside Spanish poetry and treatises on mythology—was Latin literature" (251). "The French poetry of her time, to say nothing of the English, was *terra incognita* for her," Paz adds (251).[24] In philosophy and science, "the intellectual movement that began in the Renaissance with the new science and the new political philosophy is not represented in that collection of books" (260).[25]

Paz points out that the great Spanish baroque writers of the first half of the century had been informed of the literary developments in the rest of Europe. For instance, "Quevedo and Gracián mentioned . . . [Michel de Montaigne] . . . openly" (255).[26] Sor Juana, on the other hand, makes no reference to any major French or English Renaissance or contemporary writer. However, some of the philosophical and scientific advances of early modernity reached her through Church-sanctioned mediators, in particular Athanasius Kircher (176).

A similar exclusion of the literature and thought produced outside the intellectual parameters of the Catholic Church and the Spanish language is found in Espinoza's writings. At the start of his *Apologético*, Espinoza lists approximately three hundred names of writers and scholars who "authorize" his text. Some of the names included are surprising and even hint at an unusually open mind for the time. Espinoza mentions, for instance, Erasmus and his Spanish disciple, Luis Vives, whose writings had been banned by the Church; Lorenzo Valla, who proved that the Donation of Constantine was a forgery; and other heterodox names.[27] Nevertheless, Espinoza's list manifests an overall distribution of authors congruent with the one Paz identified in Sor Juana's writings: classical authors, scholastic philosophers, Church Fathers, Spanish masters of the Golden Age, and even the Portuguese Luís de Camões, who was celebrated by Faría over Góngora.

Again French, English, and most Italian writers and thinkers contemporary to Espinoza are missing from his intellectual world. Espinoza claims to have written his *Philosophia Thomistica* to defend Aquinas's philosophy "from new foxes ['zorros recientes']" ("Prefacio" 328). However, these new authors are not Blaise Pascal, René Descartes, Gottfried Wilhelm Leibniz, or John Locke, all of whom predated Espinoza or were his contemporaries. They are Scotists and Nominalists who reproduced and continued medieval debates. It is therefore tempting to dismiss Espinoza's philosophical and literary production as, in the words used by Mario Vargas Llosa in an otherwise admiring portrait, "the anachronistic attempt by a parish priest from Cuzco ['el anacrónico empeño del curita cusqueño']" ("El lunarejo en Asturias" 404). But one should remember that, as the prologue to *La novena maravilla,* edited in Madrid in 1695, notes, the *Philosophia* "merited celebrity ['la celebridad que mereció']" in Rome, the center of Catholic ecclesiastic knowledge (qtd. in Tamayo xlii).[28]

Thus, from the perspective of the rest of Western Europe, seventeenth-century Spanish and the Spanish colonial cultural field were closed to the present, understood as the new science, philosophy and literature. However, if the Hispanic world had excluded the rest of the West, its boundaries were extensive. The Hispanophone cultural space included cities such as Mexico City, Lima, Cuzco, and Madrid, where Sor Juana and Lunarejo wrote and published their works.[29] In other words, it had fully incorporated the vast territories of the Spanish Empire into its cultural patterns and forced its values on vast heterogeneous populations.

Colonial Inclusiveness and the Coloniality of Power

One cannot deny the racist nature of Spanish colonialism, which, like all colonialisms, stratifies society in order to justify the appropriation of resources. As Aníbal Quijano has argued, racial classification is at the core of this "coloniality of power," a conceptual matrix that, while originating in the sixteenth century, still underlies contemporary capitalist globalization:

> One of the fundamental axes of this model of power is the social classification of the world's population around the idea of race, a mental construction that expresses the basic experience of colonial domination and pervades the more important dimensions of global power, including its specific rationality: Eurocentrism. The racial axis has a colonial origin

and character, but it has proven to be more durable and stable than the colonialism in whose matrix it was established. (533)[30]

Nevertheless, as is evident in the examples of Sor Juana, who as a criolla was not necessarily at the apex of this "model of power," and Lunarejo, who was probably mestizo or indigenous, there were restricted escape hatches to this racist structure. In part this may have been due to the fact that while there was a racist "coloniality of power," the concept of race as a biological concept was not fully developed. Race during colonial times was a complex combination of race, culture, religion, and legal status.

Two key institutions fulfilled a central role in permitting non-Spaniards to advance in colonial society: the Church and the university. As Jorge Alberto Manrique notes, "In a relatively static stratified society, it [entering the University] constitutes the only door—together with an ecclesiastic career, with which it is so closely tied—for social ascent of the lower classes" (673).[31] One must remember, however, that only the Church accepted both men and women, although in hierarchically differentiated positions. Nevertheless, as we have seen, convents constituted a space in which women were free from many social requirements and restraints. Thus the cloister frequently was "a room of their own," which "provided women with a semiautonomous culture in which they could find sustenance, exert influence, and develop talents they never could have expressed as fully in the outside world" (Arenal 149). Without denying the structural injustice of Spanish colonization, the Spanish cultural field, like the Catholic Church with which it was imbricated, was, at least intermittently, able to incorporate at its highest strata talented individuals regardless of gender or race.

THE LIMITS OF DISSIDENCE IN THE HISPANOPHONE LITERARY FIELD

The cases of Sor Juana and Espinoza are of interest also because despite their acceptance and celebrity within the Hispanophone literary space, their works can be interpreted as embryonic attempts at modifying colonial culture, even at constituting alternative fields and spaces. We have seen how Sor Juana in her "Response" undermines the misogynistic premises of the colonial cultural field. A similar case can be made for Espinoza as a critic of colonial society.

As we already know, Lunarejo was acutely conscious of the marginalization of American authors within the Hispanic literary world and attempted to undermine the intellectual grounds on which this discrimination was based. Thus in the preface to his *Philosophia,* he notes, "Europeans seriously suspect that the scholarship of men from the New World is the product of barbarians" ("Prefacio al lector de la lógica" 325),[32] and erects an erudite defense of the Americas based on quotations from Aristotle and St. Thomas Aquinas. Also, his theatre work—he wrote a few plays in Quechua and Spanish—implied the existence of audiences capable of interpreting texts outside the parameter of the colonial cultural field. For instance, according to Raquel Chang Rodríguez, in the case of *Amar su propia muerte* (*To Love One's Own Death*) (1645), he presented indirect criticisms of Spanish colonial society. This play, based on a story from the book of *Judges,* narrates the defeat of the Canaanites at the hand of the Israelites led by Jael, a woman, and uses the biblical plot to speak about local conditions:

> *El Lunarejo* brings to the fore problems of the mining industry and the exploitation of the Indian population as well as the vices frequently associated with corrupt and powerful members of the judicial elite. The heterogeneous theater-going public that attended the performances of colonial plays, dramas, and interludes surely was able to understand the hidden meaning offered by the author's play on words. (92)

Thus Espinoza's plays, which include two Sacramental acts in Quechua, addressed specific Andean audiences and were able to take advantage of a shared cultural knowledge different from that characteristic of the Hispanophone literary space, and can, therefore, be seen as pointing in the direction of local, regional, viceregal, and even proto-national audiences and readerships. Moreover, as Chang Rodríguez points out, Espinoza's writings, on occasion, are opposed to the racial and cultural hierarchies that underlaid not only the culture of the colony but also its social structures.

However, despite the radical potential implicit in Sor Juana's and Espinoza's texts, the incorporation of their writings into the colonial and Spanish cultural and literary fields tended to eliminate the possibility of its actualization. As we have seen, Sor Juana's "Athenagoric Letter" and "Response," by presenting the theological speculations of a woman and an intellectual defense of a woman's right to intellectual activity, undermined the ideological justification for patriarchy. However, these texts, the "Response" for the first time, were published in 1700 as part of the third volume of Sor Juana's complete works, prefaced by a biography of the Mexican nun by Diego Calleja, who interpreted the Mexican poet's life as "a gradual ascent towards saintliness ['un gradual ascenso hacia la santidad']" (Paz, *Sor Juana* 3 [Paz, *Sor Juana Inés de la Cruz* 13]). Sor

Juana's biography was thus presented as "an edifying tract ['un discurso edificante']" (3 [13]). Calleja's interpretation of Sor Juana's life blunted the subversive content and context of her writings, presenting them as steps toward the full acceptance of the most retrograde aspects of colonial society.

In a similar vein, Espinoza's plays were performed only while he was a student at San Antonio de Abad seminary and remained unpublished until 1932 (Chang Rodríguez 90). In fact, by the twentieth century, only his *Apologético* was known. Even a critic as acute as José Carlos Mariátegui could argue that he belonged exclusively to the field of Spanish literature:

> Lunarejo, despite his indigenous blood, only achieved renown as a Gongorist, that is in an attitude characteristic of an old literature, that exhausted the Renaissance, arrived at the baroque and culturanism. The *Apologético* is, from this point of view, part of Spanish literature. (*Siete ensayos* 238–39)[33]

However, the flaw in Mariátegui's criticism of Espinoza resides in his belief that Espinoza could have done other than incorporate and be incorporated into the colonial and Hispanophone literary culture and space. Mariátegui retroactively applies to the colonial world a romantic or postromantic view of literature as national—or ethnic, cultural, or racial—expression. The only way Espinoza or Sor Juana could enter the cultural field of the Spanish Empire was by having fully assimilated and, at least in appearance, accepted its basic literary and intellectual traits. As we have seen, even aspects of their writings that could be seen as contradicting central traits of the colonial Hispanophone space, such as Sor Juana's proto-feminism or Espinoza's veiled criticisms of the colonial system, were either silenced, ignored, or reinterpreted in such a manner that they were no longer threatening.

According to Casanova, a similar practice still characterizes the consecration of writers from the periphery, "which . . . served to ennoble, internationalize, and universalize . . . at the same time, ignored everything that made the emergence of such a work possible. Paris, the denationalized capital of literature, denationalized texts so that they would conform to its own conceptions of literary art" (155). Like Casanova's later peripheric writers, for Sor Juana to become an international writer in the Hispanophone literary space, her work had to be capable of being read within the cultural parameters of the Empire. And it is no accident that Espinoza's plays, which, at least to a degree, were critical of Empire, were never published.

CONCLUSION

After the dynastic transfer from the Hapsburgs to the Bourbons in 1701, the colonial Hispanophone space did not remain unchanged; or to the same degree disconnected from that of the rest of world literature. Spain will end up as a mediator, a kind of customs office, through which innovations such as neoclassicism or romanticism will reach the Americas. Given the determining role played for so long by Spain, there will always be voices defining Spanish American literature as part of the literature of the Peninsula. But as we will see in the following chapter, the question of how to create independent national and regional literatures, in other words, how to deal or not with the colonial literary and cultural legacy, will be paramount to many of the most significant writers in the region throughout the nineteenth and even twentieth centuries.

CHAPTER 2

RUBÉN DARÍO VISITS RICARDO PALMA: TRADITION, COSMOPOLITANISM, AND THE DEVELOPMENT OF AN INDEPENDENT LATIN AMERICAN LITERATURE

INTRODUCTION

The meeting in 1888 between Rubén Darío, the great Nicaraguan poet, and Ricardo Palma, the author of the *Tradiciones peruanas,* has recently attracted critical attention outside the field of Spanish American literature, where both writers, especially Darío, have long been acknowledged as major figures. Although, surprisingly, he does not mention Palma by name, this encounter has been singled out by Perry Anderson in his *The Origins of Postmodernity* as the moment when "the term and idea" of modernism was born (3).[1] There is, as Anderson insinuates, an element of irony in that the origin of a concept frequently seen as defining some of the most adventurous artistic and literary trends of the twentieth century would be linked to Lima, where the two writers met. This city, once the capital of the Spanish Empire in South America, is correctly described by Anderson as, at the end of the nineteenth century, "a distant periphery . . . of the cultural system of the time" (3). If one looks at the text in which Darío actually coined the term in 1890, a brief essay that recounts his encounter with Palma, one discovers the colonial, that is, premodern, nature of the city is stressed.[2] For instance, Darío notes, "There floats over Lima still some of the good old time of the colonial period" ("Ricardo Palma" 100).[3] However, it could be that the distance between Lima and modernity is precisely what permits Darío to name and theorize his movement, modernismo, and, indirectly, international modernism.

But if Darío's visit to Palma is of significance in the history of international modernism, it arguably also represents a central moment in the evolution of Spanish American literature. The meeting between Palma and Darío can be seen as the encounter of two alternative approaches to the creation of independent national and regional literatures. Palma, as the author of the *Tradiciones peruanas* frequently set in the viceregal period, can be identified with the construction of a Peruvian and, by implication, Latin American literature by means of the reinterpretation and extension of the colonial cultural and literary legacy. As his coinage of the term modernismo attests, Darío can be linked to the incorporation of the region's literature into what Pascale Casanova has called a world republic of letters, characterized by cosmopolitanism and continuous innovation. Despite their divergent literary approaches, Darío presents the meeting as a kind of passing of the torch in which the Nicaraguan poet and explicitly modernismo is validated by a Palma described as a patriarch of the region's letters.

PALMA AS A (NEO) COLONIAL WRITER

In Darío's description of this encounter, the poet is presented as a fan, maybe even a pilgrim, going out of his way to visit his literary hero. In fact, the Nicaraguan poet describes this meeting as the fulfillment of a long-cherished fantasy. As he says, "I remembered that in my early youth being in front of the poet of *Armonías* had seemed to me to be a sweet, unrealizable, dream" (97).[4] Moreover, there is a strong element of pride in the fact that Palma, in early 1888, "understands and admires the new spirit that today animates a small but triumphant and proud group of writers and poets of Spanish America: *modernismo* [modernism]" (97–98)—the precise moment where Darío uses for the first time this then neologism.[5]

Darío's admiration for Palma is not surprising given that he was the author of a tradición, "Las albóndigas del coronel" ("The Colonel's Meatballs") (1885).[6] Nevertheless, it is also clear that just three years later—the precocious Darío was only twenty one when he published

Azul—his writing changed considerably. No longer is he "sowing in the most fertile field of the master Ricardo Palma ['meterme a espigar en el fertilísimo campo del maestro Ricardo Palma']" that is producing stories concerned with local characters and history (85). On the contrary, his writings are, now, as Juan Valera, the Spanish writer and *Azul*'s first critic, noted, "saturated with a cosmopolitan spirit ['impregnado de espíritu cosmopolita']" that led Darío to write stories and poems "that seem written in Paris, and not in Nicaragua or Chile ['parecen escritos en París, y no en Nicaragua ni en Chile']" (xvi; xxix).

Darío's cosmopolitanism did not dampen his esteem for Palma, despite the Nicaraguan's full awareness of their profound differences as writers, and the fact that he associated the author of the *Tradiciones* with the colonial cultural and literary system he was rejecting. He notes that Palma "is decidedly aligned with classical correction and respects the Academia [de la Lengua]" (97).[7] Moreover, Palma is described as "the foremost Limeño of Lima ['primer limeño de Lima']" (100)—the city that, as we have seen, Darío associates with the colony. Even the final and laudatory mention of Palma, whose memory Darío claims he will "keep with pride, forever ['guardaba con orgullo en mi memoria, para conservarlo eternamente']" (101), reinforces the links of the Peruvian writer with the traditional Hispanophone cultural field: Palma is called "glorious prince of wits ['glorioso príncipe del ingenio']" (101). This epithet, as we all know, is associated with Cervantes, the most celebrated figure in all Hispanic letters. Not surprisingly, Palma was pleased with Darío's comments, including the Nicaraguan poet's article in several editions of the *Tradiciones peruanas*.

Darío was not alone in identifying Palma with the colony. In fact, in 1888, the same year the Nicaraguan poet met Palma, Manuel González Prada, a Peruvian poet and essayist and himself a "precursor or forerunner of modernismo ['un precursor o un adelantado del modernismo']" (Cornejo Polar, *La formación de la tradición literaria en el Perú* 95), argued regarding his country's literature that "the bad tradición reigns, that monster born out of the tragicomic falsification of history and the microscopic caricature of the novel" ("Discurso en el Teatro Olimpo" 27).[8] Two years earlier, González Prada, implicitly aiming at Palma, had stated in a public speech, "If a writer leaves her time, it must be to divine the future, not to unearth dead ideas and words" ("Conferencia en el Ateneo de Lima" 15).[9] A generation later, younger conservative intellectuals, such as Ventura García Calderón and José de la Riva Agüero, would agree with González Prada's association of Palma with colonial cultural values, but interpreted this linkage in positive terms. For them, Palma's literary emphasis on the colonial period made him "one of the principal and most efficient agents in the formation of our nationality" (Riva Agüero "La gran velada" 359).[10]

In the second half of the twentieth century, González Prada's claim that Palma consciously falsified history from a colonial or colonialist perspective was subtly transformed into the accusation that, "despite his liberal affiliation ['no obstante su filiación liberal']" and, therefore, probably unwittingly, the *Tradiciones* depicted the "colonial period idealized as an Arcadia ['la época colonial, idealizada como una arcadia']" (Salazar Bondy 13). According to Sebastián Salazar Bondy, who first proposed this interpretation in 1964, the *Tradiciones* function as a "literary stupefacient ['estupefaciente literario']" that helped forestall any political attempt at eliminating the unjust social structures that had originated in the colony (13). This position was restated in 1989 by Antonio Cornejo Polar, one of the most influential contemporary Peruvian literary critics, who argues, "For the middle classes on up, the colonial world of Palma was like a childhood without worries.... This criollo arcadia served conservatives to criticize republican excesses and was useful to disguise regressive social projects" (*La formación de la tradición* 59).[11]

PALMA AND THE SUBVERSION OF COLONIAL VALUES

But one can question whether the *Tradiciones*, which are often, though not exclusively, set during the viceroyalty, necessarily celebrate colonial cultural and social values, or nostalgically recreate the colony as an arcadia, to use Salazar Bondy's expression. This is especially true because, as the historian Alberto Flores Galindo writes, Palma is not "an aulic writer ['escritor áulico']" nor does he "exalt the colony ['exalta la colonia']" (99). In fact, already in 1925, the populist politician Víctor Raúl Haya de la Torre had claimed that "Palma was a writer of *tradiciones* but not a traditionalist" and that "no institution or person of the colony... escaped the frequently accurate bite of the irony, sarcasm, and always ridicule of Palma's criticism" (qtd. in Mariátegui *Siete ensayos* 247).[12] On occasion, the *Tradiciones* go beyond mockery. For instance, in "El corregidor de Tinta," about Tupac Amaru's indigenous revolt (1780–1781), Palma justifies the execution of colonial authorities. This anticolonial posture of Palma is not surprising given that the Peruvian writer had, after all, claimed to have striven for the independence of his country's literature. In his memoirs of his literary youth, "La bohemia de mi tiempo," he claims, "I belonged to the small group of Peruvian writers after its independence. Born under the shadow of the republic's flag, it was our obligation to break with the mannerisms of colonial writers, and we boldly set out to fulfill this enterprise" (71–72).[13] In fact, Palma invented the tradición precisely because a new country and identity required new literary forms in order to be represented. However, as the title of the genre attests, there were limits to the kind of literary independence that Palma envisioned.[14]

Despite the need he felt to develop a literature independent from that of Spain, he did not believe in breaking with a cultural tradition that, for him, constituted the ground on which national literary innovation had to rest. Peruvian cultural independence was to be achieved as part of an Ibero-American cultural and linguistic community, not against it. Palma, who belonged to what José Carlos Mariátegui called the "criollo demos ['el demos criollo']" of nineteenth-century Lima (248), saw in the colonial past of his city and Peru the cultural resource with which he could develop an independent literature. These contradictory aims—community, continuity, and independence—would lead Palma in his *Tradiciones* to expand and, therefore, test the limits of what remained of the Hispanophone cultural field.

One can almost choose any one of Palma's *Tradiciones* and see the manner in which he develops the colonial cultural inheritance, while, at the same time, wryly subverting its central values. The colonial world and its political and ecclesiastic authorities; the Catholic religion, its theology and beliefs; the racial and ethnic hierarchies of the colony; and even its literature, especially the foundational genre—the *crónica*—provide the thematic material and frequently the formal structures that are consistently reproduced and lampooned in the *Tradiciones*.

An example of this subversion of colonial models and ideology is "Dónde y cómo el diablo perdió el poncho" ("Where and How the Devil Lost his Poncho"). This tradición, like many others, attempts to explain the origin of a still used expression—*donde el diablo perdió el poncho* (where the devil lost his poncho)—that describes an extremely remote location. In this case, Palma claims to transcribe (more probably he invents) a humorous, tongue-in-cheek, story in which Christ and his disciples visit Ica, a small city on the southern coast of Peru. After a week of peace, joy, and wine—Christ, the disciples, and the citizens of Ica are described as experiencing "a version of heaven ['un remedo de la gloria']" (659)—Christ finds it necessary to return to Jerusalem, in Palma's words, "to keep the Samaritan woman from pulling out Mary Magdalene's hair ['para impedir que la Samaritana le arrancase el moño a la Magdalena']" (659). Soon after, the devil, jealous of Christ's reception, decides to impersonate him and visit the city. Inflation, taxes, and familial discord are among the results of Satan's stay. As Palma writes, it "was anarchy with all its horrors ['la anarquía con todos sus horrores']" (661). At the end of the tradición, the devil is unmasked by a young bride, who, surprisingly, given the supposed moral depravity into which the city had fallen, still "was in a state of grace ['estaba en gracia de Dios']" (661). She grabs him by the poncho he is wearing and utters, "You are evil. I make the sign of the cross ['¡Y qué malas entrañas había su merced tenido! La cruz le hago']" (661). The reference to the cross forces Satan to flee, leaving his poncho behind.

This tradición presents the complete subversion of the central values that characterized the colonial cultural field in its heyday. The Catholic religion, the core of identity in Spain and its colonies, is a source of gentle, though still blasphemous, amusement. The rigid asceticism prescribed, or at least presented as exemplary, by the colonial Church, is substituted by the representation of Christ as a benevolent bon vivant. Moreover, the role played by the virginal bride and the reason given for Jesus' return to Jerusalem—to maintain peace between the Samaritan woman and Mary Magdalene—contradict the frequently extreme ecclesiastic misogyny, which, for instance, reached an apex in the behavior of Francisco de Aguiar y Seijas, Sor Juana Inés de la Cruz's persecutor, who, according to colonial sources quoted by Octavio Paz, "tried to avoid even a glimpse of a woman's face" (Francisco Sosa qtd. in *Sor Juana* 408).[15] In fact, the manner in which Palma describes Jesus, the apostles, and their relations among themselves and with the townspeople is, more than a parody, an inversion of the ideal of holiness found, for instance, in the hagiographies still popular in the nineteenth century. (However, as should be obvious, Palma's narration is not free from patriarchal female stereotypes.)

But in addition to satirizing the religious values of the viceroyalty, Palma's revision of the colonial literary system also includes the incorporation of popular language into literature, as exemplified in the title of this tradición, as well as in the names used for the devil, such as *Cachano* (from *cacho,* meaning horn) or *Patudo* (a reference to *pata,* in this case, meaning hoof) (660, 661). If colonial literature had been often linked to the viceregal or ecclesiastic courts and, therefore, frequently reflected their putatively "elevated" language, Palma's writings, as befits one identified with republican values, were open to popular discourses and words. Alfredo Bryce Echenique, himself a master at incorporating orality into literature, writes about Palma:

> I have always thought that Ricardo Palma occupies in Peruvian literature (and I would dare to claim that, in a manner, also in Latin American literature as a whole) a very similar position to that occupied by Mark Twain in that of North America . . . Ricardo Palma and Mark Twain decided to abandon the salon where one wrote like in Madrid or London,

entered the tavern . . . and listened carefully to what their contemporaries considered the trash can of popular language and ended up writing the way it was spoken and as one ought to write. (xvii)[16]

(One must note, however, that there were partial colonial precedents to Palma's demotic language, such as the poet Juan del Valle y Caviedes, who was, in fact, rediscovered by the author of the *Tradiciones*.) Palma's *Tradiciones,* like, in a different manner, the gauchesque poetry of Argentina can thus be seen as early Latin American attempts at incorporating local words, oral narrative styles, and popular history into literature. In fact, Palma presents his writing style as a development of popular storytelling arguing that his *Tradiciones* are "popular narrative ['narrativa popular']" and a century before Virno, Hardt and Negri claiming that they "reveal the spirit and the expression of the multitudes ['revelan el espíritu y la expresión de las multitudes']" (qtd. in González 459).

But the *Tradiciones* mine not only the words but also the forms associated with oral narratives. Julio Ortega notes that in the *Tradiciones,* "Palma recalls the more interior, more familiar voice of an old aunt whose incantatory stories have the power of fable" (xxi).[17] In "Dónde y cómo el diablo perdió el poncho," the link with popular narration is presented not by this aged aunt but by an old royalist friend Don Adeodato de la Mentirola who, despite his antirepublican sentiments, described as a "weakness ['debilidad']" and his name that clearly derives from *mentira* (lie), is presented as authorizing the narrative. (But the source's name—Mentirola—also justifies the play with history and religion that characterizes this tradición.) Popular oral storytelling is thus the ground on which the *Tradiciones* is constructed.

Palma's literary populism is consonant with his biography. He was after all the son of Pedro Palma and Guillermina Carrillo, described in their birth certificate as *pardos,* that is, as partially of black ancestry (Flores Galindo 100n90). Palma's face was truly one of the "faces of the plebe" studied by the historian Flores Galindo in his study of late colonial Lima. One can argue that Palma's contradictions between continuing and debunking the colonial traditions can be seen as originating in his personal and artistic links to this plebe of Lima, a group both dependent on and resistant to the criollo elite's cultural and political projects. As Mariátegui notes in his study of Palma, given its ambiguous position within early republican society, this social group "could not produce any other literature ['no podía producir otra literatura']" and "the *Tradiciones* exhaust its possibilities ['las *Tradiciones* agotan sus posibilidades']" (248). However, as Mariátegui also points out, Palma's writings "sometimes surpass themselves ['A veces se exceden a si mismas']" (248).

Palma's concern with local, national, and regional difference was clearly expressed in his participation during the meeting in Madrid of the Real Academia de la Lengua commemorating the quatercentenary of the arrival of Columbus in the Americas. Palma proposed and defended the incorporation of Americanisms and Peruanisms into the dictionary of the Academia in terms that made clear the importance he ascribed to popular language: "Let's speak and write in American; in other words, in the language for which we will create the voices that we consider appropriate for our social being, to our democratic institutions, to our natural world" (*Neologismos y americanismos* 12).[18] Palma's balancing act between the creation of a national literature, in this passage, American, and a simultaneous belonging to a Hispanophone tradition, which includes that of Spain, is reproduced here at a linguistic and lexicological level. After all, his defiant defense and call for an American or Latin American linguistic difference is framed by a discussion of the inclusion of the region's words into the authorized dictionary and by the development of a more democratic version of the Academia itself that would see all of its national branches as equal.[19]

It is important to keep in mind that Palma's incorporation of popular narrative styles, or to be more exact, his use of popular narrative as a way of undermining the colonial values frequently present in his source materials, finds its limit in his concern with what Darío calls "classical correction." The Peruvian writer uses popular language, as well as narrative styles, within traditional grammatical and even stylistic frameworks. Palma's writings can, therefore, be seen as a populist revision of the genres, values, and ideology of the colonial literary field. Needless to say, while by doing so Palma undermines practically every central colonial value, his writing is still dependent on those models being modified. Arguably, this fact is textually represented in "Dónde y cómo el diablo perdió el poncho" in the ascription of authority, no matter how undermined, to a royalist source, which is one identified with the colony.

Palma frequently attested to his problematic but still intimate relationship with the literature of Spain. For instance, when writing about the literary influences on the *bohemios,* the would-be anticolonial literary movement of Peru in the 1850s to which Palma had belonged, he argues, "We of the new generation, captured by the newness of the freest Romanticism, then in fashion, disdained anything that stank of tyrannical classicism and we fed on Hugo and Byron, Espronceda, García Tessara and Enrique Gil" ("La bohemia de mi tiempo"5).[20] However, despite the near balance between Hispanic and French influences in the list, one must note that the Lima Romantics were led by the migrant Spanish poet, Fernando Velarde, described by Palma as "the great captain of Lima's bohemia ['gran capitán de la bohemia limeña']" (5). "Velarde fascinated us with his genius ['Velarde nos fascinaba con su genio']," continued Palma, despite acknowledging that his work was characterized by "infinite defects ['infinitos defectos']" (6). Velarde's inordinate influence among the bohemios is but one of many evidences of the mediatory role played by Spanish literature even in a case, such as that of Romanticism, in which the creative centers were located in other Western European countries. (One must remember that by the time of the bohemios—according to Palma, between 1848 and 1860—Romanticism had long passed its heyday in Spain, as well as in the rest of Europe.)

Moreover, although Palma later mentions major Romantics such as Lamartine or Leopardi as being among the favorite writers of his bohemio comrades, his personal list of influences is exclusively Spanish. According to Palma, "To talk to me of Larra's *Macías* or Fray Gerundio's *Capilladas* was to hit the spot ['hablarme del *Macías* de Larra o *Las capilladas* de Fray Gerundio, era darme por la vena del gusto']" (5). Despite Palma's knowledge of mainstream European literature—Darío, for instance, admired "his magnificent translation" of Victor Hugo's "La conscience" ("Ricardo Palma" 98–99)—his preferred authors and main influences were from Spain. In other words, to a degree greater than the other bohemios, Palma's early Romanticism is grounded in Spanish literature and in authors frequently tied to earlier styles. But if Palma remained within the then-renovated Hispanophone cultural field, he also strove to create a national and Latin American space within it.

Darío and the Embrace of the Modern

While Darío identifies Palma with Lima and the colonial past, he describes modernismo, as we have seen, as "a new spirit that today animates a . . . group of writers and poets of Spanish America" ("Ricardo Palma" 97–98).[21] Rather than being associated with a specific country, Darío links his movement with Spanish America as a whole. The supranational aspect of modernismo is made clear in the list Darío provides in the article recounting his visit to Palma, which includes the Mexicans Salvador Díaz Mirón and Manuel Gutierrez Nájera, the Argentine Rafael Obligado, the Guatemalan Domingo Estrada, and the Chilean Narciso Tondreau, among other writers (98).

However, despite modernismo's evident appeal to up-and-coming Spanish American poets, Darío's writings appear at first to have little relationship with the region's realities, especially during the period of *Azul*, before he reacted to the accusation of "involuntary anti-Americanism ['anti-americanismo involuntario']" made by José Enrique Rodó (8), before the Spanish American war (1898), and before the awareness of U.S. imperialism led him to attempt to become a specifically Ibero-American poet. The titles of the poems and stories in *Azul* evidence how deracinated Darío's literary world frequently seems: "La ninfa: cuento parisiense" ("The Nymph: A Parisian Story"), "El velo de la reina Mab" ("Queen Mab's Veil"), "El palacio del sol" ("The Palace of the Sun"). Even the section one could expect to emphasize local color, titled collectively "En Chile" ("In Chile"), does so only in a highly aestheticized manner. Unlike earlier Spanish American writers, Darío in his narrative and poetry directly represents not the region's nature, history, or society but "cultural landscapes ['paisajes de cultura']," that is, "Hellenic recreations, *galant fêtes,* versions of earlier texts ['recreaciones helénicas, las fiestas galantes, las versiones de textos del pasado']" (Rama "El poeta ante la modernidad" 98). In fact, the "Chile" of *Azul,* like other geographic locales in Darío's poetry and prose, is an example of these "cultural landscapes." Thus the Chilean setting of some of these stories is only relevant as a background for the search of a pure beauty, in which local identifying marks or traces are only of secondary value.

But despite appearances, Darío's cosmopolitanism was rooted in his condition as a Spanish American living during the last quarter of the nineteenth century. As Rama notes, "Rubén Darío's aim was practically the same that was proposed by the last neoclassicists and the first romantics of the Independence period: the poetic autonomy of Spanish America as part of the general process of continental liberty" (*Rubén Darío y el modernismo* 5).[22] Thus Darío and the modernistas will again claim the achievement of literary independence from Spain as their goal. In a 1901 article, Darío states, "Our modernismo . . . is beginning to give us a place apart, a place that is independent of Castillian literature" ("El modernismo" 315).[23] But unlike Palma, who believed, as we have seen, that cultural independence could be built on the colonial legacy, Darío's writings can be interpreted as an attempt at plugging directly into a modernity identified with French literature and compared to which the Hispanophone heritage was seen as obsolete. Thus Rama describes modernismo as attempting "the tardy incorporation of a long century of literature, seen from the symbolist culmination toward which it had been moving" ("El poeta frente a la modernidad" 83).[24] For Darío, it is only by bringing Spanish American literature up to date with the newest and most experimental trends in Europe that true cultural independence from Spain could be achieved.

The need to link up directly with European culture and, in particular, that of France and its capital, Paris, seen during the nineteenth century, in Casanova's phrase, as, "the Literary Greenwich Meridian," was in part the result of a profound unease among many Spanish Americans regarding Spain's apparent cultural incompatibility with modernity. The Argentine politician and writer Domingo Faustino Sarmiento, for instance, had already argued in 1848 that "South American republics tend to distance themselves, to the extent that they make progress, from the nation that was once their mother country—not only from its institutions, which they have repudiated with good reason, but also from its very way of thinking and even from its literary tastes" (331).[25]

González Prada, with characteristic brutality, expressed in his unpublished "Memoranda" this frequent association of Spanish culture with a premodern, even medieval, ethos: "Blessed are the Spaniards! They are born in the XIX century and breathe the air of the year one thousand" (184).[26] Even if Darío would never personally express such clear-cut anti-Spanish sentiments, there is to be found in his writings an implicit rejection of Spain's cultural and literary heritage that is congruent with this significant tendency among many of Spanish America's nineteenth-century intelligentsia.

Thus if Palma, though knowledgeable of European trends—he visited Paris in 1864 and, as we have seen, translated Victor Hugo—used the Spanish American and Peruvian colonial cultural traditions as the starting point for his attempt at creating a national republican literature, Darío, despite not having traveled outside Spanish America before publishing *Azul,* attempted to become a version of a French writer. In fact, he adopted as a virtue Valera's accusation of "mental gallicism ['galicismo mental']" (xxiii). Darío would even state, "My dream was to write in French . . . And this is how it came about that thinking in French and writing in a Castilian whose purity the academicians of Spain approved, I published the slender volume [*Azul*] that was to initiate the present American literary movement" (qtd. in Casanova *The World Republic of Letters* 19). (However, in the paradoxical passage cited above, the influence of French is seen as leading to Castillian linguistic purity.) But, as Casanova has noted, the recourse to French literature in Darío was not an attempt at creating a new cultural dependency, but rather, in her words, "an extreme (and yet, owing to the prestige of Paris, literarily acceptable) form of a larger revolt against the literary order of the Spanish-speaking world" (96). The utopian urge in Darío's poetry is that of being able to convert Spanish American literature not into a peripheric or subordinate member of the republic of letters, but into an equal of the central literatures, fully capable of autonomous innovation.

Darío's goal is the achievement of a modernity contemporaneous with that of the center. Octavio Paz thus correctly argues that "the modernistas did not want to be French, they wanted to be modern . . . For Rubén Darío and his friends, modernity and cosmopolitanism were synonymous. They were not anti-Latin American; they wanted a Latin America that would be contemporaneous with Paris and London" ("El caracol y la sirena" 94–95).[27]

But, as we have known since Rama, the rise of modernismo and its general acceptance by the Spanish American writers, as well as readers, is linked to the economic and social changes experienced by Latin America. (One must remember that the last quarter of the nineteenth century is characterized by a real, even if only partial, and ultimately truncated, process of economic and social modernization.)[28] If Palma grew up within a Lima that still maintained its colonial walls and buildings (Flores Galindo 100), Darío began his mature poetic career in Santiago de Chile, at the time, not only a Spanish American cultural center but also a rapidly growing city, and, enamored of modernity, moved to Buenos Aires in 1893 and then to Paris in 1903. Darío was fully aware of the links between modernismo and the modernizing processes experienced by Spanish America. The Nicaraguan poet, in fact, proposed the region's incorporation into the world economy as among the basic reasons why literary modernity had developed earlier in Spanish America than in Spain. Thus he argued, "In Latin America, we had this movement before Castillian Spain for reasons of the utmost clarity: our immediate material and spiritual commerce with the many nations of the world, and also because there is, in the new Latin American generation, an immense desire for progress" ("El modernismo" 314).[29]

ORIENTALISM AND SOCIAL REALITY

One of the most explicit examples of the links between literary modernismo and the specific process of modernization and incorporation into the world economy and culture as experienced in Latin America, and in particular Chile, is found in Darío's short story "La muerte de la emperatriz de la China" ("The Death of the Empress of China") first published in 1890 in the second edition of *Azul*.

In this story, the main characters are Recaredo, a sculptor, and Suzette, his wife. Deeply in love, they have their idyllic life threatened by the receipt of a gift: a small Chinese statue called the *Empress of China*. Recaredo is an admirer of Asian art and (arguably) culture. According to the story, "His great passion: Japanese and Chinese exotica . . . I don't know what he would have given to speak Japanese and Chinese" (81).[30]

Recaredo develops literally fetishistic feelings toward the *Empress of China* that make Suzette jealous. After Suzette destroys the statue, the couple begin "the ardent reconciliation ['la ardiente reconciliación']" (87), their past happiness apparently recovered.

It is tempting to see this story as just another example of modernismo's dependence on French literary fashions and innovations. The references to Chinese and Japanese art in this story are in fact another instance of the *fin de siècle* literary orientalism exemplified by writers such as Pierre Loti and Judith Gautier, authors mentioned by Darío (81). It is undeniable that for Darío, despite Recaredo's wish to know Chinese or Japanese, it is French culture that acts as a mediator for the cultures of Asia.

However, without denying the centrality of the story's French influences, the specific historical context in which Darío writes and publishes his story adds an additional dimension to the reading of the story. Not just an example of the orientalism of the time, "The Death of the Empress of China" delineates a kind of economic space that reflects Spanish America's "immediate material commerce." In other words, the specific manner in which the region and, in particular, Chile opened their boundaries to trade and influences from throughout the world is reproduced in the story. The figurine had been sent as a wedding present by "Robert, a great friend ['¡Robert, un grande amigo!']," who, according to the story, "had left two years ago for San Francisco in California ['había partido hacía dos años para San Francisco de California']" (82). Moreover, Robert had ended in China as an "agent of a California import house of silk, lacquer, ivories and other chinoiseries" (83).[31] The locations mentioned in the story, a city supposedly in Chile, possibly Valparaiso, the country's major port, San Francisco, and Hong Kong, reflect the Pacific Rim economy, which existed at the time. In fact, according to Jay Monaghan, "The end of the Opium War against China, as well as the negotiation of treaties opening Japanese ports after Commodore Perry's visit in 1854, increased the exciting Pacific trade. Thus the California Gold Rush started a period of long economic prosperity for Chile" (259). But, more than goods were exchanged. Economic commerce also led to important populational and, arguably, cultural exchanges.

Robert's trip to San Francisco, the beginning of the journeys and exchanges that would bring the *Empress of China* into Recaredo and Suzette's home, is but one of the many trips taken by Chileans to that city in the second half of the nineteenth century. The beginning and the high point of Chilean migration to California were during that state's Gold Rush. Between 1848 and 1852, about fifty thousand South Americans immigrated to California, the vast majority Chilean (Monaghan 250). In fact, by 1851, San Francisco had its own "Little Chile" located near Telegraph Hill (Walker 225). Despite the existence of a deep anti–Latin American bias in nineteenth-century California, which on many occasions led to acts of violence, many Chileans stayed in the United States after the Gold Rush ended, "establishing themselves as North American businessmen" (Monaghan 250). Robert, while a relative latecomer to the U.S. business world, is, thus, far from an isolated example. Moreover, implicit in the story is the central economic role of the United States in late nineteenth-century Spanish America—it acts as an intermediary in the exchange of goods between China and Chile—and its role as a magnet for immigration.[32]

Thus, in spite of their obvious cosmopolitanism, Darío's writings reflect the actual breakdown of Spanish cultural hegemony in the region, as well as the expansion of the region's economic and populational contacts with the rest of the world. As we have seen, "The Death of the Empress of China" is linked to some of the key locations of nineteenth-century Pacific Rim economic exchanges: Chile (Valparaiso), California (San Francisco), and China (Hong Kong). In fact, even Darío's frequent references to giants of nineteenth-century culture, such as Wagner, or minor figures, for instance Loti, to mention names found in the story, reflect the opening of Spanish America to non-Spanish cultural products—high, middle, and low brow.

CONCLUSION

As exemplified by "The Death of the Empress of China," Darío inaugurates in Latin American literature a particular way of incorporating literary modernity that is rooted in specific peripheric locations, and therefore dislocates and breaks down hierarchical classifications that are hegemonic in the center. This lack of propriety in his cultural appropriations is at the core of what Federico García Lorca once called Darío's "enchanting bad taste ['mal gusto encantador']" (21). It is not an accident that Jorge Luis Borges, who will fully theorize this approach to writing, and whose stories are probably the most developed examples of writing as appropriation in world literature, saw in Darío the writer "who made everything new again" (qtd. in Casanova 97). Not only Borges, as we know, but also much of Spanish American literature derives from Darío. As Paz, one of his most distinguished successors, claims, "If we understand *modernismo* for what it really was—a movement whose foundation and primordial goal was movement itself—we can see that it has not ended: the avant-garde of 1925 and the efforts of contemporary poets are intimately linked to that great beginning" ("El caracol y la sirena" 89).[33]

Like Darío, Palma has also had numerous, if occasionally unaware, progeny. After all, his *Tradiciones peruanas* can be read—together with the Argentinean gauchesque poem, *Martín Fierro*—as the most successful nineteenth-century attempt at creating a literature rooted in local literary traditions.[34] And this desire to write a literature grounded in Latin American local and popular cultures underlies many of the region's later literary movements. For instance, the case can be made that, despite its rejection of Palma's colonial world and of the literature, values, and ideas that he both made use of and subverted, Andean indigenismo developed in part from his example. The claim for a relationship between Palma and indigenismo may seem surprising given the traditional opposition between coastal and Andean cultures and writers in Peru: an antagonism that, it need be pointed out, is far from exhausted.[35] The role played by Palma's *Tradiciones* as an influence on the origins of indigenismo has a historical and textual basis: Clorinda Matto de Turner, the author of what is generally considered to be the first indigenista novel, *Aves sin Nido* (*Torn from the Nest*) (1889), began her literary career as the author of the *Tradiciones cuzqueñas* (1884). In fact, Palma penned the introduction to Matto de Turner's first book, where he calls her "my beloved disciple ['muy querida discípula']" ("Tradiciones del Cuzco" 470). In a similar manner, anyone who has read the indigenista writings of the Peruvian Ciro Alegría, best known as the author of *El mundo es ancho y ajeno* (*Broad and Alien Is the World*) (1941), in particular his earlier novels, *La serpiente de oro* (*The Gold Serpent*) (1935) and *Los perros hambrientos* (*The Hungry Dogs*) (1939), can recognize the influence of Palma in the conscious effort at incorporating oral popular narrative techniques and language.[36] But Palma's influence extended beyond the Andean region. As Ricardo González Vigil points out, the *Tradiciones* exerted influence on "authors of the importance of the Guatemalan Miguel Ángel Asturias . . . the Argentineans Roberto J. Payró (his famous tales of the Pago), Ricardo Güiraldes (closer, it is true, to the orality of gauchesque poetry) and M. Mujica Láinez (the reconstruction of the Argentinean past in books such as *Misteriosa Buenos Aires* and *Aquí vivieron*)" (202).[37]

One can, therefore, interpret Darío's visit to Palma as the encounter between two of the basic approaches to the creation of a Latin American "postcolonial" literature: one based on the development of local cultural resources and the other on the incorporation, modification, and intensification of international innovations. While, at least in appearance, antithetical, and seen as such by González Prada, a precursor of modernismo, these approaches would be frequently combined in later writers. After all, despite its links to Lima and the colony, Palma's early work had been impacted by international Romanticism, even if mostly mediated through Spanish literature. And, as we have seen, Darío, even at his most ethereal, developed a poetic and narrative discourse that was also rooted in the specific social and cultural reality of the Latin America of his time. Thus the mutual admiration between Darío and Palma can serve as an example of a frequent compatibility hidden behind the facades of cosmopolitanism and regionalism, of the universal and the local.

CHAPTER 3

THE INTELLECTUAL MERIDIAN DEBATE AND COLONIALIST NOSTALGIA

INTRODUCTION

In 1927, Guillermo de Torre, the Spanish avant-garde poet, published without signature in *La Gaceta Literaria* an editorial titled "Madrid, meridiano intelectual de Hispanoamérica ['Madrid, Intellectual Meridian of Spanish America']."[1] As we will see, this article generated an acrid polemic in which many of the foremost Spanish and Spanish American writers participated. (In addition to de Torre, an incomplete list of these participants includes Gerardo Diego, Salvador de Madariaga, Miguel de Unamuno, and Ramón Gómez de la Serna, from Spain; and from Spanish America, the Argentines Leopoldo Lugones and Jorge Luis Borges, the Cuban Alejo Carpentier, and the Peruvian José Carlos Mariátegui.) Given the importance of the writers involved, it is not farfetched to see in their responses a representative sample of the opinions held by some of the writers who would help shape the literature and the intellectual life of both Spanish America and Spain for the rest of the century.[2]

De Torre was close to the Spanish American and, in particular, Argentine avant-garde. Ironically, given the role the Argentine writer was to play in the polemic, he had been a friend and arguably mentor of the young Borges, during the latter's stay in Spain in 1920. De Torre's ties with Borges would become even closer in 1928 when he became Borges's brother-in-law.[3] In addition to his participation in *La Gaceta,* de Torre was well-known throughout the region as the author of *Literaturas europeas de vanguardia* (*European Avant-Garde Literatures*) (1925), which had been declared by Mariátegui as "the best . . . source for an excursion through all of the avant-garde schools" (*"Literaturas europeas de vanguardia"* 113).⁴ Mariátegui had not been alone in his praise. Borges, in *Martín Fierro,* the foremost Argentine avant-garde journal, had called it "honest ['honesto']" and "great ['grande']" (*"Literaturas europeas de vanguardia"* 210).⁵ Moreover his excellent reputation as a critic was enhanced by his frequent participation in the Spanish philosopher José Ortega y Gasset's widely read and highly influential journal *Revista de Occidente.*

However, the fact that the editorial was published anonymously raises a number of questions.⁶ While de Torre had published other unsigned articles in *La Gaceta,* one wonders whether he was aware that the article's content, clearly described in the title's claim that Madrid was, or better, should be, the "intellectual meridian of Spanish America," that is the center and arbiter of the region's culture and literature, could be seen as provocative and, therefore, decided not to personally face any controversy. However, another interpretation of this anonymity is that the article was meant to represent the point of view of the journal, *La Gaceta Literaria,* in which it was published. In fact, Ernesto Giménez Caballero, the editor of *La Gaceta,* in one of his responses calls it "our editorial ['nuestro editorial']" (De Torre et al. "Un debate apasionado" 82). Regardless of what interpretation one prefers, and needless to say they are complementary, given the importance of this publication and the tenor of the participation of Spanish intellectuals in the debate, "Madrid, meridiano intelectual de Hispanoamérica" can be seen as expressing a collective point of view rather than exclusively the point of view of de Torre. In fact, the major dissenting voice among Spanish writers was that of the great public intellectual Miguel de Unamuno, who rejected the article's argument that Spain was the necessary center of Hispanic culture, arguing, instead, that the true question was whether Madrid was the book publishing meridian of Spanish America (128). While significant, Unamuno's was an isolated voice. One can, therefore, see in "Madrid, meridiano intelectual de Hispanoamérica" an example of the implicit nostalgia for the colonial literary and cultural system characteristic not only of de Torre or even *La Gaceta* but also of much of Spanish intelligentsia.

THE ARTICLE

In the article, de Torre claimed that his proposal was "pure and generous and did not imply political or intellectual hegemony of any kind ['puro y generoso y no implica hegemonía política o intelectual de ninguna clase']" (66). To his credit, he attempts to differentiate between his vindication of

Hispanic cultural links and earlier versions of what he calls *hispanoamericanismo*. This was a chauvinistic pan-Hispanism, which he describes as obsolete, redolent of colonial nostalgia, as only "banquets, flag waving, rhetorical fire works, and magnesium lights ['banquetes y cachupinadas, tremolar de banderas, fuegos de artificio retórico y disparos de magnesio']" (67). Unlike this superficial and uncreative pan-Hispanic ideology, de Torre describes his proposal as being based on "the instauration of a new friendly spirit between two fraternal worlds ['la instauración de un nuevo espíritu amistoso entre dos mundos fraternos']," made possible because of the existence of a "new spiritual state which . . . begins to consolidate an unofficial and efficient hispanoamericanismo ['el nuevo estado de espíritu que aquí empieza a cristalizar en un hispanoamericanismo extraoficial y eficaz']" (66, 67). Given the stress made by *La Gaceta* on Spanish and international modernist and avant-garde cultural and literary developments, there is the clear implication that cultural modernity is to be seen as a priori inoculating his arguments for any residual colonialism.

De Torre's core proposal is to see the "Spanish American intellectual area as a prolongation of that of Spain ['el área intelectual americana como una prolongación del área española']," a statement that while denying significance to regional and/or national differences is presented as implying cultural horizontality (66). Despite his explicit opposition to the maintenance of cultural hierarchies, de Torre's article evidences a clear abhorrence of any position that could be seen as undercutting the linguistic and literary hegemony of the Spanish (Castillian) language. In fact, the article begins with an affirmation of the Spanish nature of Catalonia and other non-Castillian areas of the Iberian Peninsula, in spite of the existence of independent linguistic and literary traditions in those regions. De Torre calls this common peninsular identity *iberismo* (65). De Torre's implicit comparison of Catalonia, and other non-Castillian areas of the Iberian Peninsula, with the former colonial regions of the Americas makes clear his point: In the same way that iberismo would supposedly overcome cultural, historical, and even linguistic divisions, his new version of hispanoamericanismo would help put behind colonial and postcolonial strife. The assimilation of heterogeneous areas under identities that necessarily stress commonalities rather than differences can be taken as in itself a colonialist gesture—in the article directed at historically subjugated areas in the Peninsula, as well as to the former colonies. But de Torre argues that this de-emphasizing of differences is the keystone on which new nonhierarchical relations between the former metropolis and Latin America can be built.

De Torre's explicit proposal of a horizontal relationship among all Spanish speaking cultural centers was shared by many "modern"

Spanish intellectuals and was actually part of the editorial practice of their best-known and representative journals: *Revista de Occidente* and *La Gaceta*. In fact, there were close links between both. *La Gaceta*'s first issue included a "presentation" describing its editorial goals written by none other than Ortega y Gasset, the director of *Revista de Occidente*. Ortega y Gasset in his presentation claims that "if Madrid, Barcelona, Lisbon, Buenos Aires get to feel as neighborhoods of a gigantic city of letters, they will neutralize each other's intimate provincialisms and will live and work with an ecumenical radius" (1).[7] Given Ortega y Gasset's ideas, which, at least to a degree, were shared by de Torre and the editorial staff of *La Gaceta*, it is not surprising that many important Latin American writers, such as the future Chilean Nobelists Pablo Neruda, and Gabriela Mistral, collaborated in *La Gaceta*, while Jorge Luis Borges and Oliverio Girondo, the major Argentine avant-garde poets, wrote for *Revista de Occidente*. Moreover, as Karina Vásquez points out, *Revista de Occidente*, Ortega y Gasset's publication, was "directed to a Spanish American readership due to which the corresponding collaborations and bibliographic notes are seen sharing a common space . . . in fact, neither Borges nor Girondo are 'presented' [to the readers], a courtesy that in general the magazine reserves for *foreign* collaborators" ("De la modernidad y sus mapas" 17; emphasis in the original).[8]

It is not an exaggeration to claim that Ortega y Gasset, de Torre, and other Spanish intellectuals of the time were actually attempting to reconstruct the Hispanophone cultural field that had, to a degree, broken down after the independence of the former American colonies. However, unlike the colonial and early postcolonial versions of the Hispanophone space, it is now seen as incorporated into, even based on, modernity rather than resistant to it.

One can also argue that de Torre's hispanoamericanismo and, even more so, Ortega y Gasset's polycentric view of the Hispanic world resemble in their apparent horizontality the Peruvian writer Ricardo Palma's vision of the cultural relationship between Spain and its former colonies formulated three decades earlier.[9] In fact, at the start of the article, de Torre acknowledges what could be called a multicultural, yet still, Hispanic community by noting that in Spanish America "all the best historical, artistic, and highly significant cultural values—yesterday and today—that are not Spanish, are autochthonous, aboriginal" (65).[10] However, this apparent egalitarianism is contradicted by his celebration of Madrid as the necessary core of the Hispanonphone world.

La Gaceta's and *Revista de Occidente*'s pan-Hispanism is not incompatible with economic interest. For instance, Ortega y Gasset had spent time in

Argentina and was aware of the commercial potential that Spanish America offered to Spanish publications (Vásquez, "De la modernidad y sus mapas" 5–6). In fact, half of *Revista de Occidente*'s printing was sold in Spanish America, especially Argentina (1).[11] De Torre's hispanoamericanismo, that is, the development of a Hispanophone cultural commonwealth, is closely linked with a desire to expand the market for Spanish cultural products.

But the claim of cultural commonality between the former metropolis and its colonies is, as we have seen, not the only one made in the article. In "Madrid, meridiano intelectual de Hispanoamérica," de Torre's disavowal of any imperialistic ambition is to be seem as somehow compatible with the titular claim "to propose and exalt Madrid, as the new intellectual meridian of Spanish America ['proponer y exaltar a Madrid, cómo el meridiano intelectual de Hispanoamérica']" in order "to attract to Spain legitimate interests that correspond to us ['atraernos hacia España intereses legítimos que nos corresponden']" (66, 67). In other words, de Torre simultaneously argues for a nonhierarchical cultural space in which Spanish and Spanish American writers would be equal and proposes the notion that Spain had "legitimate interests" in its former colonies, that is, the precise definition of neocolonialism. It is not surprising, therefore, that in a signed follow-up to the original article, de Torre will back down from some of its most egregious colonialist statements criticizing the "editorialist"—who was himself!—for "using the term [meridian] haphazardly ['empleo aquel término un poco al azar']" and noting that it was probably done "without any desire to support imperialisms ['sin animos de apadrinar imperialismos']" (De Torre, et al. "Un debate apasionado" 83). De Torre even attempts to placate his Argentine friends by arguing that Buenos Aires was also a meridian "simultaneously and independently from Madrid ['pareja e independientemente de Madrid']" (84).

In the original article, underlying de Torre's belief in the necessary cultural centrality of Spain is anxiety over the supposed existence (regarding America) of French and Italian "obscure annexationist maneuvers ['turbias maniobras anexionistas']" (65). (He also mentions briefly the dangers posed by a pan-Americanism linked to the hegemony of the United States [66].) Since in the 1920s there was no conceivable military threat to the region from France or Italy, de Torre's "annexationism" can only be cultural. This threat was enhanced by "the great attraction that Paris exerts on Spanish speaking intellectuals ['la gran imantación que ejerce París cerca de los intelectuales hispanoparlantes']" (66). The manifestation of this French and, to a lesser degree, Italian influence was seen by de Torre as the hidden reason for the widespread adoption of the "false and unjustified name of Latin America ['el falso e injustificado nombre de América Latina']" (65). De Torre is obviously correct in pointing out the arbitrariness of the use of Latin to denote a continent in which neither French nor Italian was generally spoken, in which there was a majority population of mixed, black, and indigenous origins, and, in which, with the exception of Argentina, there had been only limited migration from those European countries.[12] However, his emphasis on the necessary association of the names *Iberoamérica*, *Hispanoamérica*, and *América española* (Spanish America) with "feeling identified with the vital atmosphere of Spain ['sentirse identificados con la atmósfera vital de España']" (66) reminds one of the colonialist connotations frequently present with these terms. For de Torre, the true justification for seeing Madrid as the cultural center of Spanish America was the cultural continuity between the two Hispanophone regions. More problematically, this pan-Hispanic embrace was seen as "exalting and lifting its [Spanish America's] best expressions ['exalta y potencia en sus mejores expresiones']" rather than as leading to the aping of foreign cultures (66). De Torre implicitly establishes a qualitative hierarchy in which cultural production and expression that derive from Spain are seen as superior to those that exhibit non-Hispanic influences, be they "foreign" or "autochthonous." The acceptance of Peninsular hegemony, that is the reestablishment of the colonial cultural space, was, according to de Torre, a bulwark against new forms of cultural imperialism originating in France and Italy.

De Torre's article falls apart in its contradictions. It claims community and equality in the name of hierarchy and the reestablishment of colonial space. Even Ortega y Gasset's version—which is free of the explicit colonialism of de Torre's—is problematic: Why should Lisbon and Barcelona—one a Portuguese, the other a Catalonian speaking city—be incorporated into the Hispanophone cultural space?

SPANISH AMERICA IN THE 1920S

However, de Torre's article is, to a great degree, anachronistic, attempting to recover symbolically what was in reality in the process of being lost. Although the Peninsular publishing industry was still hegemonic in the region, and would remain so until the civil war, Spanish literature had lost much of its cultural prestige.[13] As we have seen, beginning with Darío and modernismo, if not earlier, the substitution of Paris for Madrid as the intellectual meridian of Spanish America had begun. It is true that during the late nineteenth century and early twentieth century, as a consequence of the Spanish American war and the colonial appropriation of Puerto Rico and Cuba by the United States, there was an increase in sympathy toward Spain and frequently claims to a pan-Hispanic identity. However, as Halperín Donghi points out, this was a reaction of "the traditional elites ['elites tradicionales']," but not that of the masses or the majority of the intelligentsia (296). By 1927, the cultural centrality of Paris for the region was a fait accompli. Moreover, as de Torre points out, other cultural centers such as Italy and the United States had arisen.

However, this decline of Spanish influence was a consequence not only of the evolution in cultural preference but also of the economic changes that had taken place in Spanish America from its independence on and that had accelerated during the first quarter of the twentieth century. At the dawn of Spanish American independence, England had supplanted Spain as a central commercial power exercising over the region's economy much greater influence than France ever did over its culture. However, during the first three decades of the twentieth century, the countries of the region progressively fell under the economic tutelage of the United States. This process of the breakdown of British hegemony accelerated notably after the opening of the Panama Canal in 1914 and the simultaneous difficulties created for Atlantic commerce by the First World War (Klarén 228). An example of the growing economic influence of the United States in Spanish America can be found in the growing percentages of U.S. investment in relationship to the total investment in the case of Peru. There it was "10 percent in 1900, rose to 40 percent in 1914, 69 percent in 1919 and to a high-water mark of 74 percent in 1924" (Klarén 243).

Without a significant economic presence in the region and without a vigorous literary culture, at least from the perspective of many in Spanish America, Spain's cultural influence had diminished, even if as the center of book production it still remained an important cultural mediator. Moreover, given that much of the region's intelligentsia was fluent in French and, to a lesser degree, in English, they were able to tap directly into the cultural innovations taking place in other countries from Europe and North America. The influence from other European countries was helped by the fact that, as de Torre himself acknowledged, "the Spanish book in most of South America cannot compete in price with the French and Italian book" (67). Moreover, de Torre was forced to admit that, despite his belief in the need to create a true Hispanophone cultural and economic space, there was little interest in Spain for the literature of the region: "Reciprocity does not exist . . . it's not possible, except by accident, to find in Spanish bookstores books and magazines from Spanish America" (67).[14] While de Torre uses these arguments—the rise of a market for books from other European countries and the lack of Peninsular interest in Spanish America—to criticize earlier "conservative" versions of hispanoamericanismo, he seems unaware that these can with equal ease be marshaled against his proposal.

Moreover, the case can be made that French influence in culture was more than the substitution of a natural center of influence for an unnatural one, as de Torre argues. As we have seen, by looking to France, Latin American writers are exhibiting a desire to be included in the world literary space, where Paris "was the center of the system of literary time" and the "Greenwich Meridian of literature" (Casanova, *World Republic of Letters* 89, 82). Thus according to Casanova:

> The only way for an Irishman around 1900 (such as James Joyce) or for an American around 1930 (such as William Faulkner) to reject the literary norms of London, to challenge its condemnation or its indifference; the only way for a Nicaraguan around 1890 (such as Rubén Darío) to turn away from Spanish academic literary practice ... was to turn toward Paris. (95)

But this turn toward Paris does not, despite Casanova's claim otherwise, guarantee an egalitarian inclusion in the world republic of letters. As we have seen, unlike Joyce or Faulkner, Darío occupies an ambiguous place in what could be called the international canon. This difference in status is reflective of the different positions accorded to Spanish- and English-language writers within this world literary space. As Walter Mignolo has acutely noted, with Portuguese and Italian, Spanish and, by implication, its literature have been racialized as inferior to English and French (17).

Without denying the existing cultural connections exemplified by *La Gaceta* and *Revista de Occidente*—as widely read journals, as venues interested in publishing writers and intellectuals from the region, and even as literary forums in which authors from the Hispanophone area could establish connections with the newest literary and cultural trends—by the 1920s, Spanish American literatures and cultures were far from exclusively dependent on Peninsular mediations for access to cultural developments in the main European countries and North America. As we have seen, major works, such as the Peruvian César Vallejo's avant-garde poetry collection *Trilce,* were being written and published in Latin America. The time lag that characterized the reception of Romanticism in the region, a measurable manifestation of the second-degree relation that Spanish America had with the international republic of letters, has been replaced by a near simultaneity. In my opinion, the rapid development of the *vanguardia*—the Spanish American avant-garde poetic movement—is an example of the region's (nearly) unmediated, though not necessarily equal, incorporation into the world literary space. In the case of Vallejo, the significance of *Trilce* is magnified when one considers that it was written in Trujillo, a relatively small city to the north of Peru, rather than in Lima, the capital of the country. Literary innovation had become possible even in the edges of the cultural periphery.

Another example of the near synchronicity of the region's literature with the literature of Europe is found in the active participation of Spanish American writers in the most radical avant-garde movements of the time. The Chilean poet Vicente Huidobro, called "the initiator of modern poetry in our language ['el iniciador de la poesía moderna en nuestra lengua']" by Octavio Paz, is a case in point (*Convergencias* 49). Fluent in both Spanish and French, he was a collaborator of Pierre Reverdy's journal *Nord-Sud* (1917), Tristan Tzara's magazine *Dada* (1918), and other major publications of the French avant-garde.[15]

The internationalization of Latin America was not limited to the literary field or even to the economy. The 1920s mark the beginning of the incorporation of the region into the international world mass cultural markets that made use of the newly perfected communication media—film, music recordings, newspapers, magazines, and even radio. Film, especially Chaplin's; North American music and jazz, not only in its classic New Orleans and Chicago styles, but even more in its popularized if not bastardized Tin Pan Alley and sweet versions; and even advertisement become central cultural events that mark the region's societies and its intellectuals. Beatriz Sarlo writes about Buenos Aires in the 1920s.

> The new urban landscape, the modernization of the communication media, the impact of these processes on customs, are the frame and the point of resistance regarding which the answers produced by intellectuals are articulated. Within a few years, these must process, even in their own biography, changes that affect traditional relationships, manners of making and disseminating culture, styles of behavior, modalities of consecration, functioning of institutions. (*Una modernidad periférica* 26–27)[16]

And despite the uneven degree of modernization, Sarlo's comments are applicable to the region as a whole. If Borges and Roberto Arlt, two of Sarlo's principal examples, work in journalism in Buenos Aires, the largest and most modern Spanish American city, so do Mariátegui and Vallejo, in Lima and Trujillo, cities which in comparison can only be seen as provincial. In fact, it is this incorporation into these hierarchical world disseminative networks that makes the establishing of a cultural or intellectual meridian, by an act of will, particularly difficult. For Madrid to become the intellectual meridian of the Spanish-speaking world would imply a modification of the economic and creative structure of the world economic and cultural networks. Thus the still prevailing commercial hegemony of the Spanish book industry, a fact not addressed by de Torre, is in reality Madrid's strongest claim as a meridian.

Film, to take maybe the most important new narrative art form that came of age in the 1920s, became a major influence in the region's cultural production. Mariátegui, despite his serious health problems and his intense cultural and political activity, was a rabid film buff who dedicated one of his most important essays to Chaplin. Borges claimed Josef von Sternberg as an influence. Several major writers not only were cinephiles but also became film critics.[17] It is not an accident that in the independent but frequently parallel cultural environment of Brazil, the avant-garde poet Oswald de Andrade would state in the "Manifesto Antropófago" ("Anthropophagite Manifesto") in 1928 that "the American cinema will inform ['O cínema americano informará']" (3), thus granting the new artistic medium a paradigmatic position in the development of new cultural products. The influence of North American culture, especially film and other mass media, is but another element that complicates *La Gaceta*'s desire for a renewed Hispanophone cultural field centered in Madrid.

De Torre's proposal also contradicted the political and cultural ethos of the time. The 1920s are precisely a period in which an intense sense of regional identity was reborn as a result of three key historical events that helped free the imagination and desires of a whole generation. The first was the Mexican Revolution that seemed to promise the possibility of overcoming the cultural and, especially, the political and social stasis that had characterized Latin America until then. In fact, it would become for many in the region "the prototype for nationalistic revolutionary change in twentieth century Latin America" (Burns 196).

Moreover, Mexico, in addition to symbolizing the possibility of radical politics in the region, represented for many in Latin America and throughout the world a cultural revolution that combined artistic modernity with local traditions, topics, and political concerns. The prime example of this possibility was the muralist movement, which, for a time, became one of the central influences on artists in the Americas and beyond.[18] The impact of Mexico on many writers and artists at the time is made explicit by Carpentier, in his contribution to the "Intellectual Meridian" debate. Giving Diego Rivera as his principal example, Carpentier argues, "From the Rio Grande till the Magellan straits it's very difficult for a young artist to think seriously of making pure or dehumanized art ['Sobre el meridiano intelectual de Nuestra América']" (96).[19] But not only in Cuba is the impact of the Mexican Revolution felt. The young Argentine intellectuals of the twenties also see "Mexico as example ... as paradigm ['México como exemplo ... como paradigma']" (Vásquez, "Redes intelectuais" 61). To the influence of the Mexican Revolution must be added that of the Russian Revolution, which progressively began to shape the desire for change felt by many in the region.

The influence of Mexico and its revolution, as well as the revolution in Russia of which the news at the time was fuzzy, can be seen as helping inspire the student reform movement of 1918, which beginning in Cordova, Argentina, soon spread throughout the continent. As Halperín Donghi notes, "The student movement exhibits the double influence of the Mexican and the Russian Revolutions. These examples led to the demand that University statutes be modified diminishing the power of the professors (recruited most frequently from among the oligarchy) forcing them to share governance with the students (who came from less privileged social sectors, though only exceptionally from popular ones)" (298).[20] While not all of the new intellectuals went to college—curiously, although coming from different classes, both the proletarian Mariátegui and the somewhat impoverished patrician Borges were autodidacts—the radical, though heterogeneous, intellectual ferment brought about by the student reform helped create a sense of continental solidarity as students organized in local and regional associations. Needless to say, this intensification of a Spanish American and Latin American sense of identity made de Torre's proposal even more anachronistic.

SPANISH AMERICAN RESPONSES

Given the underlying social realities—French cultural influence and the development of North American mass cultural media, the Mexican and Russian Revolutions, the radicalization of the young Spanish American intelligentsia, a heightened sense of Spanish American identity, and so on—de Torre's proposal can be described, in Rodriguez Monegal's blunt word, as "grotesque" (*Jorge Luis Borges* 193). The absurdity of the debate is reflected in the aggressive and parodic response posted in *Martín Fierro,* titled "To a Meridian Found in a Pot ['A un meridiano encontrao en una fiambrera']" and signed by a pseudonymous Ortelli y Gasset, a name that echoes Ortega y Gasset, and which some claim was partly authored by Borges.[21] The article written in *lunfardo,* the Buenos Aires urban slang, ends with the request: "*Che* Meridian: move to a side, I'm gonna spit" (74).[22]

Under his own name, Borges provided a more reasoned response that lays out in the strongest possible words the sense of distance from Spain that many of the younger Latin American intellectuals felt in the 1920s. Despite the influence of de Torre and other Spanish writers on the Argentine avant-garde, Borges argues that the cultural links that had once existed had by now eroded and, therefore, any claim of commonality was moot.[23] In fact, for Borges it is not only a drift in culture but also the existence of a different political evolution in both Hispanophone areas that has made notions of hispanismo or of Madrid as intellectual meridian untenable. Thus for the Argentine writer, "Madrid does not understand us. A city whose orchestras cannot play a tango without losing its soul . . . a city whose Irigoyen [mildly progressive Argentine political leader and president] is Primo de Rivera [Spanish fascist] . . . how is it going to understand us?" ("Sobre el meridiano de una gaceta" 71).[24] If, in Borges's argumentation, Argentina and Spanish America are, as we have seen, marked by a sense of political progressiveness, Spain is described as being under the spell of political reaction.[25]

Mariátegui, who followed closely the discussion in *Martín Fierro*, developed Borges's arguments, as well as added some new and important points that in retrospect can be seen as central to a fuller understanding of the intellectual meridian question. In his article, "La batalla de *Martín Fierro*" ("The Battle of *Martín Fierro*"), Mariátegui notes that cultural independence is necessary for the region to continue "a vast cosmopolitan experiment that has helped us vindicate and revalue what is ours ['un vasto experimento cosmopolita que nos ha ayudado a reinvindicar y revalorar lo más nuestro']" (113). Then the Peruvian Marxist points out:

> The time is not propitious for Madrid to solicit recognition as the spiritual metropolis of Spanish America . . . For our developing peoples it doesn't even represent capitalism . . . Under the dictatorship of Primo de Rivera it is inconceivable that we could be invited to recognize Madrid as our supreme authority. The 'intellectual meridian of Spanish America' cannot be at the mercy of a reactionary dictatorship. In the city that aspires to coordinate and direct us intellectually one needs to find, if not a revolutionary spirit, at least a liberal tradition. (113)[26]

In addition to the obvious political differences between a liberal Spanish America and a fascistic Spain, Mariátegui notes the tension between capitalistic cultural markets and a presumed meridian, which, given the hegemony of antidemocratic and antimodern ideologies, is bound to suffer continuous political interference. Needless to say, the independence of market decisions is one of the requirements of capitalism and Mariátegui is aware that this is impossible under fascism.[27]

Mariátegui, however, acknowledges the still prominent role played by the Spanish book industry. In a March 1928 essay, which in its title betrays its links with his contribution to the polemic, "La batalla del libro," he notes that "when it comes to the stocking of books, the countries of South America are still Spanish colonies ['en lo que concierne a su abastecimiento de libros, los países de Sudamérica continúan siendo colonias españolas']" (118). In the earlier "La batalla de *Martín Fierro,*" the Peruvian critic identifies two Latin American cities that possessed the political and economic requirements needed to become a meridian: Mexico City and Buenos Aires. Despite its natural hegemony in the north, from a Peruvian perspective, Mexico is described as "closed and distant ['cerrado y distante']" (113). However, "Buenos Aires, more connected with the other centers in South America, combines more material conditions to become a metropolis. It is already a great literary market. An 'intellectual meridian,' to a great degree, is nothing else" (113).[28] The question is then, why is not Madrid, as the principal producer of books, the intellectual meridian?

Maybe the key to understand what seems to be a contradiction resides in comparing key passages in both texts—"La batalla de *Martín Fierro*" and "La batalla del libro." While in the former he describes the intellectual meridian as a "literary market"; in the latter, he notes that "from the point of view of booksellers, the writers of *La Gaceta Literaria*" were correct when they declared Madrid to be the literary meridian of Spanish America ("La batalla del libro" 118).[29] Thus Mariátegui establishes a clear difference between the production and selling of books and a literary market. The concept of the market is presented not only as defined by the buying and selling of books, but also as described as a location for cultural exchange. According to Mariátegui, while Madrid is hegemonic in the volume of books produced, it is not a location where literary products from all over the Spanish-speaking world arrive, or where cultural producers from the Peninsula and Latin America come together to exchange products and ideas.

In his comments, Mariátegui brings up one of the major subtexts of the debate: the possibility of Buenos Aires as an alternative site for the intellectual meridian. But Mariátegui is aware that despite "the editorial development of Argentina—which is consequence not only of its economic wealth but also of its cultural maturity ['este desarrollo editorial de la Argentina—que es consecuencia no sólo de su riqueza económica sino también de su madurez cultural']," the country is only "the one that has advanced the most towards its emancipation ['el que más ha avanzado hacia su emancipación']" (118, 120). In other words, Mariátegui sees in Buenos Aires the potential rather than the reality of a meridian.

Nevertheless, several of the participants in the debate will argue as if Argentina had already fully achieved this economic and cultural emancipation. Thus for the Uruguayan Ildefonso Pereda Valdés, "the intellectual meridian of America is not Madrid, but Buenos Aires ['El meridiano intelectual de América no es Madrid, es Buenos Aires']," while the Argentine Nicolás Olivari even declared the latter city, "the capital of South America ['capital de Sud América']" (Pereda Valdés 70; Olivari 71). Thus if Spanish writers were given to colonial nostalgia, Argentine and Southern Cone writers were frequently guilty of national or regional chauvinism.

It is clear that Mariátegui's support for regional as well as national cultural autonomy within the international networks of cultural modernity makes him receptive to the possibility of Buenos Aires becoming a meridian. According to the Peruvian Marxist, Buenos Aires would be connected to other countries in the region and, therefore, would incorporate voices from other South American centers. But few other Latin American intellectuals were sympathetic to the possibility of Buenos Aires becoming the hegemonic cultural center. For instance, Carpentier argued for the "annulment of any meridian ['anulación de todo meridiano']" rather than for the predominance of any Spanish American city (96). And an editorial from the Uruguayan literary journal *Cruz del Sur*, which clearly states "We do not want nor ought to recognize as intellectual meridian Madrid, Paris, Moscow, nor Hong Kong ['Nosotros no queremos ni debemos reconocer como meridiano intelectual ni a Madrid, ni a París, ni a Moscú, ni a Hong-Kong']," was humoristically titled "Montevideo, Intellectual Meridian of the World ['Montevideo, meridiano intelectual del mundo']" (77).

CONCLUSION

The case has been made that the true purpose of de Torre's article was the attempt to reclaim control over *ultraísmo* in Argentina, which, he felt, had drifted too far from the Peninsular movement (Alemany 27). While ultraísmo had originally been a Spanish poetic avant-garde school led by, among others, de Torre, it had been brought to Buenos Aires by Borges, who together with other Argentine avant-gardists had attempted to incorporate local topics and settings into their writings. According to Alemany, "Guillermo de Torre felt offended by the labor exerted and the new directions that literature on the other side of the Atlantic had taken" (26); and "in addition to a problem of latent nationalism in the editorial 'Madrid, Intellectual Meridian of Spanish America,' the paternity of the avant-garde is in play" (27).[30]

I believe it is possible to correct Alemany: De Torre's "hidden agenda" of vindicating his importance as the originator and arbiter of the Spanish language avant-garde—if this was his intention—and his explicit purpose to remind Spanish Americans about the need to see Madrid as the intellectual center of the Hispanophone world are perfectly compatible. In fact, the first is an instance of the second. In both cases, the hegemony of the Peninsular cultural world over that of Spanish America is proposed. Moreover, the absurdity of the debate is heightened by this possible "secret agenda." A cultural discussion about the nature of the Hispanic cultural world and the roles of the former metropolis and colonies within it is transformed into a family squabble. Future in-laws (de Torre and Borges) fight over cultural leadership under the cover of discussing cultural neocolonialism and anticolonialism.

Despite the obvious limitations of the "intellectual meridian debate," it is important in that it showed the degree to which the new generation of writers who had come of age in the 1920s saw themselves as fully incorporated into the world literary system free of any subordination to Peninsular culture. In fact, even writers of an earlier generation, such as Leopoldo Lugones, at the time the best-known Argentine poet, went out of their way to emphasize their autonomy from Spanish culture, while criticizing the rhetorical excesses of some of the articles published in *Martín Fierro* (145). If, on the one hand, the debate showed the way in which Spanish American writers were embarked on a quest to create truly postcolonial literatures responsive to their regional and local situations; on the other, with the exception of Mariátegui, the participants in the debate exhibit a certain naiveté regarding their participation within the world republic of letters. This unequal position of Latin America within the world literary system is something that is unfortunately not addressed by the majority of the discussants at the time, but which will become central to Borges's later essays, as well as to his literary praxis.

CHAPTER 4

JORGE LUIS BORGES AND (WESTERN) TRADITION

INTRODUCTION

Jorge Luis Borges has achieved a central position in the Western canon. Not only have his celebrated *ficciones* influenced writers as different as John Barth and Umberto Eco, but also have his stories and, to a lesser degree, his essays been central to the development of the critical theories of Michel Foucault and Harold Bloom, among others. It is not surprising that in the introduction to the English-language translation of *Ficciones*, a text written in 1962, when Borges was only beginning to be known outside Argentina, Anthony Kerrigan argues, "The work of Jorge Luis Borges is a species of international literary metaphor" (9). However, as the distinct, though not incompatible, works of Beatriz Sarlo and Edna Aizenberg have demonstrated, this "international metaphor" was also rooted in the specific Argentine and South American locations from which he wrote.

In this two-part chapter, I first analyze the manner in which Borges made use of Eliot's classic essay "Tradition and the Individual Talent." As John Guillory has argued, this essay "lies behind every subsequent reflection on tradition in twentieth-century criticism" (*Cultural Capital* 142–43). Therefore, an analysis of Borges's rewriting of "Tradition and the Individual Talent" becomes reflective of the Argentine writer's take on the Western cultural tradition and the appropriative logic that characterizes his innovative fictions.

The second part of the chapter turns to "El escritor argentino y la tradición" ("The Argentine Writer and Tradition"). This text is of particular importance not only for being, as the title indicates, a rewriting of Eliot's essay, but also because it is the clearest acknowledgment of the centrality of Borges's Argentine and South American location to his writing practice.

JORGE LUIS BORGES REWRITES T. S. ELIOT

Several of Jorge Luis Borges's celebrated short stories have been interpreted as sophisticated and frequently surprising rewritings of earlier European and Argentine canonical texts. Emir Rodríguez Monegal, for instance, convincingly argues that "'The Aleph' is a parodic reduction of the *Divine Comedy*" (*Jorge Luis Borges* 414), while Gene Bell-Villada maintains that "La lotería en Babilonia" ("The Lottery in Babylon") and "La bibloteca de Babel" ("The Library of Babel") "are conscious homages to the type of narrative crystallized by Kafka in such stories as 'The Great Wall of China' and 'Josephine the Singer, or the Mouse-Folk'" (115). We can, therefore, conclude with Efraín Kristal that Borges discovered "a way of writing that willfully adopts, transforms, and adapts the work of others" (*Invisible Work* xix).

But while Borges's practice of writing as rewriting has been analyzed with regard to his fiction, the intertextual transmutations to be found in his essays have not received the same kind of scrutiny. In this section, I shall study the manner in which Borges developed T. S. Eliot's argument about tradition into personal and innovative views on literature and literary history. In fact, Eliot's "Tradition and the Individual Talent" provided the basis from which the Argentine writer generated a theoretical justification for the "vampiristic" narrative practice found in much of his fiction.[1]

However, in making the case that Borges was influenced by Eliot, we cannot ignore the significant ideological differences in the way both authors relate to "tradition," regardless of how this term is defined. Eliot, as Cornel West reminds us, "posed a return to and revision of tradition as the only way of regaining European cultural order and political stability" (9). Eliot's conservative idealization of the earlier stages of European and British cultures was more of an ideological construction impelled by the cultural and political revolutions that shook Europe in 1917 than a valid representation of the historical record. By contrast, as an Argentine and Spanish American, Borges had no appealing cultural and political order to return to, even if his works frequently exhibited nostalgia for the urban underworld of his youth or for the heroic military deeds of his ancestors. Borges's appropriation of Eliot's critical argument reflects this central ideological difference between the two authors. Despite Eliot's call to order, Borges finds in "Tradition and the Individual Talent" an antihierarchical potential, justifying artistic innovations in Argentina, South America, and, by extension, the periphery—innovations that would ultimately undermine the authority of the European tradition so eloquently defended by the Anglo-American poet.

On Meridians and Dictators
Borges's rewriting of "Tradition and the Individual Talent," as, indeed, most of his major stories and essays, was marked by his involvement in two cultural events: the so-called "Polemic of the Intellectual Meridian of Spanish America," which took place in 1927, and his prolonged controversies with Peronist intellectuals during the late 1940s and early 1950s.[2] As we have seen, the first of these interventions in the cultural public sphere was motivated by Guillermo de Torre's article "Madrid, Intellectual Meridian of Spanish America." The article decried the influence of French literature on that of Spanish America, while claiming for Madrid the role of "intellectual meridian." In his contribution to the debate, Borges proposed that the claim of cultural links between Argentina and Spain was fallacious; but by arguing so, he contradicted his own personal history. The Argentine writer was first known for bringing *ultraísmo,* a Spanish variant of the avant-garde, to Buenos Aires. The mediatory role played by Spanish literature in Borges's own discovery of the international avant-garde undermined this purported separation between Spanish and Latin American literatures and cultures. However, it is also true that by 1927, France and, to a lesser degree, England and the United States had substituted Spain as literary centers. Moreover, the political evolution of Spain, culminating in the defeat of the Republic in 1936, and the establishment of the fascist dictatorship of Francisco Franco had broken the remaining links that existed between the literatures of Spain and Latin America. Of course, Borges had never been a *hispanista,* as proven in the moderate nationalism and regionalism reflected in his early poetry's descriptions of local neighborhoods and characters. Nevertheless, the debate crystallized an idea—the existence of an unbridgeable cultural distance between Argentina and Spain—that would be central to his rewriting of "Tradition and the Individual Talent."

Unlike the short-lived debate on the intellectual meridian, Borges's polemic with Peronism lasted for the years that Juan Perón was in power (1943–1955) and beyond. According to Rodríguez Monegal, Borges "sincerely believed Perón was a Nazi" (*Jorge Luis Borges* 391). Thus his public defiance of the Argentine dictator was part of his principled opposition to fascism and anti-Semitism. Borges paid a personal price for his anti-Peronism: He was demoted from librarian to poultry inspector and rather than inspecting chickens, he resigned. His experience with Peronism led to a profound skepticism regarding mass participation in politics, culminating in his belief that Latin America was not yet ready for democracy.[3] Borges's political evolution, which began with his endorsement of the (limited) middle-class populism of Hipólito Irigoyen in the 1920s, reached its lowest point—and there were many low points—in his support for the Southern Cone dictatorships of the 1970s. (He recanted his pro-dictatorship stance in 1980 as he became aware of the magnitude of the human rights violations of the Argentine military government.) Nevertheless, it is significant that Borges not only wrote his best stories but also brought to fruition his most characteristic ideas about literature during a period when he was in opposition to a regime that in its cultural policy was tolerant of fascism.

Another consequence of his opposition to Perón was his progressive abandonment of literary nationalism and his denial of a foundational or defining role to gauchesque poetry—a poetic genre that attempts to reproduce the experiences and the oral poetry of the gauchos—two stances common among Peronist intellectuals. His skepticism regarding the existence of a clearly defined or even definable Argentine literary tradition implied a substantial change from his early writings with their celebration of local settings, lifestyles, and histories exemplified in the title of his first poetry collection, *Fervor de Buenos Aires.*

Borges developed these two key ideas—the lack of relevance of Spanish heritage to the culture of Argentina and the nonexistence of a defined national tradition—in his essays "Kafka y sus precursores" ("Kafka and His Precursors") and "El escritor argentino y la tradición" ("The Argentine Writer and Tradition"), both written in 1951. Borges's belief in the absence of a tradition for Argentine letters—whether Hispanic or national—is the premise from which his rewriting of Eliot's "Tradition and the Individual Talent" proceeds. As we will see, the series of intellectual positions that led Borges to become, in Aizenberg's phrase, a "postcolonial precursor" began with his endorsement of the European tradition, a fact that gave rise to the frequent and mistaken characterization of Borges as an "extraterritorial," if not implicitly European, writer.

Eliot and Eternity
Eliot was the subject of a few marginal texts by Borges: reviews of Eliot's "Swinburne as a Poet" (1937) and F. O. Matthiesen's *The Achievement of T. S. Eliot* (1936); a biographical note, "T.S. Eliot," written for the popular magazine *Hogar* (1937); and brief entries on the poet in his *Introducción a la literatura inglesa* (1965) and in its companion *Introducción a la literatura norteamericana* (1967). Yet his first and most explicit tryst with the thought of the author of *The Waste Land* happened in a

short essay titled "La eternidad y T. S. Eliot," published in 1933. Despite its brevity and marginal position within the Borgesian canon, the essay can be seen as a blue print for one of his most influential critical texts, "Kafka and His Precursors." Indeed, "La eternidad y T. S. Eliot" functions as the crucial link between the ideas proposed by Eliot in "Tradition and the Individual Talent" and their transformation in Borges's best-known essays, "Kafka and His Precursors" and "The Argentine Writer and Tradition," in which acknowledgment of Eliot's influence is kept to a minimum: a bibliographic reference to Eliot's *Points of View,* a collection of essays including "Tradition and the Individual Talent," in the former, the word "tradition" in the title of the latter.

In "La eternidad y T. S. Eliot," Borges brings attention to what he considers a novel idea found in "Tradition and the Individual Talent": "an eternity . . . of aesthetic character ['una eternidad . . . de caracter estético']" (50). Borges's essay begins with a brief history of the notion of eternity, whose origin he traces back to the attempt by Church father Irenaeus in the second century to eliminate any whiff of hierarchy from the Christian trinity: "if the 'generation of the Son by the Father, the emission of the Spirit by the two . . . did not take place in time ['el Verbo es engendrado por el Padre, el Espíritu Santo es producido por el Padre y el Verbo . . . no aconteció en el tiempo']," chronology no longer determines preeminence (49). Similarly, Eliot's aesthetic eternity leads to the disappearance of hierarchical classifications originating in chronology in this case, among works of literature and art.[4]

Borges's privileging of "eternity" as Eliot's central intellectual contribution may appear somewhat surprising, since "Tradition and the Individual Talent" is primarily a defense of the Western literary tradition. Significantly, however, Eliot keeps the tradition itself abstract and undefined. With a few exceptions—Homer, Aeschylus, Dante, and Shakespeare—the authors and works that constitute this tradition are not identified, leading John Guillory to conclude: "Eliot's polemic is offered on behalf of this order, an order which looks rather like form without content, but in which content is signified by the heightened valuation of order itself—the idea of order" (*Cultural Capital* 144). Eliot saw this abstract order as a bulwark against the chaos that he felt threatened the republic of letters, and society at large, in that fateful year of 1917 when "Tradition and the Individual Talent" was first published. In spite of its abstractness, however, Eliot's concept of tradition still implies the existence of a history of concrete writers who read and learn from their predecessors. When Eliot emphasizes the perennial importance of the "existing monuments of Western Civilization" (526), thereby granting them a kind of eternity, he does not abolish chronology. On the contrary, as Jan Gorak has argued, Eliot's concern with tradition and its development implies an acute awareness of literature's "continuously unfolding narrative pattern," and its "narrative order" (79). Eliot's tradition can only be understood in reference to a "historical sense, which is a sense of the timeless and of the temporal" (526); Borges's "eternity," by contrast, annihilates history, denying any relevance to temporality. Thus Borges ignores Eliot's uneasy balancing of tradition as a contingent, evolving, and changing body of writings, and as an eternal canon of unimpeachable "monuments."

Eliot's main concern in "Tradition and the Individual Talent" was to theorize the possibility and limits of literary agency within the European literary tradition rather than to provide an innovative conceptualization of eternity. Since, as Eliot stipulated, the creation and reception of literary works are intrinsically linked to tradition, a writer must be aware of the basic characteristics of that tradition: "The poet must be very conscious of the main current and must be aware that the mind of Europe—is a mind which changes, and that this change is a development which abandons nothing *en route*" (526; emphasis in the original). Moreover, while maintaining that all new works are "judged by the standards of the past" (526), Eliot considers tradition, not a detriment to innovation, but the ground from which new work must spring, "a stimulus to creation rather than . . . a pedagogic list" (Gorak 78). Aware that his interpretation of Eliot's essay is not entirely faithful, Borges describes the notion of eternity he claims to have found in "Tradition and the Individual Talent" as a "thesis formulated by Eliot ['una tesis formulada por Eliot']" rather than as an exact summary of its key ideas (52).

Borges justifies this rather idiosyncratic interpretation of Eliot's key concept by quoting in Spanish two brief passages from "Tradition and the Individual Talent." The first of these quotations in "La eternidad y T. S. Eliot" is one of Borges's characteristically free translations since it conjoins sentences and phrases from separate paragraphs in Eliot's essay.[5] Through these loose appropriations, Borges created the Eliot he needed in order to make his own contributions to criticism. Given the importance of the first of these passages quoted in "La eternidad y T. S. Eliot," I shall compare Eliot's text with Borges's version, retranslated from the Spanish.

> The historical sense compels a man to write not merely with his own generation in his bones, but with a feeling that the whole of the literature of Europe from Homer and within it the whole of the literature of his own country has a simultaneous existence and composes a simultaneous order. This historical sense, which is a sense of the timeless as well as of

the temporal and of the timeless and of the temporal together, is what makes a writer traditional. And it is at the same time what makes a writer most acutely conscious of his place in time, of his own contemporaneity. (Eliot 525–26)

The historical sense compels a man to write not merely with his own generation in his *blood,* but with a feeling that the whole of the literature of Europe and within it the whole of the literature of his own country, has a simultaneous existence and composes a simultaneous order. *The appearance of a new work of art affects all those works of art that preceded it.* The order is complete before the new work arrives; for order to persist after the supervention of novelty, the whole existing order must be, if ever so slightly, altered. *The past is altered by the present* [. . .] the present is directed by the past. (Borges "La eternidad y T. S. Eliot 50)[6]

Borges's most significant intervention is his elimination of all references to literary praxis and to the role played by tradition as the source of literary production and the standard for judging new works. By means of these elisions and word changes, italicized in the retranslation, Borges presents in a more concise and direct manner ideas that in Eliot's essay are subordinated to his notion of tradition. In addition, according to Borges's essay, the truly innovative aspect of Eliot's aesthetic eternity is not that the "present is directed by the past," but its "corollary—the influence of the present on the past ['corolario—la influencia del presente en el pasado']," which Borges argues is of "literal veracity, even if it seems a relativist prank ['es de una verdad literal aunque parece una travesura relativista']" (52). While Eliot stipulates a reciprocal relation between innovation and the ideal order of tradition, between present and past, Borges uses the notion of aesthetic eternity that he "discovered" in Eliot as a circuitous way of freeing himself from conventional hierarchical orderings that situate the past over the present. Thus his interpretation of Eliot's essay singles out ideas that acknowledge the possibility of a Latin American writer making substantial contributions to the Western literary tradition.

Kafka and Chaos
Borges developed the idea he identified in "La eternidad y T. S. Eliot" as Eliot's main critical contribution in his 1951 essay "Kafka and His Precursors," in which he admits regarding his changing interpretation of the Czech author's writings: "I thought, at first, that he [Kafka] was as unique as the phoenix of rhetorical praise; after spending a little time with him, I believed I could recognize his voice, or his habits, in the texts of diverse literatures and periods" (145).[7] Among these he lists the writings of such heterogeneous authors as Zeno, Han Yu, Soren Kierkegaard, Robert Browning, Léon Bloy, and Lord Dunsany.

Any assumption that the authors mentioned by Borges were aware of Zeno's teaching and that most of them had been read by Kafka is immaterial for Borges's conceptualization of influence, which neither implies nor requires evidence of an author's direct engagement with an earlier writer. Thus Kafka's precursors do not constitute an actual chain of influences whereby authors learn from their predecessors. Borges writes, "The word 'precursor' is indispensable in the vocabulary of criticism, but one should attempt to purify it from any connotation of polemic or rivalry. The fact is that each writer creates his precursors. His work modifies our conception of the past, as it will modify the future" ("Kafka y sus precursores" 145).[8]

Of course, Borges's progressive erasure of Eliot's name from his own essays attests to an "anxiety of influence" that contradicts his "purified" definition of precursor and suggests instead his success at eliminating traces of Eliot's influence while appropriating the poet's key critical concept for developing an idea—the influence of the present on the past—that inaugurated a novel approach to literary history. Commenting on Browning's "Kafkaesque" poetry, Borges writes, "Robert Browning's 'Fears and Scruples' prophesizes the writings of Kafka, but our reading of Kafka noticeably refines and modifies our reading of the poem. Browning did not read it as we read it" (147–48).[9] It thus becomes possible to claim texts as belonging to a shared tradition without considering either direct literary influence or the conditions surrounding the creation and contemporary reception of a given text.

As the above passage suggests, the "Kafkaesque" tradition, while apparently rooted in textual features, is ultimately dependent on the reader's ability to perceive these shared characteristics. Only after "spending a little time" with Kafka, Borges notes, was he able to identify the Czech author's precursors; in other words, only after identifying Kafka's signature traits and innovations was Borges subsequently able to "discover" their presence in earlier texts. Kafka's innovations lead Borges to a "refined" reading capable of identifying hitherto ignored aspects of Browning's poem.

Borges develops this notion of the influence of literary innovation on the act of reading in his 1979 lecture "El cuento policial." There he argues that "the detective novel has created a special type of reader . . . because if Poe created the detective narrative, he then created the reader of detective fictions" (72).[10] This reader of detective fictions is capable of bringing a specific gaze to literary texts that permits the identification of characteristic traits of the detective tradition, to classify a text as belonging to this tradition, and subsequently to identify the presence of literary innovations. The influence of Kafka on Browning, or any of his other "precursors," then, is an effect of the way literary innovation modifies the way we read, enabling us to identify elements present in earlier texts that had not come to the attention of previous interpreters. Thus, Borges maintains that Kafka's innovative style created a new kind of reader who was able to identify Kafka's precursors.

While extending and applying the ideas he developed from his reading of "Tradition and the Individual Talent," Borges's redefinition of tradition in "Kafka and His Precursors" also implies an inversion of Eliot's core concept. Eliot had indeed argued that "the difference between the present and the past is that the conscious present is an awareness of the past in a way and to an extent which the past's awareness of itself cannot show" (526). Eliot's primary concern, however, was to establish a continuity between literary and artistic production of the present and that of the past, as writers "develop or procure the consciousness of the past," and incorporate this awareness into new works (527). Borges, by contrast, argues that current innovations, rather than developing that which already exists, lead to the discovery of contemporary difference in earlier texts, that is, within the past. This transforms Eliot's notion that "honest criticism and sensitive appreciation are directed not upon the poet but upon the poetry" (527) into a critical approach based on the act of reading. For Borges, innovative texts create new ways of reading, which in turn create and recreate the way we approach earlier texts, thereby shaping our construction of tradition.

Tradition and the Location of Writing

If in "Kafka and His Precursors," Borges examined how the "past is altered by the present," his other 1951 essay, "The Argentine Writer and Tradition," considers the way the "past directs the present," or more precisely the manner in which literary praxis relates or should relate to tradition. In a significant departure from the title of Eliot's classic essay, Borges inverts its key terms, thus modifying the hierarchy between them. Moreover, by substituting "Argentine Writer" for "individual talent," Borges designates a specific agent and location rather than the putatively universal, though implicitly Eurocentric, subject of Eliot's essay. In one of his rare acknowledgements in his criticism of a Latin American or, in his words, South American writerly location, Borges elaborates on both the identity and the location of the writer, referring to the situation of "Argentines, South Americans in general ['argentinos, los sudamericanos en general']" (161). Therefore, the title can be read as a statement of belonging to Western culture—the tradition—while at the same time staking a distinct location—Argentina and implicitly South America—within it.

Therefore, Borges's starting point is the acknowledgment that Argentina and South America are full-fledged participants in Western culture. Borges's stress on the participation of Argentina in Western culture is part of his then ongoing polemic with Juan Domingo Perón's government and its chauvinistic supporters. As we have seen, for Borges's Peronist critics, Argentina had already achieved cultural autonomy as evidenced by the existence of undeniably local topics, such as that of the gaucho.

One must note, however, that at the time, the notion of a South or Latin American national or regional culture separate from that of the West was held only by few, if any, of the region's major intellectuals. Even José Carlos Mariátegui, who was one of the promoters of indigenismo, that is, of a literature centered on the representation of Amerindian cultures, was convinced that, in his words:

> Peru, like the other peoples of America, revolves within the orbit of this [European] civilization, not only because its countries are independent in politics, but colonial in economics, tied to the car of British, American, or French capitalism, but our culture is European and our institutions are derived from those of Europe. ("La crisis mundial" 16)[11]

Borges's stress on the participation of Argentina and South America in European culture is, therefore, consistent with the opinions held by a majority of the region's intellectuals.

Borges's vision of Argentine culture avoids what Neil Larsen has called, in his reading of "The Argentine Writer and Tradition," the "fallacy of essentialism, that is, the false idea that the nation or its 'tradition,' etcetera, is a fixed, freestanding and pre-existing content or 'essence'" (*Determinations* 84). In fact, in his classic short story "El sur" ("The South"), originally published in 1953, Borges parodies constructions of nationality associated with specific cultural products, no matter how rooted these may be in local history. In this story, which describes the real or imagined death of Juan Dahlmann at the hand of a gaucho—"The South" can be interpreted in both manners—the narrator describes the protagonist's development of a sense of national identity: "A locket with the daguerreotype of an inexpressive and bearded man, an old sword, the joy and courage of certain songs, the habit of reciting the verses of the *Martín Fierro,* the passing of time, the lack of energy, and solitude promoted the development of a voluntary, though never ostentatious, *criollo* identity" (123).[12]

Borges here presents Dahlmann's Argentine identity as rooted in a haphazard collection of cultural artifacts, even in an aleatory set of emotions. Thus, unlike his Peronist critics, Borges does not see nationality as expressed in specific topics or tropes, in which a history of cultural mixture is believed to have crystallized. One can note in passing that "The South" seems to anticipate Benedict Anderson's notion of nationality as imagined, in part, on the basis of selected and isolated elements of the past. In "The Argentine Writer and Tradition," Borges's criticism of the "essentialist fallacy" is couched in an attack on the belief that an immutable "Argentineness" is necessarily expressed through "local color," that is, certain specific topics or figures that are seen as exclusively linked to Argentina. This criticism of "local color" is illustrated with a reference to Gibbon's mistaken remark that camels are not mentioned in the Quran.[13] Based on the English historian's assertion, Borges argues: "Mohammed as an Arab did no have to know that camels were especially Arab. For him they were part of reality. He did not have to single them out. On the other hand, the first thing a falsifier, a tourist, an Arab nationalist, would have done is to present camels, caravans of camels, on every page" (156).[14] His basic argument is, thus, against the identification of any environmental or cultural trait, whether "superficial" or not, as connotative of "Argentineness" or, for that matter, "Arabness." In fact, Borges designates the poetics of nationalism, with its emphatic lists of national topics, as a kind of exoticism. Only by assuming the gaze of the foreigner can a specific trait seem "different" from the "norm," and, therefore, define the national in relation to other countries and cultures. There is an obvious polemical thrust to this aspect of Borges's arguments. As I have mentioned, he was criticized by Peronist intellectuals for his supposed lack of nationalism. But in "The Argentine Writer and Tradition," by identifying the stress on regional topics with exoticism, Borges ends up describing his critics as "foreign" while implicitly presenting his own position as truly Argentine, even if he redefines what is meant by these two terms.

However, Borges's criticism of essentialism does not lead him to a celebration of a cosmopolitanism that denies the existence of regional or national difference. In a gesture that probably infuriated the often anti-Semitic Peronist nationalists, Borges presents Jewish culture—together with that of the Irish—as exemplary of the Argentine condition. For Borges, Jews "act within that [Western] culture and at the same time are not tied to it by special devotion ['actúan dentro de esa cultura y al mismo tiempo no se sienten atados a ella por una devoción especial']" (161). Thus Borges's emphasis on his country's participation in Western culture is rooted not in a belief in the perfect identity between an Argentine subject position and the position of Europeans or North Americans, but, paradoxically, in its difference. Borges writes about the role played by the Irish in English literature and culture: "It was enough that they felt Irish, different, in order to innovate in English culture. We Argentines, South Americans, are in an analogous situation; we can handle all European topics, handle them without superstition, with an irreverence that can have, and already has had fortunate consequences" (161).[15]

A sense of distance from the Western center lies at the core of Borges's definition of "Argentineness." But by participating in and contributing to Western culture, national or regional groups such as the Irish, Jews, Argentines, and South Americans show that their difference is balanced by a sense of belonging.[16] Thus Borges presents Argentines, South Americans, Jews, and Irish as being situated and as participating in Western culture in an alternative manner to that of individuals belonging to the "central" cultures. Rather than the perfect identity between the Argentine and a hypothetical "mainstream" Western subject position Borges is arguing for what could be called identification in difference. For Borges, national or communal identity is defined not by a list of cultural icons, not even by the development of a truly "independent" cultural tradition, but by the position in which the individual, through his or her community, is inserted into what could be called the Western cultural system. According to Borges's analysis, in the case of Argentines, South Americans, Irish, and Jews, whose cultures are by definition marginal to the larger national or regional cultures within which they act, the position is that of the periphery.

The Argentine Writer and Dependency
From the above description of "The Argentine Writer and Tradition," one can argue that Borges simultaneously predicts and corrects the later "leftwing" theory of dependency in vogue during the 1960s and 1970s. Despite the obvious fact that different fields are analyzed—literature and economics—both "The Argentine Writer and Tradition" and dependency theory see South America as part of a world system in which the experiences of the center and the periphery are differentiated. Dependency theory, however, argues that this international division leads to—in the words of one of its principal theorists, Theotonio dos Santos—"a situation in which the economy of a certain group of countries is conditioned by the development and expansion of another economy to which the former is submitted" (45). In other words, at its core, dependency theory implied the lack of agency of the periphery. For many theorists of dependency, the only manner in which this condition of subordination could be changed resided in a socialist revolution—a

paradoxical proposal in that the only manner of achieving agency is for the periphery to assume it in the most radical manner imaginable: the overthrowing of the world economic system and the replacement of its institutional structures. Borges, on the other hand, while not denying the importance or the strength of the central traditions, designates the periphery as the locus of cultural possibility.

But an additional point of contact between Borges and the later dependency theorists can be found in that his reflections on the Western tradition imply—even if they do not state—political and economic considerations as the ground on which he constructs his theorization of cultural agency. For instance, the relationship between Ireland and England was, as we all know, not limited to the cultural field. Ireland, despite its literary vibrancy, had been a British colony for centuries and at the time of the writing of "The Argentine Writer and Tradition" still belonged to the English sphere of economic influence.

Similar implicit political and economic arguments can be found in Borges's depreciation of the links between Spanish and South American cultures. According to Borges, there is little or no connection between Spain and Argentina or, for that matter, South America. The Western, but not Spanish, character of Argentine and South American cultures is illustrated, with some exaggeration, by Borges in the fact that:

> On many occasion I have loaned French and English works to people without any particular literary training, and those books were enjoyed immediately, without any effort. On the other hand, when I have suggested that my friends read Spanish books, I have found that these books were difficult for them to enjoy without special training. (158–59)[17]

Underlying Borges's emphasis on the distance between Spain and Argentina is the fact that Spain had, since the eighteenth century, become peripheral culturally and economically to the rest of Europe. And, as we have seen, England, France, and the United States had replaced Spain as the economic and even cultural centers of influence in the region. The weakness of the cultural links between contemporary Spain and South America can be seen as one of the consequences of the withering of the economic connections between the former metropolis and its colonies.[18]

The Advantage of the Margins
Based on the peculiar relationship he identifies between South America and what had been its colonial metropolis, Spain, Borges proposes a significant difference between Argentine and South American writers and those of the center: the capacity to see Western culture as a whole.

In "The Argentine Writer and Tradition," Borges makes the following statement: "I believe that our tradition is the whole of Western culture, and I also believe that we have a greater right to this tradition than that of the other inhabitants of other countries in the world" (160).[19] Implicit in this statement is Borges's belief that central authors, such as those of France or England, work within clearly defined national cultural and linguistic traditions that paradoxically limit their capacity to access Western culture as a whole. Likewise, given the strength of the specific "national" and linguistic tradition of the British metropolis, the field of innovation of Irish writers is described by Borges as limited to that of English culture. And one could add that the nature of the Jewish diaspora would, according to the logic of Borges's arguments, similarly lead Jewish writers to participate and innovate within specific European "national" cultures. In the case of Argentina and South America, the economic and cultural weakness of Spain made it possible for this field of innovation to be linked to the whole of Western culture.

Despite such departures, a superficial reading of the essay might give the impression that Borges's position is similar to Eliot's in "Tradition and the Individual Talent." After all,, Borges still stresses that "our tradition is the whole of 'Western culture.'" However, clear differences between Eliot and Borges emerge when we look at how each describes the manner in which a writer should relate to this Western tradition. While Eliot is concerned with defining the limits of individuality and artistic change, Borges embraces innovation. Borges views the European tradition as something that does not exact a writer's "continual surrender" of self (Eliot 527) but calls for the display of "irreverence"—by which he means both freedom and a kind of superiority. Furthermore, tradition, as Borges uses the term, includes all of European culture without the sense of hierarchical ordering present in "Tradition and the Individual Talent." Borges's "irreverence" toward tradition is richly exemplified in the use of detective and science fiction elements in his stories and his appropriation of authors high and low, such as Kafka, G. K. Chesterton, James Joyce, and Ellery Queen.

Departing even further from Eliot's understanding of tradition, Borges expands his earlier comments about the relationship between the Argentine writer and tradition toward the end of his essay: "We must believe the universe is our inheritance" (162).[20] Here Borges's antihierarchical, but still Eurocentric, proposal of employing Western subjects with irreverence is replaced by a defense of the Argentine writer's freedom to engage all topics regardless of their cultural provenance. Tradition has become the cultural inheritance bequeathed not only by Europeans but also by humanity as a whole. Therefore, for Borges, the Argentine and

South American position within the Western cultural system enables a horizontal and nonhierarchical view of this tradition.

One can, therefore, find in "The Argentine Writer and Tradition" a "theoretical" analogue to Borges's masterful short story "El aleph" ("The Aleph"). In this story, "the Aleph" is described as "the place where without confusion can be seen all places in the world from all angles ['el lugar donde están, sin confundirse, todos los lugares del orbe, vistos desde todos lo ángulos']" (70). In the story, by looking at the "Aleph," the homonymous character "Borges" is able to simultaneously view every single event, object, and individual in history. In a similar manner, the Argentine and South American writer, as described in Borges's essay, is able to freely view and then select elements from the totality, not only of Western but also of universal history and cultures.

Conclusion

More than Eliot's Eurocentric and rather abstract literary order, Borges's tradition is a "library, where ideally everything is preserved and where the system of preservation makes no distinction at all between good books and bad" (Guillory, "Canon" 240). The library is one of the central figures in Borges's writings.[21] Indeed, in the "Poema de los dones" ("Poem of the Gifts"), he claims, "I imagined paradise as a library" (146). Borges explored the notion of the "total library"—a library that includes every possible book—in his essay of the same name and, in nightmarish terms, in his story, "La biblioteca de Babel" ("The Library of Babel"). The library and its market analogue, the bookstore, appear in "Tlön, Uqbar, Orbis Tertius," "The South," and "El inmortal" ("The Immortal"), among other stories. Yet libraries are not the only symbols for total inclusion in Borges's writings. As we have seen, there is the Aleph; but also the encyclopedia in "Tlön"; in "El jardín de senderos que se bifurcan" ("The Garden of Forking Paths"), the apparently chaotic Chinese book that is finally decoded as "an incomplete, though not false, image of the universe ['una imagen incompleta, pero no falsa del universo']," which "includes all possibilities ['que abarca todas las posibilidades']" (127); and the mind of Funes, whose "perception and memory were infallible ['su percepción y su memoria eran infalibles']" in "Funes el memorioso" ("Funes, the Memorious") (117).

In his essays and stories, Borges has made thorough use of Western cultural elements without becoming an epigone to the European literary tradition. Instead, his manner of employing the Western tradition deconstructs the hierarchical relations between original and copy, master and epigone, Europe and the postcolonial peripheries. Borges's conceptualization of tradition as a library implies a denial of classifications based on influence, content, place of origin, language, or putative quality. Moreover, he hints at the possibility of a non-Eurocentric version of literary tradition that would include, but not be limited to, the literary monuments of Europe. His denial of chronology and his privileging of the act of reading in the constitution of tradition is designed to empower writers from apparently marginal or supposedly new countries. In this, as in his ability to combine European cultural elements with local Argentine and non-Western elements, Borges is indeed, as Aizenberg maintained, a "postcolonial precursor," who is "for postcolonial writers... a reference point beyond his general preeminence in a European-North American repertoire of culture" (*Books and Bombs in Buenos Aires* 109).[22]

As should be obvious, by undermining notions of originality, by emphasizing the creative possibilities present in the periphery, and by describing South America as a kind of margin of the margins, an Aleph-like location from which European, North American, and other cultures can be viewed, free from the hierarchical orderings present in established cultural traditions, and by proposing a literary practice that takes advantage of these regional characteristics, he clears the ground for a new valorization of the region's agency and, therefore, of its cultural productions. But what must also be kept in mind is that while Borges undermines hierarchical relations between "original" and "non original" works, he does not do so in order to create a new hierarchy in which the "copy" is now valorized over the original. On the contrary, what Borges does is to find the possibility of agency in what has generally been considered an abject position.

CHAPTER 5

CAETANO VELOSO: *TROPICAL TRUTH* AND TROPICAL QUESTIONS

INTRODUCTION: THE ISLAND BRAZIL

In 1996, Caetano Veloso, the Brazilian singer-songwriter, published his memoirs detailing his youth and his rise to fame as a leader of *tropicalismo,* the musical movement of the late 1960s and early 1970s.[1] The book, *Verdade Tropical* (*Tropical Truth*), begins with a brief discussion of the commemoration of the 500th anniversary of the so-called discovery of Veloso's country by the Portuguese. In his text, Veloso emphasizes the manner in which for Brazilians, unlike the other inhabitants of the Americas, it is not "enough to have been discovered together by Christopher Columbus in 1492" (3).[2] According to Veloso, Brazil is presented in schools and the country's media "as an independent continent, a huge island in the middle of the South Atlantic" discovered on its own by Pedro Cabral, the Portuguese explorer (3).[3]

The image of the "island of Brazil, ever floating, barely suspended above the real ground of America" is central to Veloso's narrative (9).[4] It permits him to establish, as he points out, "a parallel with the United States" (4), bypassing any reference to Brazil's Spanish-speaking neighbors.[5] In fact, in *Tropical Truth,* despite mentioning numerous Brazilian, North American, and British singers and songwriters, Veloso singles out only one Spanish American musician by name: the Peruvian composer of criollo music Isabel "Chabuca" Granda (192). This separation between the two regions is contradicted by Veloso's recordings, which include two albums principally dedicated to Spanish-language tunes, *Fina estampa* (1994) and *Fina estampa ao vivo* (1995); collaborations with Spanish

American singers and songwriters; covers of well-known Spanish-language songs; and original compositions influenced by Hispanic music. However, this belief in the lack of a direct cultural connection with Spanish America may lie behind Veloso's stress, presented in other texts, on the dramatic uniqueness of the Brazilian condition, what he calls "the loneliness of Brazil ['a solidão do Brasil']" ("Don't Look Black" 23).[6]

The belief in the cultural distance between Brazil and Spanish America signaled by Caetano Veloso is far from an idiosyncratic opinion of the *tropicalista* songwriter. Writing about the development of a regional identity among the criollo intelligentsia, Walter Mignolo reminds us that "Brazil was marginal to the idea of 'Latin' America" (159). Brazilian difference, when taken into account, is simply assimilated by Spanish American criollo intellectuals into a putative regional commonality. Exclusion and assimilation clearly mirror each other. In neither case is actual Brazilian cultural and historical specificity considered. The cultural separation between both regions of Latin America, implicit in Veloso's reflections, is thus verified by this disregard for Brazilian difference.

Nevertheless, the radical distance between the two regions proposed by Veloso is not an exact description of the true state of their musical and cultural relations. It is, as we have seen, a rhetorical device that permits Veloso to focus on what truly matters to him: the contrast between the Brazilian musical tradition and the popular music produced in the central countries, which, after all, defines modernity. In fact, as we know from Veloso's recordings, as well as from some of his other statements, Spanish American music has been of interest to him.[7] Moreover, Spanish American misperceptions of Brazil are examples of an incomplete and marred communication not absolute isolation. This imperfect communication, linked to limited commercial interaction between the regions, is bound to improve as collective economic projects, like the Southern Cone's Mercosur, become consolidated.

Despite the above, I cannot resist taking into account Brazilian culture and, more specifically, Veloso's music in this analysis of the literary and cultural spaces of Latin America. It is well known that there are significant historical and structural similarities between the regions. Brazil, like much of Spanish America, originated as a settler colony, dependent on an extractive economy and slave labor and characterized by significant racial and cultural admixture. Furthermore, contemporary Brazilian society, like that of Spanish America, has not been able to overcome the founding social inequality nor modify the central economic structures of colonial origin. One can add to these foundational points of contact, parallel political histories in which, for instance, Brazil, like Southern Cone countries, has during the last fifty years experienced populism, military dictatorships, and the neoliberal realignment of its economy and culture. Thus, despite possible pitfalls—partial knowledge, use of critical paradigms different from those generally used by Brazilian intellectuals, and so on—the analysis of Brazilian culture and, in particular Veloso, gives an additional dimension to this attempt to examine the relationship between Spanish American (now Latin American) cultural production and that of the Western centers. From a Spanish American perspective, the analysis of Brazilian culture permits a look at many of the questions faced by the region from a slightly different angle. It is like looking at a long-separated twin with many of the same physical features but with an independent life history.

THE SINGER AS INTELLECTUAL

An additional reason for my interest in Caetano Veloso originates in a characteristic of Brazilian music and, in particular, of the generation that came after the early 1960s bossa nova revolution: the intellectualization of its music. As Charles Perrone notes:

> Popular music gained new status and dignity among the Brazilian arts. Song came to be recognized as one of the nation's richest and most significant cultural manifestations. Composers and performers were involved in sociopolitical mobilization and actively participated in intellectual debate about the paths of the creative arts. (*Masters of Brazilian Song* ix)

It is tempting to see in this intellectualization, which, as Perrone argues, is linked to the lyric quality of the songs ("certain songwriters came to be considered . . . as the best young Brazilian poets" [ix]) a trait characteristic of the music of the times not only in that South American country but also throughout the world.[8] After all, John Lennon and, in particular, Bob Dylan have been recognized as important cultural figures. However, the careers of major Brazilian singer-songwriters, such as Chico Buarque, who is also a celebrated novelist, and Gilberto Gil, currently minister of culture in Luiz Inácio Lula da Silva's government, exhibit a more consistent commitment than their Anglophone counterparts to cultural debate and public action that includes, but is not limited to, popular music. And of all these musicians, Veloso best exemplifies the popular musician as a serious artist and public intellectual.

From the start of his career, Veloso was acknowledged by major cultural figures as an intellectual whose influence and relevance went beyond the field of MPB (*Musica Popular Brasileira*/Brazilian Popular Music). As early as 1968, Augusto de Campos, the Brazilian concrete poet, referred to Veloso as "gifted with an implacable critical lucidity ['dotado de uma implacável lucidez crítica']" (n.p.). What distinguishes Veloso from his singer-songwriter peers is the critical erudition shown in his writings, musical and others. For instance, while *Tropical Truth* is primarily a musical and biographical memoir, it also includes reflections on neoliberalism, Samuel Huntington's notion of the "clash of cultures," gay rights, and globalization, among other topics. Moreover, Veloso has been an active participant in the Brazilian public cultural scene since he came to fame in the 1960s. He has written articles for Brazilian journals and, beginning in the late 1990s, even occasionally the *New York Times;* given public lectures; published polemical liner notes and manifestos; and written forewords to books on varied topics.[9] Veloso's innovations in song are the result of an intensity of analysis unusual in the realm of popular art. In his musical and critical writings he has been particularly concerned with the problem of the relation between tradition and modernity; or, what in the case of any cultural production in the periphery would seem to be its synonym, the relation between the local and the foreign. In other words, Veloso openly addresses questions regarding hegemony and subalternity within what could be called the "world republic of commercial music."

THE UNIQUENESS OF BRAZILIAN MUSIC

Any analysis of Brazilian music must begin by taking into account the fact that Brazil, as Fredric Jameson has correctly pointed out, possesses a "unique status as an immense market of virtually continental dimensions" ("Globalization" 70). Unlike musicians from the countries that make up Spanish America—with the partial exceptions of Mexico and Argentina—those from Brazil have benefited from the existence of a discrete market large enough to permit at least the lucky few to make a living without needing to appeal to larger Latin American or international audiences. One of the consequences of this symbiotic relationship between national market and national industry is the fact that musical production has been responsive, to a greater degree than in other Latin American countries, to internal cultural, social, and economic developments. As Christopher Dunn and Charles Perrone point out, "Except for the United States and Japan, Brazil consumes a greater percentage of national music than any other country with a major music market" (30).[10] The economic solvency of the Brazilian music industry helps explain the existence of a continuous and identifiable national musical tradition throughout most of the twentieth century, as well as of the options opened for continuous experimentation to some of its representatives.

Caetano Veloso's career has benefited from the strength of the Brazilian music industry: he managed to become a star in Brazil and stay one for over twenty years before his slow ascendancy to international canonization took place.[11] Underlying Veloso's career—as well as giving plausibility to the notion of Brazil as a cultural island—is the existence of a solid and, at least in part, independent music industry.

But, at the economic level, this autonomy is, as I have intimated, relative. Foreign capital is a major factor in the Brazilian music industry. For instance, of the "top ten" songs for the period ending August 27, 2005, only one is not on an international label.[12] Moreover, given that Brazil has been progressively incorporated into the globalized mass media industry and market, foreign musical styles still provide producers and consumers with the benchmarks of modernity. Nevertheless, the existence of a relatively autonomous national market also means that local tastes are frequently attached to regional and national traditions. Thus Brazilian music, rather than developing autonomously or merely repeating central styles, has for decades responded to North American and, to a lesser degree, European musical styles by rejecting, imitating, assimilating, or modifying them.

It is possible to see in this fact, as Dunn argues, both an example and a geographical expansion of Paul Gilroy's notion of a "Black Atlantic" counterculture. From this perspective, the contact with the rhythm and blues, soul, disco, and rap produced by African Americans leads Brazilian music to become "the primary vehicle for the circulation of oppositional values" (Dunn 178). (But do these oppositional values extend to the relatively "white" North American and British rock that played such a central role in the development of tropicalismo?) In the unidirectional character of cultural influences, a clear instance of the limitations of Brazilian cultural autonomy is also visible.

The relationship between Brazilian music and the international pop music industry can be best described as one of partial dependency. As we will see, Frank Sinatra, the swinging pop of the 1950s, and the cool jazz of the same period, played a central role in the development of bossa nova. And tropicalismo was impacted in a similar manner by the rock of the 1960s. Despite occasional fads for Brazilian styles—Carmen Miranda, bossa nova, and more recently tropicalismo—there has not been a similar consistent influence of Brazilian music on the music of the United States.[13]

Thus the questions in Spanish American literature regarding the relationship of national, regional, and linguistic spaces with those of the hegemonic West are repeated for Brazilian music. But here the center is occupied by the heterogeneous and ever-evolving Anglophone mass popular music rather than by French or European literature. However, as we will see in chapter 6, in this regard Brazilian music may not be that different from much contemporary Spanish American or Brazilian literature.

Blame it on the Bossa Nova
It is tempting to classify tropicalismo—the Brazilian music movement of the late 1960s and early 1970s, as a local version of the rock of the era. After all, the foundational moment of tropicalismo, when its differences with earlier local musical styles were made public, is Caetano Veloso's performance of his "Alegría, Alegría" ("Happiness, Happiness") at the 1967 Record Music Festival. Backed by a visiting Argentine rock band, the Beat Boys, Veloso's incorporation of rock instrumentation and, to a degree, rhythms, costumes, and stage attitudes associated with the then-burgeoning mass youth culture was correctly seen as challenging the politically progressive and nationalist student audience, for whom the dissemination of North American music was synonymous with cultural imperialism.[14] Moreover, the fact that the Beat Boys were not even Brazilian and reproduced, in Veloso's words, "the typical sound of British neo-rock" seems to situate tropicalismo in an international youth rock culture (*Tropical Truth* 102).[15]

Despite the apparent alignment of the song and, therefore, tropicalismo, with international trends—evidenced in the name "universal sound," given by the tropicalistas themselves to the new musical style—Caetano Veloso and Gilberto Gil, and their companions also claimed to be following the "evolutionary line" of Brazilian music exemplified by the master bossa nova singer João Gilberto.[16] For Veloso, João Gilberto and his bossa nova represented a "radical process of cultural transformation, which led us to revaluate our tastes, our heritage and—even more important—our possibilities" (22).[17] In fact, in a joint interview with Gil given to Augusto de Campos in 1968, Veloso claimed that "bossa nova (João Gilberto) led me to compose and sing and to become interested in the modernization of Brazilian music" ("Entrevista a Augusto de Campos" n.p.).[18] Thus the repertoire of Veloso and Gil, both during and after their tropicalista period, included both "modern"—if we define their attempt at a "universal sound" as such—and more traditional Brazilian music, including bossa nova. In fact, Veloso and other tropicalistas exhibit a continued, though far from exclusive, loyalty to bossa nova. It is, therefore, not an accident that in 2000 a CD with Veloso's recording of classic bossa novas as well as his own was titled *A Bossa de Caetano*.

But Veloso, Gil, and their tropicalista comrades not only attempted to create music that is both Brazilian and universal, they also aimed at producing songs that simultaneously belonged to the "high" and "mass" poles of artistic production. In other words, the tropicalistas wished to create high art within what Veloso describes as "the befouled and healing guts of the global entertainment industry" (*Tropical Truth* 9).[19] If, on the one hand, this interest in "high" culture can be seen as continuing bossa nova—Antonio Carlos Jobim before becoming a bossa nova icon had composed classical music—on the other hand, tropicalismo exhibits an interest in literary and artistic movements that had, until then, rarely been within the purview of popular art, such as concrete poetry or atonal music. (However, there is little doubt that the dalliance of the Beatles in concrete music was a direct example for Veloso, Gil, and other tropicalistas.) It is thus not far-fetched to see in tropicalismo an early, but aesthetically realized, example of postmodernism; if we define the latter, in Jameson's words, as characterized by "the effacement . . . of the older (essentially high-modernist) frontier between high culture and so-called mass or commercial culture" ("Postmodernism" 189–90).

As Veloso's statements about Gilberto exemplify, the influence of bossa nova on the tropicalistas, as well as on other musicians who came of age in the Brazil of the 1960s, was enormous. This is because bossa nova had attempted to modernize Brazilian music by bringing it into contact with what seemed to its practitioners the most advanced innovations in the international popular music of the late 1950s, such as the recordings of Sinatra or Stan Kenton. In fact, for many, the "apparently strong influence of American jazz" on the music is central to any attempt at understanding or defining bossa nova (Mc Gowan and Pessanha 53). The importance attached by these Brazilian musicians to the "pop jazz" that still dominated the North American hit parade of the time is exemplified by Ruy Castro's imaginative listing of the influences on João Gilberto: "The natural enunciation of Orlando Silva and Sinatra. Dick Farney's velvet tone and style of breathing. The timbre of Frank Rosolino with Kenton's orchestra. The soft enunciation of the Page Cavanaugh trio, Joe Mooney, and Jonas Silva" (102).[20] In this list, even the Brazilian musicians are, to a greater or lesser extent, linked to North American musical styles. Jonas and Dick Farney, and even, to a degree, Silva, were local practitioners of North American pop at the time.[21]

Given that bossa nova did not limit itself to replicating Sinatra's swinging pop, but instead attempted to incorporate into a samba framework elements from North American popular music, it can be seen as an example of what the Uruguayan theorist Ángel Rama defines as transculturation. According to Rama, who took the concept from the writings of the Cuban anthropologist Fernando Ortiz and adapted it to the analysis of regional Latin American literature, transculturation means

> to take hold of the contributions of modernity, use them to revise regional cultural content, and use both regional and modern elements to compose a hybrid capable of transmitting the inheritance received. It will be a renewed inheritance, but one that can still identify with its past. (29)[22]

While Rama is interested in the manner in which regional authors integrate modern literary techniques and genres into their own cultural background, his ideas are applicable to bossa nova, even if now it is "national," rather than "provincial" or regional, culture that is supposedly being brought up to date.[23] João Gilberto's interpretative and rhythmic innovations, Tom Jobim's use of sophisticated classical and jazz harmonies in his music, and Vinicius de Moraes's modernist lyrics are all attempts at incorporating "modernity" in order not to replicate North American pop but, rather, to create a hybrid still identifiable as Brazilian.

Bossa nova's interest in the pop music of its time can be seen as an attempt at rescuing a heritage potentially in danger of being rendered obsolete by the inroads of international music. Bossa nova, therefore, presented to many younger musicians, such as Caetano Veloso, the possibility of producing a sound that would be simultaneously Brazilian and universal; thoroughly modern without breaking its links with local musical traditions. In fact, Veloso describes the achievement of Gilberto in terms that are fully compatible with the passage from Rama quoted above. For Veloso, samba is renewed and transmitted by Gilberto. For instance, contrasting Brazilian singer Maysa's earlier version of the bossa nova standard "Caminhos Cruzados" with João Gilberto's, he notes that:

> João's interpretation is more introspective than Maysa's, also markedly less dramatic . . . one can hear—in the mind's ear—the big *surdo* drum of the street samba, beating with a relaxed bounce from beginning to end. It is a lesson in how samba can be wholly present even in the most seemingly improvable of forms; by radicalizing the refinement, it finds a way of locating the black man's hand beating the leather of the first conga in samba's birthplace (and this in the context of a string arrangement by the German Klaus Ogerman). (25)[24]

In the first text he published after becoming a recording musician, the liner notes to his debut bossa nova recording *Domingo* (1967), made with Gal Costa, the soon-to-be-fellow tropicalista, Veloso notes: "Gal shares in the mysterious quality that is found in the great samba singers: the capacity to innovate, to do violence to contemporary taste, moving samba to the future, with the spontaneity of one who remembers old songs" (202).[25] Here, before the public unveiling of tropicalismo, Veloso makes explicit the concern with the relationship between modernity and tradition that would soon become central to his musical practice. Therefore, like Gal Costa and the mythic samba singer, Gilberto "moves samba to the future" with the "spontaneity of someone remembering old songs." In all of these cases—Gilberto, Gal, and the hypothetical samba singer—modernization and tradition are presented as compatible. Roberto Schwarz has noted about the role played by Gilberto in *Tropical Truth*:

> Veloso's theory is that João Gilberto aesthetically made explicit and modernized an evolutionary line that had been evolving from the rhythms of Bahia and Rio and that now, in their new João-Gilbertian form, came into circumstances in which it interacted with the best of contemporary popular music without debasement. ("Resolving Doubts" 179)

Veloso's comments on Gilberto and Gal, as well as Schwarz's description of Veloso's "theory," emphasize the linkage between cultural continuance, even revitalization, and modernization characteristic of Rama's version of transculturation. (Schwarz, however, does not refer to Rama.)

But bossa nova's transcultural modernization, like any process of modernization, is by definition time-bound. The obsolescence of the modern is accentuated by the fact that the dynamic center is located outside Brazil. Despite the brilliance of its main practitioners—Gilberto, Jobim, and de Moraes—bossa nova was, as we have seen, subsidiary to a specific period in international pop music: cool jazz and, especially, Sinatra and other post-swing singers and instrumentalists of the 1950s. In fact, the case can be made that bossa nova appealed to a pop-music sensibility that was on the wane by 1958, the time of João Gilberto's first landmark recordings. Already in 1954, Bill Haley and the Comets had enjoyed breakthrough commercial success with "Rock around the Clock." Elvis Presley, in turn, had become a superstar in 1956. And by the early sixties, especially after the explosion of the Beatles in 1963, the mainstream of the world pop market had already distanced itself from the musical styles that had nourished bossa nova. Despite its "Brazilianness," the international success of "The Girl from Ipanema" in 1964, like that of Louis Armstrong's "Hello Dolly" in the same year, or Sinatra's "Strangers in the Night" in 1966, can be interpreted as one of the last commercial gasps of the musical styles associated with an earlier generation.

Tropicalismo's interest in rock, particularly in the Beatles, Bob Dylan, Jimi Hendrix, and the Rolling Stones, can, therefore, be seen as an attempt at updating bossa nova; of moving the "evolutionary line" forward from the swing pop of Sinatra to the psychedelic rock and pop of the Beatles.[26] Given the change in the nature of pop music—from pop jazz to pop rock—by 1967, bossa nova could only be seen as an obsolete example of modernization. Moreover, it was one that had lost its local audience. As Castro notes, "young people were the biggest market. And the music they were now listening to was rock'n'roll" (Castro 321), even if in its Brazilian *Jovem Guarda* version.[27]

Implicit in the preceding discussion is that transculturation is associated not only with modernization but also with a reevaluation of the elements that make up regional or national culture. Thus Rama argues: "After self-reflective examination and the selection of its still valid elements, one attends to the rediscovery of aspects, that, while belonging to the traditional inheritance, had not been used previously in a systematic manner and whose expressive possibilities become evident from the modernizing perspective" (30).[28] The incorporation of folk instruments—such as the *berimbau*—and the reemphasis on regional and traditional styles—such as those associated with Afro-Brazilian religions—exemplify this aspect of transculturation. In bossa nova, the best example of this reevaluation of earlier musical styles is de Moraes's and Badem Powell's 1966 *Afro-sambas*. This recording, which includes the now classic "Canto de Ossanha," uses topics, rhythms, and instruments associated with Afro-Brazilian religion within a bossa nova musical framework. Another instance of this folk-tinged bossa nova is *Louvação* (1967) by Gilberto Gil, Veloso's closest collaborator.

Thus, paradoxically because of the passion of many of its creators for the international pop music of the time, bossa nova is the transcultural Brazilian musical genre par excellence. Moreover, it underlies Veloso's notion of an "evolutionary line" to which tropicalismo would supposedly belong. For Veloso, bossa nova is an example to be followed not in its specific musical traits but, rather, in its ability to process and incorporate international popular music within a Brazilian framework. As Veloso stated about tropicalismo's relation with bossa nova in an interview with the North American critic Christopher Dunn, "We wanted to be better disciples than those who were merely imitating it or perpetuating it" (121). Thus one can interpret Veloso's concept of an evolutionary line as an argument for an unending process of transculturation in which new trends in foreign pop are continuously incorporated into Brazilian music, which is somehow able to maintain a recognizable national and regional difference.

Because transculturation is, as we have seen, not limited to an outward glance toward new, modernizing trends, the tropicalistas not only looked "forward" to Jimi Hendrix or the Beatles, but also "back" to samba or *baião*. After all, "regional identity was an important dimension of the tropicalist project" (Dunn 47).[29] This preoccupation with recovering local musical traditions is frequently forgotten due to the emphasis placed on tropicalismo as a universal sound.

A clear example of tropicalismo as transculturation is Veloso's and Gil's "Bat Macumba," according to Dunn, "perhaps the most hybrid song in the entire tropicalist repertoire" (105). While "Bat Macumba" was composed by Gil and Veloso, it was sung by the former and is included in the key manifesto recording *Tropicália ou panis et circencis* (1968).[30] Critics have noted the manner in which the song fuses rock, Afro-Brazilian music, and, through the lyrics, concrete poetry and elements from Afro-Brazilian traditions and international mass culture.[31] Moreover, the lyrics are not only an example of concrete poetry—the transcription resembles a pair of wings—but are constructed out of one verse—"batemacumbaiêiê batemacumbaobá"—that, as Dunn points out, incorporates "semantic units pertaining to popular comics Batman Brazilian rock (iê-iê-iê), and Afro-Brazilian religion, sometimes referred to as *macumba* (bá, obá)" (Dunn 105).[32] (One need point out that the pronunciation of bat in Portuguese is "ba-teh.") Thus elements of highbrow and lowbrow, Brazilian and foreign, and art and mass provenance are present in both lyrics and music.

"Bat Macumba" brings Brazilian music up to date by incorporating elements and styles that had been outside the purview of bossa nova in high culture (concrete poetry) and mass culture (rock, Batman). By tapping into pre–bossa nova sounds and instrumentation—such as the *berimbau* and the musical styles associated with Afro-Brazilian religions—while using "Beatlesque" harmonies and a seamless combination of rock and Afro-Brazilian rhythms, the song exhibits a perfect homology between music and lyrics. Furthermore, the unusual cohesion of "Bat Macumba" as a transcultural product can be seen in the fact that its appropriation of concrete poetry, a style hegemonic in the São Paulo of the 1950s and 1960s, is directly linked to the song's reference to Batman, a foreign, modern, mass- (low-) culture product. As we have seen, the transcribed lyrics have the form of a pair of wings, possibly those of a bat. And this solidity of form in which any immediate distinction of the provenance of the elements fused—whether foreign or national, high or low cultural, modern or traditional—is eliminated can be seen as reflecting the vision of culture implicit in the concept and practice of transculturation. Thus one can describe transculturation, in words from the title of a book on Gilberto glowingly prefaced by Veloso, as dealing with "contradictions without conflicts" ("Bim Bom" 89).[33] By incorporating modernity and tradition, rock and baião or samba, concrete poetry and macumba, transculturation ultimately reconciles all the cultural tensions that cut across peripheric cultures.[34]

The Trouble with Transculturation
Transculturation has come under strong and valid criticism. As the late Antonio Cornejo Polar argues in his critical testament, the essay "Mestizaje e hibridez: el riezgo de las metáforas," ("Mestizaje and Hybridity: The Risk of Metaphors") transculturation has become "the principal emblem of the false harmony in which a process of multiple mixture would have concluded." He criticized the idea, which he felt was implicit in the concept, that the history of racial and cultural struggle had ended "harmonized in the pleasant and peaceful spaces ... of our America" (8).[35] For Neil Larsen transculturation proposes "a return of writing to its oral, cultural roots what may just as well be understood as its inversion—the return that marks the final phase of domination and expropriation" (*Modernism and Hegemony* 59). Thus transculturation becomes a theoretical expression of the desire held by many Latin Americans to deny the violence and injustice of the region's past and present. Transculturation would thus appear to suture all of Latin America's social and cultural wounds while obscuring and, according to Larsen, actually participating in class and racial violence.

Nevertheless, it is possible to defend transculturation—at least to a point. After all, Cornejo Polar and the other critics of Rama tend to forget that transculturation as presented in *Transculturación narrativa* is based on the existence of a split between a potentially popular regional culture and that of the capital, described as aligned with international literary and cultural styles. For Rama, writers such as the indigenista José María Arguedas, his principal example of transculturation, are of value because they permit the survival of the central traits of cultures threatened by an aggressive, homogenizing, and alienating process of modernization. While Cornejo Polar and, implicitly, Larsen associate transculturation with mestizaje, that is, the belief that racial and/or cultural mixture can create a homogeneous society, Rama's is ultimately a peculiar version. Unlike "mainstream" mestizaje, which has frequently served as a cover for elite domination, Rama's version would be one in which rural and indigenous cultural areas are privileged in the creation of nationality. Thus Misha Kokotovic notes: "To equate transculturation with mestizaje is to simplify and misrepresent Rama's nuanced theorization of Latin American narrative responses to modernization" (*The Colonial Divide* 11).

Transculturation is an ambiguous concept and cultural practice. Rather than erasing intra- and intercultural tensions, it conceptually reduces them to "contradictions without conflict," to again use the title of the book prefaced by Veloso. Transculturation imagines that, ultimately, the indigenous and the foreign, the local and the global, can be brought, at least temporarily, into some kind of equilibrium. One can, therefore, see transculturation as applicable not only to local cultural spaces but also to national and regional ones. In fact, because transculturation implies both modernization and the suture of all intractable intracultural contradictions and oppositions, it is possible to see in it the cultural logic of developmental capitalism, to paraphrase Jameson's well-known phrase. In the same manner and to the same degree as the developmental state—a source of resistance to external economic imperialism, but one that also internally promotes and guarantees capitalism—transculturation can be seen as both "progressive," in that it resists global homogenization, and as an illusion that hides the truth of class and other domination.

Transculturation and the Developmentalist State

Juscelino Kubitschek's government (1956–1961), in power during the rise of bossa nova, is a prime example of the developmentalist state. As Schwarz notes, the state and the policies it promoted "reorganized the space of imagination and critical thinking around an internal axis ['reorganizava o espaço da imaginação e do pensamento en torno de un eixo interno']" ("Fim de século" 156). This reorganization led to "a new social imaginary which for the first time refers to the nation as a whole, and that aspires, for the first time, to a certain internal consistency" (157).[36] The Brazilian governments of the late 1950s and early 1960s promoted the idea of a process of modernization that would lead to an integrated and, therefore, more just nation, in which class differences would be, if not eliminated, at least ameliorated. In fact, the correlation between national and popular interests had been at the core of the ideological framework that supported the Brazilian developmentalist state. For instance, in his *O nacionalismo na atualidade brasileira*—a text that can be seen as having an official imprimatur, having been published in 1958 by the Ministry of Education and Culture—Hélio Jaguaribe promotes the idea that "it is necessary to take conscience of Brazil's own interests in relation to other nations, and of the popular masses in relation to the internal sphere" (32).[37]

In an analogous manner, transcultural artistic styles like bossa nova created cultural products that were identifiable as being modern and national, and, equally important, reconciled the contradictory artistic styles into a coherent whole. Thus, by incorporating foreign forms and rejuvenating partially obsolete national traditions, transcultural music such as bossa nova or "Bat Macumba" expresses the imagined capacity of the national culture to fully assimilate modernity on its own terms. Underlying transculturation is a social imaginary that sees the regional and, often, the national culture, despite its being made up of diverse elements, ultimately as forming a clearly identifiable totality capable of modernization.

Despite this belief in the solidity of national or regional culture, there is an implicit ambiguity in transculturation regarding the direction of the process itself. As we have seen, Rama presents the Peruvian indigenista Arguedas as the paradigmatic example of a regional author appropriating modernity and using it to revitalize regional culture—in his case, the hybrid Quechua culture characteristic of the Peruvian Andes. However, Arguedas on occasion presented his literary practice in very different terms. In his stirring intellectual testament "No soy un aculturado" ("I Am Not an Acculturated Man"), included in his novel *El zorro de arriba y el zorro de abajo* (*The Fox from Up Above and the Fox from Down Below*), he claimed that his "sole ambition was to pour into the current of wisdom and art of criollo Peru that other stream of art and wisdom [of the Quechua people]" (256).[38] Thus, in this instance, Arguedas presents his literary practice as permitting the modernizing urban criollo culture to absorb Quechua culture, making regional culture compatible with modernity rather than incorporating modernity into traditional cultural frameworks, even if this assimilation is linked to a modification of the basic epistemological structures of criollo culture.

A similar ambiguity can be found in bossa nova as a transcultural product, though now expressed at the level of national and international rather than regional cultures. If bossa nova is a perfect example of the appropriation of certain pop music of the 1950s into a national musical tradition, it can also be seen as leading to the assimilation of Brazilian musical styles by foreign musicians. Dunn, for example, has described bossa nova as being "received abroad as a jazz-related idiom" (30). But as any one who's had the opportunity to listen to lounge versions of the bossa nova classics is fully aware, these North American appropriations de-emphasize the specifically Brazilian traits in the music.[39]

By incorporating foreign elements, transculturation also makes it possible for the modified national cultural product to become part of international modernity and can, therefore, be seen as contributing to the international assimilation and, arguably, disappearance of the national difference that it purportedly attempts to preserve. As Jean

Franco notes: "Singers like Caetano Veloso express their concern about the authenticity of regional music as it becomes appropriated by the global music industry and transformed into 'world music' while contributing precisely to this transformation" ("Globalization and the Crisis of the Popular" 213).[40]

The developmentalist state, which girded the social imaginary of transcultural practice and which in Brazil had been in power since Getúlio Vargas's second administration (beginning in 1951), was brought to an end in 1964 with the coup d'état that deposed João Goulart. If, as Dunn points out, "the bossa nova movement might be regarded as a cultural expression of what Thomas Skidmore calls 'the years of confidence'" of the Kubitschek government (30), tropicalismo developed in a very different intellectual and social climate. While, as Schwarz points out, the developmentalist illusion had not fully disappeared, "the democratizing dimension of the process ended ['a dimensão democratizante do processo chegava a seu fim']" ("Fim de século" 158). Given the centrality of the homology between nation and populism during the developmentalist period, one can add to Schwarz's analysis the obvious fact that this pluri-classist understanding of development became difficult to maintain after the coup. One could no longer imagine a unified nation after having experienced a coup that had its roots in the existence of sharp and irreconcilable class differences in the "internal sphere."

"Saudosismo" as Metasong

Caetano Veloso has referred to his musical relationship with João Gilberto and more generally with bossa nova not only in *Tropical Truth,* articles, and interviews, but also in song. As Augusto de Campos argued in 1971: "In truth, Veloso and his comrades have gone on to use progressively more a metalanguage, in other words, a critical language, based on collages, parodies and quotations" (n.p).[41] As an example of this musical metalanguage, de Campos singles out "Saudosismo," first recorded live by Veloso with the Tropicalista-influenced rock group Os Mutantes in 1968 in an EP titled *Caetano Veloso e os Mutantes ao vivo.* The best-known version of "Saudosismo," is Gal Costa's, released in 1969. The popularity of Gal's version is probably due not only to her superb singing but also to the by-then unusual format in which Veloso's and Os Mutantes version was released.

In "Saudosismo," a truly beautiful bossa nova melody, the poetic persona meditates about his and his lover's past and future while they listen to João Gilberto "spinning on the turntable endlessly."[42] The links with bossa nova are made clear in the first line, which is an exact repetition of the melody and lyric with which Jobim's classic bossa nova "Fotografia" begins: "I, you, we two." Moreover, in its chorus "Saudosismo" quotes the titles of the main tracks of the first four singles released by Gilberto: "A felicidade," "Lobo, bobo," "Desafinado," and "Chega de saudade."[43] "Saudosismo" is, therefore, a song that explicitly refers to and comments on the bossa nova of the late 1950s and early 1960s.[44]

There is a close relation between the title of the song and its content. As *A Portuguese-English Dictionary* indicates, the meaning of *saudosismo* is: "a longing for the return of former days, especially as under a given political regime." Despite this definition, the word is frequently used without any political connotation. Moreover, the same dictionary gives the root of the word saudosismo as *saudade*—"longing, yearning (for someone)." Scott Saul describes *saudade* as "the emotional baseline of Brazilian music, and indeed of the Luso Brazilian-lyric since the Middle Ages" (65). In fact, Veloso in *Tropical Truth* claims *saudade* as a "word . . . emblematic of our experience and our language" (146).[45] With only slight exaggeration, Saul defines the word *saudosismo* as "a kind of meta-*saudade*" and as the "discourse of longing" (Saul 66).

The *saudade* present in the song for bossa nova and its corresponding social, political, and cultural environment is implied by its references to Jobim's "Fotografia." The situation described in "Saudosismo" is similar to that of "Fotografia," but in Jobim's song the lovers describe their romantic and idyllic present, while, as we will see, in Veloso's, the lovers live in a degraded world. The fact that "Saudosismo" was composed and performed in 1968 is also relevant. In 1967 a coup within the coup had brought an even harder-line military group into power. Therefore it is not difficult to imagine that a longing for the days of political freedom and hope for progress was shared by Veloso and his audience as well as by contemporary listeners of the EP. "Fotografia" can be seen as representing the ideal and idealized romantic past that in "Saudosismo" is contrasted to the brutal and brutalizing reality of late 1960s Brazil.

In fact, there are political connotations to the lyrics in "Saudosismo." The second stanza refers to an ominous "Ash Wednesday," which, as we will see, seems to have marked a moment of change in the world described in the song. Veloso's reference to Ash Wednesday is of special significance given that it is a time of fasting and meditation on the fragility of human life immediately after Carnival, the Brazilian celebration par excellence. It is tempting to see in Veloso's lyrics an implicit identification of the pre-dictatorship days, those not only of the romantic bossa nova but also of political populism and developmentalism, with Carnival, a time of joy, freedom, and free expression. In contrast, Veloso links Ash Wednesday with the darker, repressive society created by the military regime. Furthermore, the reference to a day of reflection that is followed forty days later by Easter seems to imply the promise of a resurrection, which could be understood as a return to freedom.

However, the song should be interpreted as referring primarily to the cultural politics of the time, not the military dictatorship, although this regime is clearly present as the context within which the cultural politics are set. In fact, the lovers find solace, a moment of respite from an ashen world, not only in their intimacy but also in the music of Gilberto. Veloso's description of the basic situation in the lyrics—"I, You, João/ spinning on the turntable endlessly"—seems to present the music of Gilberto with its nonending rotation as an atemporal achievement, beyond contamination by the degraded reality outside the lovers' haven. More than a song about politics, it is a song about the power of music and art to resist politics. What type of music is listened to, written, and performed is, therefore, of enormous cultural and even political importance.

Veloso's song is both a remembrance of the early bossa nova and an aggressive meditation on how this music is to be developed in the contemporary world of Ash Wednesday. "Saudosismo" begins with the following verses:

> I, you, we two
> We already have a past, my love
> A packed guitar
> That flower
> And other little things

The song insinuates a prelapsarian, pre–Ash Wednesday João Gilbertoan and Jobimian past in which music and life were beautiful. (Not only does the first verse refer to "Fotografia" but also the mention of "love" and "flower" are direct references to the lyrics of Jobim's "Meditação.") Curiously, this beauty is linked to dissonance. The song continues by referring to "the dissonant world we tried to invent," followed by the repetition of the title of the Gilberto hit, "A felicidade" ("Happiness"), composed by Jobim and de Moraes for their play *Orfeu da conceicão*. The emphasis on dissonance rather than on bland and perfect harmony as characteristic of this edenic past recalls the notion of "contradictions without conflict." However, as mentioned above, this happy reminiscence is interrupted in the lyrics by the irruption of "Ash Wednesday."

What is peculiar is that the mention of "Ash Wednesday" is not followed directly by a reference to political and social destruction—although the lyrics refer later to "bossa, cesspool, our great pain." Instead, it is followed by a comment on the post–bossa nova produced in the 1960s and against which tropicalismo rose: "And the dissonant notes were integrated into the sound of the imbeciles." The imbeciles, that is, the politically committed bossa nova musicians, popular among students and intelligentsia, are described as appropriating, even debasing, the edenic legacy of Gilberto. If the chorus to the first stanza repeats "A felicidade" ("The happiness"), the title of another Gilberto standard, "Lobo, bobo" ("Foolish wolf"), which can be taken as a description of tropicalismo's rival musicians, serves as the conclusion to this section of the song. As de Campos noted: "['Saudosismo'] is a declaration of love and humor for João Gilberto and a criticism of institutionalized bossa nova" (n.p.).[46]

One cannot help but be surprised by the fact that Veloso's attacks are directed against his former—and future—musical comrades rather than against the dictatorship or its supporters. Schwarz's comment about Veloso's criticisms of other Brazilian musicians in *Tropical Truth* is relevant to "Saudosismo": "Relying on quarrels and hurling scorn, which in the end were more a part of show business than the class struggle, Veloso rails against the left as if it, which was being persecuted, was or had been in power" ("Resolving Doubts" 179). There is an element of displacement in Veloso's words. After all, unable due to the rigid censorship to criticize the true enemy, the tropicalistas directed their attacks to the post–bossa nova musicians. The animosity was mutual, and for some of the major singers and songwriters of what was then the mainstream of MPB, tropicalismo's embrace of international pop and rock was seen as anathema since it seemed to imply a capitulation to foreign culture parallel to the regime's close links with the U.S. government.[47]

For Veloso, the importance of musical production resided in the presence of what he regarded as the key inheritance of bossa nova: dissonance. Unlike the "imbeciles," who were content with merely incorporating the by-then conventional "dissonances" of bossa nova, Veloso describes dissonance as an ongoing and ever expanding developmental musical practice: "Ah! How good it was / but no more nostalgia (*chega de saudade*) / the reality is that / with João we learned / for ever / to be out of tune (*desafinados*)." Instead of being linked to bossa nova's specific melodic, rhythmic, or harmonic patterns, Gilberto is presented as the creator of a new way of making music and even of being. Rather than proposing a return to the past—whether in imagination or actuality—Veloso, in the words of de Campos, "reaffirms the permanent revolution of his art ['reafirma a revolução permanente de sua arte']" (n.p.). Veloso proposes the continuation and development of the dissonant project he identifies with Gilberto within and beyond the debased world of Ash Wednesday.

As noted above, the first recording of this song presents Veloso backed by Os Mutantes. In fact, the performance intelligently parallels the lyrics. Sung by Veloso in his characteristically restrained Gilberto-derived style, "Saudosismo" begins with a quiet pop-bossa backing by Os Mutantes that very slowly becomes dissonant—an acoustic guitar plays "wrong" chords in a slightly arrhythmic manner beginning in the second verse. Near the end of the performance, as he begins to sing the final chorus—"chega de saudade" ("no more nostalgia"), significantly, the title of Veloso's favorite Gilberto recording[48]—the guitarist Sérgio Dias plays an unusually intense and distorted rock guitar solo. In the recording, Gilberto's dissonance is transformed into the dissonance of rock. What Saul states about Gal Costa's version of the song is even more applicable to Veloso's and Os Mutantes's harder rocking version "that ended with a squealing acid-rock guitar riffs, which made for a harsh kiss-off to bossa nova" (68). Except that this is not a farewell to bossa nova. Rather, the song is presented as exemplifying the continuation of bossa nova under the musical, cultural, and social environment of Ash Wednesday. Despite the intense rock ending, the performance can be identified as a bossa nova that has been modified and radicalized by its incorporation of international musical elements.

The universal sound proclaimed by Caetano Veloso is here congruent with the rock/pop/folk of the international youth movement—and yet the performed song is still identifiable as Brazilian, and even as bossa nova. (In his 1986 and 1998 versions, Veloso sings "Saudosismo" as a "straight" bossa nova). It is tempting to read political connotations into the musical congruence between tropicalismo and the neorock of the youth moment. Unlike the "institutionalized bossa nova" of his rivals, linked with traditional nominally class-based left-wing politics, Veloso and the tropicalistas would therefore appear to be closer to the youth counterculture of the time and its alternative politics.[49]

TROPICALISMO AS HYBRIDITY

We have seen that the social context in which tropicalismo developed was radically different from that in which the classic Jobim and Gilberto collaboration took place. But the change that took place between 1959 and 1968 was not only political or even cultural. There were also significant modifications in production and marketing in the music industry, fueled principally by the exponential growth in television and in radio.[50] Tropicalismo is, therefore, a response to the development of a modern culture industry in Brazil, and to the concomitant establishment of a star system.

The modernization of the recording industry also led to a change in the formats in which musical products were delivered, as the international standard LP replaced the single. The foundational bossa nova songs, such as "Chega de saudade" or "Desafinado," were issued as "singles"—though later collected in LPs—but "Bat Macumba," on the other hand, is part of a manifesto LP, *Tropicália ou panis et circencis,* issued in 1967. However, the original release of "Saudosismo" as an EP is proof that the hegemony of the LP was not complete.

Tropicália ou panis et circencis is not characterized by the presence of a homogeneous hybrid musical style, as Gilberto's recordings were. (In the recordings made between 1958 and 1961, Gilberto showed himself capable of converting not only earlier Brazilian sambas and samba-canções—a slower variant of the samba—but even Tin Pan Alley novelty songs, like Mort Dixon's and Harry Wood's "Four Leafed Clover," into bossa novas.) Instead, *Tropicália ou panis et circencis* is a heterogeneous collection of songs including, among other styles, a Cuban rumba ("Tres caravelas"), a ballad ("Coração Materno"), and the "official hymm" of the Bonfim church of Bahia. *Tropicália ou panis et circencis* is, therefore, not the homogenous fusion of national and foreign musical strands characteristic of transculturation but, in words used to describe *Sgt. Pepper's Lonely Hearts Club Band,* the example followed by the tropicalistas, an "astonishingly eclectic grab bag of musical and lyrical approaches" (Stokes 370).[51]

It is, therefore, possible to see *Tropicália ou panis et circencis* as exemplifying not transculturation but, rather, hybridization as defined by the Argentinean sociologist Néstor García Canclini. His theorizing of hybridity challenges the homogeneous national/regional culture implied in transculturation. Thus, García Canclini claims to "conceive of Latin America as a complex articulation of traditions and modernities (diverse, unequal), a heterogenous continent formed by countries in each of which coexist multiple logics of development" (*Culturas híbridas* 23). In fact, García Canlini's hybridity can be characterized as juxtaposing elements, including those produced by earlier cultural fusions, belonging to different traditions.

A hybrid aesthetic, in this Canclinian sense, can also be found in "Saudosismo." As mentioned before, in Veloso's and Os Mutantes's version, the song begins as a kind of pop–bossa nova but concludes as acid rock. Despite the basic bossa nova tilt of the melody, "Saudosismo" presents melody, harmony, rhythm, and lyrics evolving together from bossa to rock. Arto Lindsay, a New York musician with roots in Brazil, defines tropicalismo in relation to the artistic practices characteristic of the Anglo-American pop of the 1960s:

> A lot of pop musicians in the U.S. and England were borrowing stuff from strange places in the 60's, but they were doing it the way musicians tend to—blending it in to make it theirs, and in that way sort of hiding it. In Tropicalia, you let the rough edges show, that was the point. The meaning was in the juxtaposition. The juxtaposition said something about the world. (qtd. in Marzorati, "Tropicália Agora" 235)

(Lindsay's description of 1960s Anglo-North American pop is also applicable to bossa nova, which blended Sinatra, jazz pop, and cool jazz with Brazilian samba.)

In *Tropical Truth,* Veloso expresses a vision of tropicalismo congruent with Lindsay's analysis. According to Veloso, "we preferred to utilize one or more sounds that were already recognizable from commercial music, so that the arrangements would be an independent element that would enhance the song, but also clash with it" (102).[52] "Saudosismo" is an example of this juxtapositional aesthetic. It is not accidental that Veloso, together with less obviously Canclinian artists such as Ruben Blades or Astor Piazolla, is singled out in *Culturas híbridas* (*Hybrid Cultures*) for "fusing" "cultivated and popular traditions ['tradiciones cultas y populares']" (14).[53]

The Persistence of a National Imaginary in Tropicalismo

Despite its variety of musical styles, *Tropicália ou panis et circencis* can still be read as implying a vision of Brazil. Like *Sgt. Pepper's Lonely Hearts Club Band, Tropicália ou panis et circencis* is a recording that can also be described as a concept album. As Stokes, despite his doubts of the success of the endeavor, writes about *Sgt. Pepper's:* "One has to remember—and one measure of the Beatles' achievement is that it is an effort to do so—that even in 1967, it was still almost inconceivable that a group could make an album that claimed, as an album . . . to be a work of art" (369).[54] Similar claims to artistic unity and value are implicit in the tropicalista LP.

Therefore, one can still argue that *Tropicália ou panis et circencis* implies a vision of the Brazilian musical tradition and of the country's culture, though one obviously different from that present in bossa nova. Tropicalismo, in its original manifesto recording, implicitly presents Brazilian culture as disaggregated; as heterogeneous; as motley; as the juxtaposition of multiple logics; and as made up of national, regional, and foreign elements and their mixtures. *Tropicália ou panis et circencis* connotes a Brazil that is resistant to the homogenization and totalization that found its political expression in the developmentalist state and its cultural representation in transculturation. In *Tropicália ou panis et circencis,* Brazilian culture is defined by rock and by bossa nova, by kitsch ballads and by Cuban rumba, by art music, and by macumba. And yet, paradoxically, by being presented as a whole by means of its framing Beatlesque borrowings—baroque trumpets, slightly dissonant guitars, strings, and so on—this stylistically heterogeneous collection of song is presented as describing a national Brazilian cultural space.

Moreover, by placing national cultural elements at the same level as international ones, a kind of flattening of cultural hierarchies takes place in *Tropicália ou panis et circencis.* Veloso's "universal sound" implies not only that rock or Cuban music is part of Brazilian culture, but also that Brazilian music is part of the world's culture and is just as important and valid as styles originating in North America or Europe. Thus *Tropicália ou panis et circencis* can be interpreted simultaneously as a nationalistic affirmation and as a Brazilian example of the international pop music of the 1960s. Tropicalismo implies a third way, or the desire for a third way, between the developmentalism of bossa nova and the wholesale and uncritical adoption of the foreign, one that reaffirms the national—seen not as unity but as diversity—and at the same time embraces foreign modernity, which it considers part of the national. But as "Batmacumba" illustrates, transculturation had become one possible artistic tactic of the tropicalistas.

The correlation between tropicalismo and the actual economic, cultural, and political structures of Brazil in 1968 can be verified by the ease with which its practices rapidly became the norm in the recordings produced even by some of tropicalismo's harshest enemies. The career of Elis Regina, generally considered Brazil's greatest singer, is an example of the manner in which a quasi-tropicalismo became the norm in the country's music industry. For instance, in her 1971 *Ela,* in addition to covering two bossa nova songs—including the classic Jobim and Dolores Duran "Estrada do Sol"—Regina sings songs by Veloso ("Cinema Olympia," "Os Argonautas"), by the *Jovem Guarda* star Roberto Carlos ("Mundo deserto"), and even a song in English by Lennon and McCartney ("Golden Slumbers"). The record includes a "soul ballad" written by Marcos and Paulo Valle in which, in the words of Nelson Motta, "Elis lets her vibrato loose, like a . . . black American woman singer" (230).[55]

The eclecticism of the tropicalista and tropicalista-influenced recordings is likely one of the reasons why Brazilian music managed to maintain a relatively firm grip on its national audience during a period when

Anglo–North American pop was rapidly increasing its hegemony in different international markets. Rather than being fully replaced by foreign musicians, tropicalismo, which incorporated the rock of the Rolling Stones and the Beatles, the soundtrack of the international youth culture, became associated with the local counterculture. In this manner, Veloso and the tropicalistas gave a new lease on life to Brazilian music. As Dunn points out: "Together with international countercultural materials, which circulated in the form of magazines, books, films, and sound recordings, *Tropicália,* was the primary point of reference for the Brazilian counterculture in the early 1970s" (170). Thanks to tropicalismo, the summer of love was also experienced in Portuguese.

It is possible, therefore, to see in tropicalismo a cultural reconversion as theorized by García Canclini: "cultural crossings . . . [that] include a radical restructuring of the links between the traditional and the modern, the popular and high culture, the local and the foreign" (*Culturas híbridas* 172).[56] However, in *Culturas híbridas* (*Hybrid Cultures*), cultural reconversion is a subaltern reaction to the implementation of the free market. This aspect of cultural reconversion is less clearly applicable to tropicalismo in that, as pop stars, Veloso and his colleagues are not subalterns but members of their country's cultural elite.

As Kokotovic points out, however, cultural reconversion is in principle a restructuring that accepts the free market as its unimpeachable starting point: "Cultural reconversion is . . . a manner of competing in the international capitalist economy, adapting cultural traditions, knowledge and practices to the implacable logic of the market, producing hybridity, but always from subordination" ("Hibridez y desigualdad" 297).[57] This interpretation of cultural reconversion describes accurately the ambiguous position of Brazil's music industry (both as music and as industry)—simultaneously independent and subordinate, creative and reactive; or, better said, Kokotovic's text captures the contradictions of practicing resistance by means of market commodities. Moreover, hybridity, as Kokotovic asserts (though referring to the case of "traditional cultures"), is precisely the way capitalism produces "profitable cultural differences ['diferencias culturales rentables']" (297). This creation of difference, that is, of hybrid musical products, is at the core of the music industry's practices not only in Brazil, Latin America, and the postcolonial periphery, but also in the United States and Europe.

CONCLUSION

In what is probably the most acute analysis of the political contradictions of Veloso's music, Liv Sovik points out that tropicalismo is characterized by the tension of being "an expression of high aesthetic purpose, on the one hand," and "a product for sale on the other" (97). We have already seen how Veloso, in a thoroughly realist gesture, saw his activity as a musician as set within the "the befouled and healing guts of the global entertainment industry" (*Tropical Truth* 9). In an interview from 1968, right before the tropicalista revolution, Veloso stated regarding the international pop music of his time: "It's a music for all classes and of no class, it's a vulgar music, it's a product made for general consumption" and "it's under the sign of merchandise that music exists" (Homem de Mello 199).[58] Despite the reference to the music's vulgarity, there is no doubt that Veloso accepts the market and the condition of music as merchandise as the precondition for his own musical production. In the interview, Veloso celebrates the music of the Rolling Stones and the Beatles as exhibiting a clear awareness of this fact (Homem de Mello 199).

This celebration of the market as the ultimate judge of musical products marks a point of contact between Veloso and neoliberalism. A corollary to the acceptance of the market in neoliberalism is the opening of borders to foreign goods in order to achieve the optimization of resources and production. The emphasis placed by Veloso on the importance of foreign music, on the need to listen to the Beatles and the Rolling Stones and to produce music that can compete successfully with the output of the cultural centers, echoes the neoliberal celebration of national competitiveness in the international market.

And yet there is in Veloso's cultural practice a refusal to become a mere mass producer. National and artistic difference is still valued. However, Veloso's emphasis on the uniqueness of his music is not incompatible with neoliberalism. Cultural reconversion is precisely a survival tactic in a market-centered world. In the case of music, Canclinian hybridity is one way in which Brazilian music managed to thrive despite globalization. Furthermore, quasi-tropicalista approaches to music making, even if devoid of the critical dimension characteristic of Veloso, have not only proven to be commercially successful, but have also permitted "peripheric" artists to enter the core music markets. Shakira and Ricky Martin are cases in point.

Instead of exemplifying resistance to a globalizing and homogenizing international pop music and culture, Veloso is, therefore, an early example of what García Canclini calls a "glocalizing" "'world entrepreneur' [who] articulates in his culture information, beliefs, and rituals deriving from the local, the national, and the international" (García Canclini, *Consumidores y ciudadanos* 86).[59] According to Canclini, the notion of the glocal, a word that combines global and local, was developed by

Japanese corporations to describe this alternative business strategy to the homogenizing saturation of international markets with mass-produced, one-size-fits-all cultural products (86). The case of MTV, a globally successful U.S. corporation, which in some of its international branches, such as MTV Latinoamérica and MTV Brasil, promotes both local and Anglo-American music as part of their market strategy, serves as a textbook example of glocalization.

Like transculturation and hybridity, glocalization can be interpreted as a strategy that permits the continuance of local culture, yet is frequently used by "foreign" capital to enter and conquer a market that may be resistant to an unmodified culturally neutral—or, more frequently, North American—product. In the case of Veloso, the embrace of the market and the conscious acceptance of his role as glocal cultural entrepreneur can be seen as an attempt to use globalization as a manner of not only preserving but also modernizing Brazilian musical traditions. But tropicalismo's glocal practices are also a significant contribution to the rise to hegemony of North American forms, such as rock or rap, within the Brazilian musical markets.

For Sovik, the story of tropicalismo is one of an emergent structure of feeling that slowly achieves dominance. Its trajectory is summarized in the fact that Veloso, who parodied Carmen Miranda and thus celebrated sexual ambiguity during the glory days of tropicalismo, now wears expensive suits and is a central establishment figure (97). A more dramatic story can, however, be penned: the rise to hegemony of tropicalismo can be summarized as going from imprisonment in 1968 to international canonization. In the case of Gilberto Gil, one could describe this narrative as going from prison to the Ministry of Culture. (In late 1968 Veloso and Gil were arrested. They lived in exile in London from 1969 to 1971.) However, I have argued that the cultural hegemony of tropicalismo in Brazil arrived much earlier, ironically, during Veloso's and Gil's exile in London from 1968 to 1971, when the music industry and establishment were forced to incorporate new musical styles in order to survive.

Veloso—and more generally tropicalismo—is thus riddled with paradoxes. Precisely by being a guardian of tradition—defined as an evolutionary line of Brazilian musicians—he has also been a major mediator of foreign musical styles. The paradox is magnified by taking into account that the "tropicalization" of Brazilian musical production in the late 1960s and early 1970s was an intelligent and creative response to the beginning of musical globalization. The adoption of a tropicalista approach to music permitted the continuance and the modernization of a specifically Brazilian musical tradition and cultural market. However, by embracing North American influence, it was also fully compatible with the economic and cultural politics of the military, and even more so of the post-dictatorial regimes. As befits his role as glocal entrepreneur, Veloso's cannibalistic embrace of Anglo–North American music permitted the development of hybrid musical forms responsive to a local social reality that included the progressive incorporation of Brazil into the world economic system.

The contradictions of Veloso are, ultimately, present in any attempt at local or national modernization in our neoliberal world.

CHAPTER 6

Reading, Publishing, and Writing Networks: The Hispanophone and Latin American Literary Spaces in the Twenty-First Century

The Liberal Pan-Hispanist Discourse

On July 14, 2006, Felipe, the crown prince of Spain, presided over the opening ceremony of the Beijing Center of the Instituto Cervantes. Although the institute's centers are best known for providing Spanish-language instruction, Prince Felipe described the newly opened institution as "a lighthouse that illuminates the path towards a fascinating, rich and enormous regions of the world, that is Ibero America, that, united by history, language and culture, is currently experiencing important developments in the field of politics and the economy" ("El principe" n.p.).[1] While the fact that the crown prince spoke for countries that are not politically dependent on Spain seems to disregard Spanish American political and cultural autonomy, it is perfectly compatible with the self-described mission of the Instituto Cervantes. According to its Web page, the Instituto Cervantes is "a public institution created in Spain in 1991 . . . for the diffusion of Spanish and Spanish American culture" (*cervantes.es* n.p.).[2] It is, therefore, not surprising that in the same opening ceremony, the director of the Instituto Cervantes, César Molina, claimed that the Beijing center would "serve as a bridge between three continents ['servir de puente entre tres continentes']" (n.p.), therefore, implicitly ascribing to the institute the representation not only of Spanish culture, but also that of Latin American culture.

This rhetorical incorporation of Spanish America has been supported by the valuable cultural activities promoted by the different branches of the Instituto Cervantes. For instance, the participation of the New York Center during the "2006 PEN World Voices: The New York Festival of Voices" exhibited this concern with Hispanophone literature and culture beyond that of the Iberian Peninsula. The two panels sponsored by the institute, "A Tribute to Juan Rulfo," and "Discovering Roberto Bolaño," dealt with two major Latin American novelists of the twentieth century—Mexican and Chilean, respectively. Among the participants were well-known writers like the Mexicans Carlos Monsiváis and Carmen Boullosa and the Argentinean Rodrigo Fresán. The promotion of two important twentieth-century Spanish American writers who have, at least until recently, been relatively ignored by North American readers, is fully consonant with the pan-Hispanic intent of the institute. In fact, with the exception of a conversation between the Chilean Antonio Skármeta and the Brazilian Paulo Lins, about the film adaptation of the latter's *City of God,* these were the only sessions out of thirty-two dealing with Latin American literature. (There were, however, a few other panels dealing with general topics in which Spanish American writers participated).[3]

Despite this interest in Spanish American culture, the institute's administrative structure is controlled by Spanish political and cultural figures. The king of Spain, Juan Carlos, is the nominal president of the Board of Trustees (*Patronato*) of the Instituto Cervantes, while the prime minister of Spain, at the time of writing, José Luis Rodríguez Zapatero, is its executive president.[4] Although there are seven positions designated "in representation of the letters and culture of Spanish America ['en representación de las letras y la cultura hispanoamericanas']," which currently include such well-known writers as the Peruvian Alfredo Bryce Echenique and the Mexican Ángeles Mastretta, these are relatively few compared to the large number of Spanish political and cultural figures among the trustees.[5] (As of August 2006, the total number of members of the board of trustees was forty-nine.) One can, however, add to this group the Spanish American recipients of the Miguel de Cervantes Prize, frequently considered the Nobel Prize of Spanish-language letters and given by the institute, who are automatically named to the board of trustees.⁶ However, the administrative council, which "approves the general plans of the institute ['aprueba los planes generales del Instituto']" is exclusively "made up by representatives of the Ministry of Foreign Affairs, Education, and Economy, as well as the Trustees ['integrado por representantes de los Ministerios de Asuntos Exteriores y de Cooperación, de Educación y Ciencia, de Cultura, de Economía y de Hacienda']" (n.p.). Given its administrative composition, it is not an exaggeration to see in the Instituto Cervantes a branch of the Spanish government and, in consequence, to see its policies as responding to the Spanish government's interests.

The Instituto Cervantes is not the only example of the concern with Spanish American culture exhibited by the Spanish government. In 1992, as part of the commemoration of the five hundred years of "Encuentro de dos mundos" ("Encounter of Two Worlds"), the supposedly politically correct name given, at the time, to the arrival of Columbus and the Spaniards to the Americas, the Casa de América was founded.⁷ (The founding of the Instituto Cervantes in 1991 is also part of this Columbine commemoration.) The Casa de América is described on its Web page as having as its objective "to promote a better knowledge between Ibero-America and Spain ['fomentar el conocimiento entre Iberoamérica y España']" and as aiming to "become a center promoting ideas and debates on economic, political, scientific, technological, and cultural topics of Ibero-America ['generar un foro de ideas y debates sobre aspectos económicos, políticos, científicos, tecnológicos y culturales de Iberoamérica']" (n. p.).⁸ The Casa's organization again shows it to be an unofficial organ of the Spanish government. According to its Web page, the Casa de las Américas "was born as a consortium between the Foreign Ministry, the Community of Madrid, and the City Government of Madrid" (n.p.).⁹ Unlike the Instituto Cervantes, however, no nominal Spanish American presence is included in the structure of the Casa. The board of trustees is also, not surprisingly, led by King Juan Carlos. The trustees and the directing council are comprised of national and local government officials together with representatives of the Spanish business sector. Despite the absence of Spanish American names, however, like those of the Instituto Cervantes, the activities promoted by the Casa are beyond reproach.

That the Casa, which, as I have pointed out, includes in its governing boards representatives of business conglomerates and the major Spanish publishing houses indicates the imbrication of cultural and economic concerns that characterizes the renewed Iberian interest in Latin America.¹⁰ Thus among the trustees one finds the CEOs of Grupo Santillana (which includes Editorial Alfaguara) and Grupo Planeta, the two prominent book publishing conglomerates in the Spanish-speaking world, together with the CEOs of Iberia Airlines and Telefónica.

The statements of Prince Felipe can thus be seen as representative not only of the cultural and political elites, but also of the economic leaders of Spain, even if the latter occasionally use blunter language. For instance, Juan Cruz, the principal editor of Alfaguara Global, the largest publishing house of Grupo Santillana, when asked by the German critic Burkhard Pohl about the commercialization of Spanish American authors in Spain, replied: "But they are Spanish, they write in Spanish ['Pero son españoles, escriben en español']" (Cruz 322). When pressed by Pohl about calling these authors "Spanish," Cruz replied: "We must eliminate the idea that one belongs to one place or the other. They belong to the Spanish language, that is my idea" (322).[11] Pohl describes these statements as representative of a "liberal pan-Hispanist discourse" developed by the Peninsula's political and cultural elites during the Columbine commemorations. According to Pohl, "this new pan-Hispanist discourse, adopted by both the left and the right, abandons the imperialist, ethnic, and religious traits found in the notion of *Hispanidad* of the Francoist ideology" ("¿Un nuevo *boom?* 275). Even if not "imperialist," this new discourse is still predicated on the centrality of Spain as "the mediator of Latin American interests regarding the European Union and the United States" (275).[12] The critic Gustavo Faverón has ironically commented on Prince Felipe's statements, quoted at the beginning of this chapter, and implicitly on the cultural and economic project that undergirds this pan-Hispanist discourse:

> Maybe Spain has a crazy plan, somewhere between directed globalization and an undercover invasion . . . a plan in which things like the Instituto Cervantes, the trips of Prince Felipe, and the . . . Real Academia [de la Lengua] Española, are the Niña, the Pinta, and the Santa María of an expansionism that bets on the idea that Latin Americans are truly prodigal children that one day will return to the fold. ("El faro y la reconquista" n.p.)[13]

The "liberal pan-Hispanist discourse" is, therefore, an explicit and conscious example of the manner in which culture and commerce frequently intersect.

Markets and Discourses

The rise of this "liberal pan-Hispanist discourse" brings to mind the "Intellectual Meridian Debate" of 1927 in which, as noted in chapter 3,

Spanish American writers, such as Jorge Luis Borges and Alejo Carpentier, among others, reacted angrily to the by-then anachronistic proposal that Madrid become the cultural center of Spanish America. (The proposal was anachronistic because, as we have seen, Madrid, despite experiencing a literary revival thanks to the avant-garde Generation of 1927, was no longer a major European cultural center and, equally important, was in the grip of Primo de Rivera's fascist dictatorship.) Like Cruz, Guillermo de Torre, who wrote "Madrid, meridiano intelectual de Hispanoamérica," the unsigned article that generated the debate about the "Intellectual Meridian," saw Spanish America's "intellectual area as a prolongation of that of Spain" (66). Like de Torre's proposal, the new "liberal pan-Hispanist discourse" combines nominal egalitarianism—"we are all Ibero-Americans" or even "we are all Spaniards"—and a de facto hierarchy in which Spain acts as both a mediator between Hispanophone culture and the cultures of the rest of the world as well as the arbiter of what is of value or what is worthy of publication and pan-Hispanic distribution.

However, unlike de Torre's proposal, this new "liberal pan-Hispanist discourse" is grounded in political, economic, and cultural reality. The promotion of cultural activities by institutions like the Casa de América, and the fact that Spanish houses have become the main publishers of the best-known Spanish American authors, brings to mind José Carlos Mariátegui's assertion during the 1927 debate that an intellectual meridian is nothing but a "great literary market" ("La batalla de *Martín Fierro*" 113). In fact, it may very well be that today, for the first time since the end of the nineteenth century, Spain has become the true "Intellectual Meridian" of the Hispanophone world.[14] As the presence of CEOs and other representatives of the Peninsula's publishing industry in the direction of the Casa de América illustrates, at its core, the Spanish elites see this "pan-Hispanism" not only as a rhetorical affirmation of a common language and a putative common culture, or even of a nostalgia for a long-dead empire, but also as the ideological justification for a new, real-life commercial and economic hegemony.

In 1997, 40 percent of all books published in Spain were exported to Spanish America, while books brought from the region to Spain amounted to only 2.5 percent (Pohl "¿Un nuevo *boom?*" 278). Moreover, in addition to this unequal exchange, many of the major, even historic, presses in Spanish America, such as Borges's publisher *Emecé* in Argentina, have been bought by Spanish multinationals.[15] In a recent development, large Spanish book publishers such as Planeta have entered smaller local markets, publishing local fiction and nonfiction, including school textbooks, the bread-and-butter source of income for small local presses throughout Latin America (Solé n.p.).

The expansion of the Spanish book industry into Latin America as a publisher of books by Latin American and non–Latin American authors is part of a larger process of Peninsular economic expansion. As the text by Faverón quoted above exemplifies, there are occasional complaints about a new cultural and economic conquest on the part of Spanish conglomerates, such as Telefónica, a government-owned corporation.[16] The case can be made, therefore, that the new pan-Hispanist liberal discourse is the ideological justification for the economic expansion of Spanish capital into Spanish America, which, despite the obvious need for investment and jobs in the region, is not conducive to egalitarian relations with the Iberian Peninsula.

The hegemony of the Spanish publishing industry raises a number of significant questions. Given that the ultimate decision to publish is in the hands of Spanish editors, even if they may be receptive to suggestions from local subsidiaries, the ideal text for publication would be one that appeals to the larger Spanish-speaking readership regardless of nationality or region. As the Mexican author Jorge Volpi, one of the main beneficiaries of this internationalization of Spanish American literature, notes:

> The problem . . . is that the greater part of the large book publishers in our language are either in the hands of Spanish or international conglomerates. There are no longer large Latin American book publishers that can compete . . . For a writer to become known in Latin America, the decision must be made in Spain. If not attractive to the Spanish public, it's difficult a writer will reach our region" ("Cuando nací el *boom* estaba allí" n.p.)[17]

This temptation to break free from local concerns is enhanced by the proliferation of literary awards offered by Spanish publishing houses, which have opened the Hispanophone market to writers who would otherwise have been unable to access it. In fact, some of the rising stars of Spanish-language literature—such as Jaime Bayly (Peru), winner of the Herralde award in 1997; the previously mentioned Jorge Volpi, winner of Seix Barral's Biblioteca Breve Award in 1999; and Santiago Roncagliolo (Peru), winner of the Alfaguara Award in 2006, among others—have benefited not only from the prestige of the prizes, but, even more important, from the international mass marketing provided by the book publishers who sponsor these awards. Moreover, Bayli and Roncagliolo have both been accused of writing texts that use their Peruvian settings merely as "local color," to use the Borgesian phrase, to enliven narratives that otherwise could have been set in any other location or cultural context.[18]

A generation of authors of an explicitly pan-Hispanic, if not world, literature characterized by an understandable rejection of a clichéd second generation Magical Realism has appeared.

LATIN AMERICAN PAN-HISPANISM

It would be a mistake, however, to believe that this pan-Hispanist discourse is without support in Latin America. Even if some of the beneficiaries of this "directed globalization," such as Volpi, are perfectly aware of the downside of the superseding of national and regional markets by a Hispanophone space centered in Spain, many writers see in this potential expansion of readership a positive development. In fact, Mario Vargas Llosa and Carlos Fuentes, two of the core "boom" writers who as a group have since the 1960s been seen as representatives of the region's literature, have played different but equally significant roles in the establishment and ideological justification of this development of a common literary market on both sides of the Atlantic.

Vargas Llosa has been a key figure in the development of pan-Hispanic book publishing. According to Alfaguara's director Cruz, the buying of the rights to all of Vargas Llosa's books was the lynchpin of their expansion plan: "We already had Donoso, in Argentina Cortázar, in Uruguay Tomás de Mattos and Omar Prego, in Mexico Carlos Fuentes. In addition we needed a great global writer, who was Mario Vargas Llosa, and we bought his complete works. This was our strategy" (Cruz 320).[19] As Pohl notes, this "global" nature is defined by "the ability of being sold in any country ['vendible en cualquier país']" (¿Un nuevo *boom?* 267). The unique position of Vargas Llosa, which is shared with only a few authors—in the interview Cruz talks of twelve "global writers," but gives no names (321)—seems to make him, from a commercial point of view, *primus inter pares* among the boom writers. After all, Cruz's list includes two core boom writers—Cortázar and Fuentes—as well as one of their major contemporaries, José Donoso.[20] One can, however, safely assume that Gabriel García Márquez is also a "global writer."

If Vargas Llosa has been the keystone of the expansion of Alfaguara Global and Grupo Santillana throughout Spanish America, Fuentes, as Pohl has noted, has been a central proponent of the pan-Hispanic liberal discourse (Pohl "¿Un nuevo *boom?* 276).[21] While Fuentes has stressed the Mexicanness of his own work and writings, he also describes it as compatible and coexisting with a parallel pan-Hispanic identity. In 1992, the year of the Columbine commemoration, his *El espejo enterrado* (*The Buried Mirror*) presented a vision of Spanish America that not only emphasized the obvious historical connections between the Peninsula and the region, but also argued in favor of strengthening contemporary links as Spain became a developed European country: "Spain is in Europe, legitimately so. But it should not forget that it is also in the nations of Spanish America, 'the cubs of the Spanish lion,' as the Nicaraguan poet Rubén Darío called us." He then adds: "Can we be without Spain? Can Spain be without us?" (369).[22] In fact, Fuentes frequently refers to a "territory of La Mancha" "that begins in the Pyrenees, ends in the Tajo, crosses the Atlantic, goes to America, begins in California, continues through Mexico, and reaches Chile and Argentina, an enormous territory is this of La Mancha" ("La Universidad de Castilla–La Mancha nombra doctor Honoris Causa a Carlos Fuentes" n.p.).[23] It must be pointed out that this linking of Spanish America and Spain has long been a characteristic of Fuentes's thought, even before the rise of the liberal pan-Hispanic discourse. In *La nueva novela hispanoamericana,* published in 1969, Fuentes includes the Spanish author Juan Goytizolo, making him a member of the boom, therefore, implicitly defining *Hispanoamérica* as including Spain.

The reasons behind Fuentes's whole-hearted adoption of the pan-Hispanist liberal discourse are insinuated in the reference to Rubén Darío's 1905 poem "A Roosevelt" ("To Roosevelt") found in the quotation from *The Buried Mirror* above. In this foundational Latin American anti-imperialist poem, Darío advises the United States, personified in the figure of Theodore Roosevelt, of the impossibility of conquering the region: "Beware / Spanish America lives! / A thousand cubs of the Spanish lion roam free" (39).[24] It is quite clear that Fuentes's espousal of the pan-Hispanist liberal discourse can be seen as a response to the ever-growing cultural and political influence of the United States. In fact, Fuentes had already expressed his concern, as well as his overall optimism, over the topic in his 1987 Cervantes Award speech. Quoting Darío again, and referring to the mass immigration of Latin Americans into the United States, Fuentes concluded: "In the century that arrives Spanish will be the principal language in the three Americas: South, Central, and North. The famous question made by Rubén Darío—will so many millions speak English?—will at last be answered: no, they will speak Spanish" ("Discurso" 2).[25] The expansion of Spain's cultural industry in the region could thus be seen as a bulwark against North American capitalism and the English language. The renewed domination of Spanish capital and cultural institutions could thus, paradoxically, guarantee the permanence of Latin American culture.[26]

Local and Cosmopolitan Markets and Writers

In addition to personal advantage—as commercially successful writers see their potential markets expand—or ideological reasons—whether out of loyalty to the free market or as a result of concern with the status of Spanish in a world mainly dominated by Anglophone media and North American capital—many in the region celebrate the expansion of Spain's book publishing market.

In part due to the worldwide economic crisis of the early 1970s, the Hispanophone book market, which had included Spain together with Argentina and Mexico as one of its centers, broke down. For instance, by the early 1990s, when the Chilean writers Alberto Fuguet and Sergio Gómez attempted to select stories for their influential anthology *McOndo,* they found the lack of distribution of Spanish American writers appalling: "In all the capitals of Latin America one can find best-sellers or authors translated in Spain, but never Ibero American authors . . . If one is a Latin American writer and wishes to be stocked in the bookstores of Quito, La Paz, and San Juan one must publish (and hopefully live in) Barcelona. Crossing borders implies crossing the Atlantic" (13).[27] The establishment of a pan-Hispanic market centered in Spain, insinuated in Fuguet and Gomez's text, was seen as a solution to the breakdown of the region's continental distribution system.

The resultant development of a pan-Hispanic market has not been, at least till now, as satisfactory for the majority region's writers as the eloquent rhetoric or the continuous expansion of Spanish book-publishing corporations in Latin America would have led one to expect. Thus, according to Jorge Fornet: "In a curious development, the editorial policies of these corporations become sometimes precapitalist and the circulation of authors is limited in the majority of cases to their respective national spaces. As paradoxical as it may seem, globalization can sometimes act in favor of parochialism" (1).[28] An example of the limitations of this Spanish-led globalization can be seen in the fact that, according to Francesc Solé, president of Grupo Planeta, twenty-five Peruvian authors will be published yearly as a result of Planeta opening a branch in Lima. However, of these, only a handful—obviously, those who sell the most copies—will have their publications sent to other branches of Planeta: "A Peruvian author, not very well-known abroad, capable of selling three thousand copies in her country, can surely sell a few hundreds abroad" (n. p).[29]

LOCAL AND PAN-HISPANIC WRITERS DURING THE BOOM

Obviously, this tension between local and pan-Hispanic markets and literatures is not new. It had already become explicit during the boom. Remember that the boom arose during an earlier moment in the growth of a pan-Hispanic market and cultural space. In *A Personal History of the Boom* (1977), Donoso rues the poor distribution of key works by Borges and Carpentier: "In each country, no one knew what was being written in other Latin American countries; especially because it was so difficult to publish a first novel or a first collection of short stories or get them recognized. All of the publishing houses were more or less poor and, in the larger countries, prejudiced in favor of foreign literature" (21).[30] The development of a pan-Latin American literary market and space, where Borges is read by Chileans and Donoso by Argentines, is one of the main reasons behind the development of the boom, which in turn helped promote a further internationalization of the book market. But, as should also be obvious, this process implies the creation of a kind of pan-Hispanic writer—precisely, the core and near-core of the boom—that is seen as superior, given their "international breath" to writers who address more local concerns (Donoso 113).

The criticisms by the indigenista novelist José María Arguedas of the boom writers in his novel *El zorro de arriba y el zorro de abajo* (*The Fox from Up Above and the Fox from Down Below*), published posthumously in 1971, serve as examples of the tension between a literature grounded in local traditions and one that is directed toward a greater regional and international readership.[31] Arguedas's attacks were a reply to the comments made by Julio Cortázar, the author of the key boom novel *Rayuela* (*Hopscotch*) (1963), in his essay "Acerca de la situación del intelectual latinoamericano" ("Regarding the Situation of the Latin American Intellectual") (1967). Cortázar states:

> I am surprised that occasionally it is not noticed to what degree the echo that my books have had in Latin America derives from the fact that they propose a literature whose national and regional roots has been exponentially developed by a more open and complex experience, and that each evocation or recreation of what is originally mine reaches its extreme tension thanks to this opening on and from a world that ultimately surpasses it and in last instance selects and perfects it. (276)[32]

Despite many qualifications introduced by Cortázar in this essay—he claims, for instance, "to speak for myself and only for myself ['en hablar por mí mismo y sólo por mí mismo'] (270)"—the logical conclusion of this passage, as well as the essay as a whole, is that the writer settled in Europe, and, by extension, the internationalized boom writer who has been able to move beyond national boundaries, has overcome intellectual and artistic limitations necessarily present in texts produced by local writers. Cortázar establishes a classification in which the cosmopolitan, pan-Latin American, maybe pan-Hispanic, boom writer is considered superior to the local writer.

This hierarchy of writers, with one group seen as valuable only when considered from a local perspective and a second of universal worth, is one of the staples of mainstream literary criticism. For instance, Pascale Casanova in *The World Republic of Letters* establishes hierarchical relationship between what she calls national and international writers. According to the French critic, "each national space"—and in the case of Latin America, the subcontinent as a whole is described as functioning as one—"is structured by the rivalry between . . . 'national' writers (who embody a national or popular definition of literature) and 'international' writers (who uphold an autonomous conception of literature)" (108). Not only does Casanova value the "international writers," who are the only ones "who know the laws of world literary space" (109), but they are described as ultimately better interpreters of their local reality than the national ones: "paradoxically it is the most international writers who, while rejecting adherence to national belief, are the best at describing the literary manifestations of national feeling" (185).

Although frequently without Casanova's critical sophistication, this two-tier classification is clearly the norm among international and Latin American critics, whether academic or popular.[33] However, the rise of pan-Hispanic writers who produce a literature that is exported not only because of its "quality," as was frequently argued before the hegemony of mass cultural conglomerates, but also because of their intelligent appeal to an international mass readership, has problematized, without destroying, this hierarchical classification.

Arguedas, not surprisingly reacted strongly to Cortázar's statements. His response pointed out the obvious arrogance in the statements by the author of *Hopscotch,* noting that Cortázar's privileging of international writers could be seen as equivalent to Arguedas claiming, regarding his indigenous mentor Felipe Maywa, to "better, much more essentially interpret the spirit, the desires of *don* Felipe, than *don* Felipe himself" (14).[34] But Arguedas's rejection of Cortázar's claim for his European location as epistemologically superior is based not only on ethical grounds. According to Arguedas: "We are all provincials, *don* Julio (Cortázar). Provincials within the nation and provincials of the supranational, that is also a sphere" (21).[35] Arguedas here points out the existence of different literary spaces embedded and communicated but rejects that they imply a hierarchy. Limitations and, one assumes, also insights are implicit in both international and "provincial" locations.

Despite the tensions between the international boom writers and those identified with local traditions and, therefore, frequently less accessible to international readers, there was, as Ángel Rama pointed out, a great degree of diversity in the publishing industry of the 1960s. After mentioning a number of smaller presses from Chile, Argentina, Uruguay, Venezuela, and Spain that published major Latin American authors during the boom period, Rama argues that "of all of these, a central role was played by Fabril Editora, Sudamericana, Losada, Fondo de Cultura, Seix Barral y Joaquín Mortiz" ("El *Boom* en perspectiva" 66).[36] A brief review of the cities where these presses were located—Buenos Aires (Fabril, Sudamericana, and Losada), Mexico City (Fondo de Cultura, Joaquín Moritz), and Barcelona (Seix Barral)—serve as proof of Rama's assertion. Rama's argument is also verified if one notes that *Cien años de soledad* (*One Hundred Years of Solitude*), the best seller of the boom classics, was originally published by Sudamericana in Buenos Aires.[37] In fact, the inclusiveness of the international space during the boom period is verified by the fact that Arguedas had three of his last four novels published by Losada, including *The Fox from Up Above and the Fox from Down Below*.

In other words, although the boom was an international movement that contributed to the development of a pan-Hispanic cultural space, it was not centralized, even if, as the 1960s and, particularly, the 1970s progressed, Spanish presses achieved a relative hegemony. In fact, the context in which the production of Latin American literature took place in the 1960s reminds one of Ortega y Gasset's inclusive vision of a policentered Hispanophone cultural and literary space.[38] The magnificent plurality of the boom novels, despite the frequent absurd lumping of these texts outside Latin America under the rubric of "Magical Realism," is an example of the many options open to authors at the time.[39] From the rigorous realism and structural sophistication of Mario Vargas Llosa in his 1960s novels—*La ciudad y los perros* (*Time of the Hero*), *La casa verde* (*The Green House*), and *Conversación en La Catedral* (*Conversation in the Cathedral*)—to the varied styles of Carlos Fuentes—realistic in *La muerte de Artemio Cruz* (*The Death of Artemio Cruz*), fantastic in *Aura*, and so forth—to the high modernism of Cortázar's *Hopscotch* or *62/modelo para armar* (*62: A Model Kit*) or the true magical realism of Gabriel García Márquez's *One Hundred Years of Solitude*, one of the hallmarks of the boom is the proliferation of narrative modes.

Underlying this internationalization of Latin American literature is the existence of canons that privilege texts, such as those of the boom, that are ultimately compatible with modern and postmodern literary norms, regardless of the specific local difference they have internalized. In fact, it is precisely because of their cosmopolitan writerly sophistication that they are ultimately comprehensible to readers throughout Latin America, Spain, and international markets. Given the explicit and, frequently, nearly exclusive commercial orientation of today's editorial industry, contemporary internationalization of texts does not necessarily correspond to the incorporation of modernist literary techniques. On the contrary, literary internationalization may frequently imply the adoption of narrative approaches closer to the commercial best seller than to those that characterized the boom. Be that as it may, "national" texts that respond primarily to problematics and traditions linked to specific communities are frequently marginalized and undervalued regardless of their originality. Access to the pan-Hispanic market is, in last resort, predicated on a partial abandonment of the local or in its transformation into an ingredient within a world (or pan-Hispanic) concoction. Thus, not without irony the critic Gustavo Guerrero notes: "Perhaps one of the great paradoxes of globalization is that, for many of our writers, the true challenge is no longer that of being read abroad, but, rather, in capturing again the local reader" (26).[40]

Conclusion

The consequences this indirect pressure on the creation of international texts—which, as I have argued, frequently implies resorting to the formulas of the best seller—will have on the long-term literary production of the different cultural areas of Spanish America are not yet clear. In fact, there are still numerous small, local presses that permit the continuance of an almost artisan literary production both in narrative and poetry, but they may not suffice to counterbalance the understandable pressures to enter—or try to enter—the larger continental and international markets. This change does not necessarily imply a lessening of quality—however this is defined—of the texts, but simply a difference in their traits, as local literary markets and readerships, and the creation of correspondent literatures, which become less important.

As we have seen, for Fuentes and others, the establishment of a pan-Hispanic literary and cultural space could be seen as a bulwark against the expansion of the English language and North American cultural patterns throughout the region. However, as recent developments in Latin American literature prove, the development of a pan-Hispanic literary space is not incompatible with the establishment of significant connections between the new literature of the region and North American mass and literary cultures. In fact, Alberto Fuguet and other members of the "*McOndo* generation" attempt in their writings to incorporate the mass and literary cultures of the United States.

CHAPTER 7

THE MOVIES OF MY LIFE; OR, A BRIDGE TO NORTH AMERICA

INTRODUCTION: MCONDO AND THE CRACK

In 1996, when the expansion of Spanish capital in Latin America was in full bloom, two manifestos shook the Spanish American literary world. Published within one month of each other and literally from the two extremes of the region, Mexico and Chile, "Manifesto Crack" (published in August) and "Presentación del país McOndo" ("Introduction to McOndo country"; published in September), the introduction to the short-story anthology *McOndo,* seemed to herald a new generation of writers who, in the most traditional of literary gestures, rejected earlier literary traditions. United by chronology and by an explicit animosity to Magical Realism, the Crack writers (Jorge Volpi, Pedro Ángel Palou, Ignacio Padilla, and Ricardo Chávez Castañeda) and the McOndo group (led by Alberto Fuguet and Sergio Gómez, but frequently seen as also incorporating the authors included in the anthology) were considered by many as seizing the torch forcibly from the hands of the boom writers.[1] The linking of these two independent movements is explicitly accepted by Padilla, who writes that the "McOndo anthology and the Crack manifesto, and everything that's happened recently with the new Latin American novel . . . were natural phenomena" (137).[2] Despite this frequent association of the two groups of writers, a closer analysis of the literary production, the founding manifestos, and the career of the movements' main writers exhibit significant differences.

As noted above, the main point the two groups have in common is their rejection of Magical Realism. In the "Crack Manifesto," which consists of four sections, each signed by one member of the group, Padilla writes somewhat mysteriously of a "dubious Magical Realism which has become transformed for our letters in a Tragic Magicism" (Volpi et al "Manifiesto Crack" 5).[3] A recent statement by Volpi, who in the actual manifesto does not refer to Magical Realism, reinforces Padilla's point: "It's negative, for instance, that Magical Realism is seen as the only option for Latin American literature" ("Los autores del boom son clásicos vivos" n.p.).[4] When asked if the Crack was formed as a reaction against Magical Realism, Volpi responded affirmatively, but added that the group also aimed "to link our literature with the more universal and cosmopolitan tradition of Latin American literature" (n.p.).[5] In a paradox, Magical Realism, one of the few Latin American literary styles that have actually gone global, is seen as the antithesis of the region's cosmopolitanism.

Fuguet and Gómez attack Magical Realism with much greater animosity. In fact, a criticism of Magical Realism is already implicit in the title of their short-story collection, *McOndo,* which, as is obvious, parodies the name of the imaginary location of *One Hundred Years of Solitude,* Macondo. Fuguet and Gómez thus contrast García Márquez's novel with a reality full of "McDonald's, Mac computers, and condominiums ['McDonald's, computadores Mac y condominios']" that has supposedly rendered Magical Realism obsolete (17). There is a strong element of indignation in their attack on Magical Realism: "To sell a rural continent when, in truth, it's urban . . . seems to us aberrant, easy, and immoral" (18).[6] In an article written one year later, Fuguet describes Magical Realism as "a formula" and complains that Magical Realists are "cranking out shamelessly folkloric novels that cater to the imaginations of politically correct readers" ("I Am Not a Magic Realist" n.p.).[7] For Fuguet and Gómez, Magical Realism depicts a rural, magical, world dissonant with the Latin American urban and, even if unequal, modern reality of 1996. Thus in McOndo, "there is more toothbrushing and trips to the countryside (well, to the apartment or the mall) than levitations" (19).[8]

Despite this common opposition to Magical Realism, critics have correctly noted significant differences between the groups. In fact, the Crack writer Ignacio Padilla, despite seeing both movements as linked in their desire to renew the region's literature, correctly claims "there is no aesthetic proposal which links the Crack and McOndo ['no hay una propuesta estética que unifique al *crack* y a *McOndo*']" (143). The Bolivian writer Edmundo Paz Soldán, a close collaborator of Fuguet, is even more emphatic about the differences between both groups. He describes McOndo as "a moment in the celebration of the creative mixture of high and popular culture ['un momento de celebración de la mezcla creativa entre la cultura alta y la popular']" while describing the Crack as having "proposed a sort of elitist reestablishment of values ['una suerte de elitista reestablecimiento de valores']" (n.p.). Burkhard Pohl agrees:

> While the Crack emphasizes the return to the totalizing aesthetic presuppositions of the generation of the 1950s and 1960s, the inventors of McOndo—as the texts collected in the anthology confirm, among them the contributions of the Mexicans David Toscana, Naief Yehya and Jordi Soler—defend a literature voluntarily youthful or at least opened towards daily life in the cultural field, a deliberate inscription in the cultural codes of the Anglo Saxon international mainstream. ("Ruptura y continuidad" 60)[9]

In fact, a brief summary of the topics of some of the novels written by Volpi—*En busca de Klingsor* (*In Search of Klingsor*), about the moral dilemmas faced by Nazi physicists; *El fin de la locura* (*The End of Madness*), dealing with May 1968 and the theories of Lacan, Althusser, and so on—and by Fuguet—*Tinta roja* (*Red Ink*), the story of a beginning journalist working the crime beat; *Las películas de mi vida* (*The Movies of My Life*), about a Chilean seismologist coming to terms with his life by means of watching commercial movies—makes clear the differences between the two writers and, by implication, the two movements.

For the Crack, a return to the complexity of the boom—Vargas Llosa's "total novel"—is the solution to the putative proliferation of inferior García Márquez clones.[10] For McOndo, and more specifically Fuguet, the embrace of a "realist" literature reminiscent in some ways of earlier and contemporary Anglophone literature—such as the writings of John Updike or Philip Roth—and a turn to North American culture, in particular popular film and music, signals the way out of this supposed creative quandary.[11] But this common diagnosis of Spanish American literature as being stuck in a creative rut linked to Magical Realism is common to both groups, even if their solutions to this supposed problem differ substantially.

Gustavo Faverón has questioned the rationale behind the rejection of Magical Realism characteristic of both the Crack and McOndo arguing that: "Latin American criticism has never confused Magical Realism with the rest of our literature, and that it has always been quite clear for us that it is only a literary mode, temporary as any, whose culminating moment was brief and is distant from us today" ("Crack & McOndo" n.p.).[12] As mentioned earlier in this book, of the major boom writers, only García Márquez can be accurately described as a Magical Realist.

Even Alejo Carpentier had by the 1960s moved beyond any association of Latin America and the magical or supernatural. The Cuban writer had in his "Prólogo" (prologue) to *El reino de este mundo* (*The Kingdom of This World*) (1948) asked rhetorically: "But what is the history of all of the Americas but a chronicle of the real marvelous" (198).[13] Carpentier proposed the "real marvelous," a concept frequently seen as the precursor to that of Magical Realism, as the defining difference between America and Europe. However, according to Roberto Ignacio Díaz, after *The Kingdom of This World,* Carpentier came to the "realization that his theories of Spanish American fiction"—and one can add Spanish America—"may be altogether artificial (52).[14] In fact, the original Spanish title of his later novel *El siglo de las luces* ("The Enlightenment"; 1962), translated as *Explosion in the Cathedral,* can serve as an example of some of the changes that had taken place in Carpentier's writing. Gone was the emphasis on a radical and exclusive Latin American difference. Instead, he explored in this novel the region as participating in global developments—the enlightenment and revolution—and as the location from which a critique of these could be elaborated. The settings of the novel are cities, such as Havana, Paris, Madrid, and even the small, though still urban, Basse-Terre.

Many of the specific criticisms of the boom by these writers echo statements made by the boom writers themselves when they, similarly, attempted to distance themselves from their literary predecessors. Like the McOndo group, the boom writers rejected the supposedly rural literature written by their predecessors and emphasized the urban and contemporary character of the "new novel." Thus Vargas Llosa, in "The Latin American Novel Today," his well-known 1970 article for the journal *Books Abroad* argues: "Just as the countryside was the immutable setting of the then primitive novel, the city is the permanent setting of the creative novel" ("The Latin American Novel Today" 10). There is little doubt that in the same manner in which the boom writers had constructed a caricature of their predecessors—evidenced above by Vargas Llosa's naming their novels "primitive"—these more recent literary groups, especially McOndo, have also simplified and misrepresented the writings of their elders.

LATIN AMERICAN LITERATURE AND MARKET EXPECTATIONS

It is important to note that despite these distortions, the attacks on Magical Realism made by the McOndo and Crack groups were rooted in the reality of Latin American and international literary markets. As Gustavo Guerrero notes: "in the last fifteen years the true Latin American bestsellers have almost all been written by notorious epigones of García Márquez" (27).[15] The McOndo and Crack criticisms were prompted by the enormous commercial success in the United States, Europe, Spain, and Latin America of novels written by Magical Realists such as Isabel Allende and Laura Esquivel. But not only best sellers were written in the Magical Realist idiom. It had also become the style used by generally respected writers like Eduardo González Viaña, Ángeles Mastretta, and Carmen Boullosa. The fact that many of these writers were women has led some critics to accuse the McOndo and, to a lesser degree, Crack writers of misogyny. Thus Diana Palaversich criticizes Fuguet's and Gómez's "virulent machismo—evident in the exclusion of women authors but also in their inclusion as characters [in the McOndo novels], without exception frivolous and superficial" (n.p.).[16] But given the market domination of Magical Realism, one can see in the Crack and McOndo attacks an attempt at opening commercial doors by writers who had different stylistic predilections. Thus Juan Poblete notes about McOndo:

> One must not forget that in an international market saturated by magical realisms produced in different parts of the global south or by its diasporas in the metropolitan countries, it would seem a good commercial strategy, in addition to an expected generational move, to offer a literary product consonant with versions celebrating indiscriminate cultural hybridization. (295)[17]

While Poblete is writing about McOndo rather than the Crack—it is difficult to describe the novels of the latter group, with their topics frequently linked to the high culture of Europe, as being concerned with "indiscriminate cultural hybridization"—his emphasis on the rejection of Magical Realism as a generational market strategy must be kept in mind. Moreover, the fact that the "literary" writers of the Crack would exhibit such a keen concern with their possible participation in the market can be seen as an implicit rebuttal of the frequent exclusion of any consideration of commerce in theories of world literature.[18]

The control of the market by Magical Realist epigones has also created a false image of Latin America. As Padilla writes about the McOndo writers, but implicitly also about the Crack:

> When in the prologue to his *McOndo* Alberto Fuguet took distance, or rather made his escape, from the universe of García Márquez, he was not doing so because it lacked value, or because the other authors in the anthology thought it did, but because other writers less skillful than the

Colombian author had begun to create its caricature, creating a work that was not only absurd as literature, but also depicted Latin America as an absurdity. (141)[19]

The success of Magical Realist novels promoted in Europe and North America a false image of the region as "magical." Magical became a signifier assigned not only to the region's literature but also, frequently, to Latin America as a whole. Thus the region and its populations were exoticized as somehow breaking the norms of Western reason. In the 1970s, this linkage of the region with the irrational was associated with the implicit belief that unlike in "reasonable" Europe or North America, radical political innovation was still possible in the region. Now, after the demise of communism, the connection of Latin America with magic has helped reinforce the image of the region as ungovernable and its problems as unsolvable. In fact, a cursory look at the titles of a few academic books written about the region or its diaspora reinforce this putative linkage between the region and the irrational: *Magical Sites: Women Travelers in 19th Century Latin America* (1999), a collection edited by a Marjorie Agosín and Julie Levinson; *Magical Urbanism: Latinos Reinvent the U.S. Big City* (2001), by the noted urbanist Mike Davis; and *Magical Reels: A History of Cinema in Latin America* (2000), by the British Latin Americanist John King.

Arguably of greater importance for the Crack and McOndo writers is the fact that Magical Realism became accepted as the canon—both in its meaning of "critical yardstick" and in terms of the actual books being accepted as having value—by the North American and European literary establishments. As we have seen, Magical Realism quickly became the signifier assigned to the texts of the boom and other Latin American writers, regardless of whether or not magic was actually present in them—and in a vicious circle helped guarantee success to those texts that reinforced this expectation. In fact, Fuguet's own career as a writer clashed with this vision of Magical Realism as the criterion with which to measure Latin American literature. In "I Am not a Magical Realist," Fuguet retells in greater detail a personal anecdote set at the University of Iowa that he had already narrated in a briefer version in his and Gómez's "Presentación."[20] Excited by the prominent place assigned to Latino and Latin American writers in the local bookstores, Fuguet believed: "There seemed to be a Spanish-language wave that I wanted to ride on my South American board" (n.p.). However, after having one of his translated stories rejected by the *Iowa Review*, Fuguet reflects:

I got the message. I knew I had done something wrong, and I had the sinking feeling that my North American glory days had come to an end before they had even gotten started. Add some folklore and a dash of tropical heat and come back later. That was the message I heard. So I went back to the bookstores and took a closer look at all those novels with Hispanic authors. Sure enough, they fit the formula. They had done their homework. Each book offered either color-by-numbers Magical Realism or the cult of the underdeveloped. Sagas of sweaty migrant farm laborers, the plight of misunderstood political refugees or the spicy violence of the barrio. All decent themes, of course, but quite removed from my middle-class, metropolitan Chilean existence. All of a sudden, it hit me: I was Latin American, all right—I just wasn't Latino enough. (n.p).

The importance of Fuguet's anecdote is that markets, canons, and the position assigned Latin America in the North American imaginary all come together to become a stumbling block to the internationalization of his career. Thus, both McOndo and the Crack can be seen as rejecting the kinds of expectations—commercial, critical, and imaginary—that limit the acceptance of Latin American writers who cannot be classified as "Latino." Latino in Fuguet's text is not the actual diasporic communities and their descendants but, rather, an exoticist construction.

McOndo's and the Crack's common animosity toward Magical Realism implies the rejection of this exoticization of Latin America on the part of the North American and European critical establishment. Therefore, the Crack writers—by dealing with European topics—and McOndo—by embracing U.S. popular culture, which has become a global cultural common denominator—deny the cultural othering implicit in the identification of Latin America with Magical Realism. Moreover, by doing so, both groups emphasize the region's full membership in Western culture. On the one hand, like Borges in "The Argentine Writer and Tradition," these writers make a full claim to their right to Western culture. On the other hand, by exclusively focusing on this participation, both the Crack and McOndo seem to ignore, or at least de-emphasize, the critical, even subversive, element that has frequently characterized the region's relationship with Western culture.

Movies and *The Movies of My Life*

References to and incorporation of mass-culture styles, genres, and, at the level of representation, products have a long history in Latin American literature. In the case of Brazil, writers such as João do Rio, Olavio Bilac, and Lima Barreto, active during the first two decades of the twentieth century, were profoundly influenced by film and other emerging media.[21] As we saw in chapter 3, film also had a significant impact on the Latin America of the 1920s. Even the boom writers, frequently seen as defenders of high culture, were marked by North American popular culture. For instance, Carlos Fuentes's *La muerte de Artemio Cruz* (*The Death of Artemio Cruz*) (1962), one of the foundational boom texts, was influenced by Orson Welles's *Citizen Kane*.[22] Gabriel García Márquez developed a parallel career as a screenwriter and as the central participant in the "Fundación del Nuevo Cine Latinoamericano" helped found a successful film school in Havana, Cuba. Closer to the aesthetics proposed by Fuguet, Manuel Puig—of whom the Chilean novelist has declared himself a fan—modeled his writings on, of all things, the Hollywood screenplay. Even Mario Vargas Llosa, once the author of intense high-modernist texts like *La ciudad y los perros* (*The Time of the Hero*) (1963) or *Conversación en La Catedral* (*Conversation in the Cathedral*) (1969), in *La tía Julia y el escribidor* (*Aunt Julia and the Scriptwriter*) (1977) playfully incorporates and parodies the radio soap operas of the 1950s.[23]

Fuguet's *The Movies of My Life* (2003) exemplifies the significant change that has taken place in the incorporation of North American film and mass cultural products in Latin American literature. After all, if Borges's literary practice is based on an antihierarchical interpretation of Western culture, most readers would still classify his work as high culture. And there is little doubt that *The Death of Artemio Cruz* develops the complexity of *Citizen Kane*, a film that has achieved a central position in the film canon. Despite Puig's passion for Hollywood films and Vargas Llosa's playful flirtation with radio soap operas, both authors are also critical of mass culture.

In Puig's *La traición de Rita Hayworth* (*The Betrayal of Rita Hayworth*) (1968), the falsely colorful Hispanic world of the Hollywood movie *Blood and Sand* (1941), with its bullfighters and exaggerated romantic situations, is contrasted with the colorless provincial life in Patagonia. His *El beso de la mujer araña* (*The Kiss of the Spider Woman*) (1976) can be seen as a meditation on the uses to which film can be put. Puig's emphasis is on the human capacity to take even the basest narratives—for instance, the Nazi film recounted in the novel—as the ground on which an imaginary resistance to the degradation of the real can be built. Puig's texts are, therefore, as much a celebration of, among other things, the capacity of filmic and other melodrama to provide a life-affirming escape from a life-denying reality and express the desires that society attempts to repress, as a criticism of the mystifications found in mass art forms. As Lucille Kerr notes, "Puig has been regarded as the celebrator of popular culture and as its critic; as the regenerator of its languages, forms, and characters and as their detractor. His work is in fact a powerful blend of both these projects." (8)

In a similar vein, Vargas Llosa's *Aunt Julia and the Scriptwriter* can only be seen as a partial recuperation of the radio soap opera genre. The titular scriptwriter Pedro Camacho's progressively demented radio plays serve as a counterpoint and commentary to the apparently autobiographical love story between the future novelist Varguitas and his aunt Julia. But there is little doubt that Varguitas is destined to write "better things"—one assumes *The Time of the Hero* and the author's other 1960s masterpieces. In this manner, despite Vargas Llosa's often-comic appropriation of soap opera "scripts," a hierarchy is established—even if one that is paradoxical and contradictory in that *Aunt Julia* is eminently enjoyable and easy to read. However, this classification, in which the difficult boom texts—the total novels—are seen as superior is implicit in a novel that itself marks a turn toward popular entertainment in the Peruvian novelist's writing.[24]

The Movies, Mass Culture, and Daily Life
In Fuguet's novel, the role played by film and its positive evaluation are already intimated in its title. The Spanish-language title *Las películas de mi vida* literally translates the French title of François Truffaut's famous collection of criticism, *Les films de ma vie* (1975). (Truffaut's book was rendered into English as *The Films in My Life*.) This echo is far from accidental. One of the many chapter epigraphs is from Truffaut's book. After all, like the coterie of critics at the film journal *Cahiers du Cinema*, Fuguet, even if only implicitly, proposes the validation of U.S. popular film and culture. Moreover, the McOndian recovery of North American culture, like that of the Nouvelle Vague, is part of a generational struggle. If Truffaut and his colleagues needed to symbolically kill their French filmmaking predecessors in order to open a cultural space for their activity, Fuguet and company needed to do likewise with their literary elders.[25] Fuguet is also a film critic and soon after the publication of *The Movies of My Life* would become a filmmaker with *Se arrienda* (2005), so one can easily imagine a personal identification with Truffaut, who, together with his confrère Jean-Luc Godard, is the prime example of critic turned filmmaker. Given the association of Truffaut, as well as the other Nouvelle Vague filmmakers, such as Godard, Claude Chabrol, and Jacques Rivette, with "high culture," it is useful to remember that they first became notorious for their debunking of the "Tradition of Quality" in French films. Thus Truffaut and his comrades will rescue a number of "commercial" Hollywood directors—including

Alfred Hitchcock—from critical disdain, claiming them as auteurs, that is, "men of the cinema and no longer . . . scenarists, directors, and literateurs" ("A Certain Tendency" 234).

Even if Truffaut and Fuguet share a common interest in Hollywood films, the constant critical evaluation characteristic of the French critic turned filmmaker is completely absent from Fuguet's *The Movies of My Life*. In fact, Fuguet borrows the form of the film review, giving information about each movie he mentions: not only the names of the director and main actors, but also where and when the main character viewed it. However, the films are not analyzed and are very rarely judged in the novel. Instead, they are mainly mnemonic devices—Fuguet is like Proust, but with movies instead of cookies—that the central character, Beltrán Soler, a Chilean seismologist in the midst of a personal crisis, uses to recall his and his family's story. (Beltrán and his family had lived in the California of the 1960s, where they moved to escape their native country; surprisingly, they returned to the Chile of the Pinochet dictatorship on a whim and out of nostalgia.) In Fuguet's novel, a film's value is exclusively personal and emotional. Hollywood classics, such as Frank Capra's *It's a Wonderful Life* (1946); widely admired films from the 1960s and 1970s, such as Peter Yates's *Bullitt* (1968) and Brian de Palma's *Carrie* (1976); or commercial fodder, like the Walt Disney productions *The Barefoot Executive* (1971) and *The World's Greatest Athlete* (1973), are only meaningful and differentiated on the basis of the personal events that are associated with them.

It is significant that in the novel the title is ascribed not to Truffaut's classic collection of reviews but, rather, to a book by the fictive "border" film director Lorenzo Martínez Romero. According to the novel, Romero's book is "not scholarly or criticism, but embarrassingly personal" (159);[26] a description also applicable to Fuguet's novel, except that there is no pretense of reviewing films. Truffaut's reviews, in contrast, are intensely evaluative and attempt to create a new canon. However, Truffaut, the fictive Romero, and Fuguet share a concern with the personal contexts in which a film is encountered.[27] As Beltrán states, after watching *Players* (1979; starring Ali McGraw and Maximilian Schell), "the movies that really speak to you are the ones that are really about yourself" (253).[28]

The Movies of My Life does not limit itself to creating connections between film and Beltrán's life. Arguably, Fuguet's main innovation is the naturalizing not only of the discourse of film but also of the discourse of advertising. In fact, references to film and advertising constitute the semantic ground on which *The Movies of My Life* is constructed. Mass culture grounds communication between author/narrator and the reader.

Fuguet assumes that the reader understands the mass culture references and frequently uses them as contrast and commentary on the facts recounted without any additional explanation. Thus the implied reader of the novel is one who has seen the films "reviewed" by Beltrán and who is familiar with the commercial products mentioned in the text.

An example of how knowledge of North American mass culture is necessary for a full understanding of the narrative is found in the chapter that is supposedly about *The Sound of Music*. This section (213–15), in addition to describing Beltrán's imperfect adaptation to Chile after his return from the United States, narrates the bizarre case of the Echaurren family. According to the novel: "Owing to the patriarch's age, the Echaur-ren Stevens family was not all well. All of the children suffered from one thing or another: one was deaf, two others seemed retarded to some degree, three were diabetic, one was blind, two were obese, and the eldest had a hip problem" (214).[29] The Echaurrens are described as a parodic version of the Von Trapps, the main characters of the film and Broadway musical, who were a real-life family of performers. The Echaurrens enter and win a TV talent contest—*Fa-Mi-La en Familia*—singing the songs from "the only movie the children have ever seen" (214).[30] However, the distance between this Chilean version—a criticism of uncritical copying?—and the Hollywood or Broadway (or Austrian) original is only apparent to those who have seen *The Sound of Music* (or the Von Trapps). At no point does Fuguet actually refer to the film, except to note that when the young Beltrán saw it a second time, "it was even tougher to stomach than I remembered" (214).[31] To add to this critique of popular culture, Beltrán links the program with the ideological promotion of Pinochet's fascism: "it was a program 'recommended' by the brains of the military regime in order to promote the family, 'which is the support and cornerstone of the regime'" (215).[32] The irony in this association of *The Sound of Music* with fascism is again apparent only to those who have seen the film or the original Broadway musical, or who are familiar with the plot (But given the popularity of the film, this group is very large.). After all, the movie and the play are ostensibly anti-Nazi, adaptations of sections of Maria Von Trapps's autobiography dealing with the family's escape from Nazi-dominated Austria. Moreover, the music and lyrics are by Richard Rodgers and Oscar Hammerstein, the impeccably liberal Jewish-American musical writing team.[33]

Another example of how the novel naturalizes mass culture is its frequent reference to Hollywood actors. Thus Lindsay, an immigration lawyer from California to whom Beltrán addresses the e-mails that make up the bulk of the novel, is introduced as "Lindsay? Like Lindsay Wagner?" (50).[34] Beltrán's father is identified with Steve McQueen, the star of the 1970s: "McQueen, like my father, almost never spoke in films" (76).[35] The personae of these movies and TV stars—attractive, active, energetic, maybe heroic, in the case of Wagner, the protagonist of the original *Bionic Woman* TV series; taciturn, independent, cool on the outside, turbulent inside, in the case of McQueen—are thus automatically associated with these two characters. It is not surprising, therefore, that Lindsay, an immigration lawyer, describes herself as "one of the good guys" (48); in *Las películas de mi vida,* "del lado de los buenos" (47). Despite her relatively brief presence in the plot, Lindsay will play the role of a catalyst in Beltrán's emotional development. And his father, like the actor's persona, is unable to assume his family obligations and in the end lives on his own, breaking off all contact with his children.

The discourse of commerce and commercials is also central to Fuguet's text. When Beltrán, motivated by his encounter with Lindsay, visits the store DVD Planet, he writes: "It was great, like a return to my youth, when I ate up movies like they were M&Ms" (59).[36] In this passage, Fuguet brings together film and commodities or, better said, uses one commodity to explain his relationship to another, thus bringing out their centrality to the discourse of the novel. Maybe the most dramatic example of the incorporation of advertising in the novel comes at the beginning in a brief introductory passage set in Los Angeles, where Beltrán says he is "dying to open a big, 2.5-liter bottle of ice-cold, refreshing Coke ['deseosos de abrir una helada y refrescante Coca-Cola de dos litros y medios (*Las películas de mi vida*)']"(4 [4]), thus reproducing the language of advertising. This quotation is from a passage in which Fuguet in a first Proustian moment compares the explosion of a Coke bottle with the unbottling of memory, which is the subject of the novel. Beltrán claims that a woman, who, as we will find out, was Lindsay, "opened up my mind and let loose the thick, viscous, gooey stuff that memories are made of ['la que abrió mi memoria y dejó escapar la viscosa sustancia de la que están hechos los recuerdos']" (4 [4]). Coke is not the only product mentioned in the novel: Funny Face Drink Mixes (99), Wonka Bars, See's chocolates, and Jean Naté perfume (108), are among the product names dropped in the novel.[37] Fuguet practices the production of meaning by means of commodities. *The Movies of My Life* describes a world in which, to quote Naomi Klein, brands "monopolize ever expanding stretches of cultural space" (16). As we have seen, Fuguet assumes that the implied reader has seen many of the movies and TV series or consumed many of the products mentioned and will be able to decode these meanings. After all, the reader knows how refreshing Coke is, or claims to be, and will probably be familiar with the attractive, masculine, and laconic characters played by Steve Mc Queen.

Mass culture is more than a narrative organizing device or a source for immediate communication and connotations. Film and advertising are both part of Beltrán's and the Solers' story. Beltrán's "Uncle Choclo" is in charge of the advertising for Milo, the soluble chocolate drink. In fact, Beltrán's cousin, Pedro Soler, is nicknamed Milo because he stars in his father's advertising campaign. This is one of the handful of passages where Fuguet, à la Puig, contrasts the world of mass culture with that of "reality." In addition to being the son of the producer, Milo had been chosen as a young boy to star in the advertisement because he was blond—"every brown-haired Latino boy wants to be blond ['todos los niñitos morenos latinoamericanos desean ser rubios']" (206 [204]). But when grown up, he is described as "alone and forgotten, and his living room was filled with posters and cans ['solo, olvidado, y su habitación estaba tapizada de afiches y tarros de Milo']" (206 [204]). Milo's loneliness is, however, representative of those of most of the characters in the novel, including Beltrán.

Film is also part of the plot. Beltrán Soler, like the real-life Alberto Fuguet, grows up in Encino, a Los Angeles neighborhood built on land that was once part of RKO Picture's back lot, where the Frank Capra classic *It's a Wonderful Life* was filmed. Beltrán notes: "I felt myself extremely fortunate to have lived the first years of my life in a place colonized by Frank Capra and Jimmy Stewart and not by a group of stinking, resentful Spaniards who escaped their native land to kill Indians and rob them of their riches at the other edge of the world" (86).[38] In a plot twist that again brings into contact fiction and reality, Yul Brynner is described as married to Beltrán's Aunt Nora (136). And the well-known Hollywood character actor Edward Everett Horton lives in Encino; makes delicious candied apples that he gives out at Halloween; and interacts, maybe in unsavory ways, with Beltrán's friend Drew (88–89).

Representing a Globalized Chile and Latin America

This wholesale, though not fully uncritical, adoption of the forms of mass media and communication is an attempt at representing the life experiences of McOndo, that is, of middle- and upper-class Latin Americans. This group, like Beltrán and Fuguet, if not necessarily beneficiaries, have at least managed to adapt to the cultural and economic changes promoted by neoliberal economic reforms, of which Chile has been the paradigmatic example.[39] With the opening of economic borders in Chile and throughout the Americas, M&Ms and other North American and international commodities have became part of the fabric of daily life. However, even if not as radically as in the case of Beltrán—after all, the novel is partly set in California—the centrality of North American mass and commercial culture is being experienced by a majority of Latin Americans at the start of the twenty-first century, regardless of class. The fact that only one of the movies mentioned in the novel—*Julio comienza en julio* (1977)—is Chilean exemplifies the lack of balance between Chilean and North American cultural production. As Fuguet notes: "I try to be a realist and if I had put only Latin American films in the novel I would have been lying. 99 percent of movies one sees in Latin America are from the United States" ("Estados Unidos es un país latinoamericano" n.p.).[40]

This cultural and commercial inequality, which is precisely what characterizes globalization in Latin America, has momentous consequences. If, according to Fredric Jameson, "whoever says the production of culture says the production of everyday life" ("Globalization" 67), the world depicted in *The Movies of My Life* is no longer fully Chilean. In fact, as Adelaida Caro Martí has pointed out, thanks to the globalization of film distribution, "the same films are seen in diverse places in the world, creating a common cultural background and a specific 'collective imaginary'" (n.p.).[41] One can add to Martí's comments that this global "collective imaginary" is produced not only through the assimilation of film but also through access, whether real or imaginary, to the same or, at least, a similar set of commodities.

This "collective imaginary" is not necessarily incompatible with the permanence of local difference, In fact, the notion of "Chilean" has become associated not only with the production of culture but with specific conditions of reception or consumption. Thus, in an interview, Fuguet argues:

> For me, *Jaws* is a Chilean movie because I will always watch it in the context of where I was and who I was when I saw it. *Brazil* is a movie about a futuristic, Orwellian world. It's a kind of social science fiction set in the future, but when it played in South America we all became convinced it was about Chile. For us, it had to be a metaphor about Pinochet—we saw the movie and made it ours. In the end for me, *Brazil* is a local film. That's the way culture works; we appropriate it. (qtd. in Guy García 263)

Fuguet's emphasis on cultural appropriation is, of course, not new in Latin American criticism or, more generally, culture. As we have seen, the issue of the cultural relation between Latin America and the mainstream of Western culture has been central to the art and literature of the region. Fuguet's argument above—which, as needs to be pointed out, is only partly illustrated by *The Movies of My Life* since it is a cultural product—does not define the appropriation of the culture of the center as a step in the production of new Latin American cultural products. Instead appropriation or consumption is an end in itself. It is through the consumption—in this case viewing—and the context in which this act takes place, that *Jaws* can become a "Chilean" film and that *Brazil* is transformed from a "social science fiction film" to an allegory about Pinochet's Chile. Fuguet's reflections are in line with much contemporary thought about consumption. Thus Canclini, in *Consumidores y ciudadanos* (*Consumers and Citizens*) defines the nation as "an interpretative community of consumers ['una comunidad interpretativa de consumidores']" (66). Nevertheless, despite the frequent "Chileaness" of Beltrán's interpretation, his idiosyncratic family and personal experiences are of greater impact in his relation to film.

It is tempting to link Fuguet's stress on appropriation as individual consumption with the individualism that characterizes his writing. Already in the "Presentación," Fuguet and Gómez write: "The stories of McOndo concern themselves on individual and private realities. We assume that this is one of the inheritances of the world-wide privatizing fever" (15).[42] As we have seen, consumption, rather than being fully privatized also has a social and even a national dimension. In the novel, references to *The Sound of Music* and *Soylent Green* (which in the novel is interpreted as an allegory of Pinochet's Chile) prove that consumption and the meanings ascribed to cultural goods are frequently determined by the specific social conditions in which the act occurs.[43] The act of interpretation itself, however, though influenced by the social context, is ultimately individual.

Another instance of McOndian "privatizing" is found in the beginning of the novel. On the first page of the novel, Beltrán asks himself a question that the rest of the narrative will try to answer: "What the fuck is going on?" (*Las películas de mi vida* 3). (Significantly, the question is in English in the Spanish original, and in Spanglish—"qué fucking pasa?—in the English translation [2]). As Poblete perceptively notes, this question can be interpreted as an allusion to the "famous Vargas Llosian interpellation in *Conversation in the Cathedral* ['la famosa interpelación vargasllosiana en *Conversación en La Catedral*']" (296). The well-known second sentence in this key boom novel asks: "At what precise moment had Peru fucked itself up?" (3).[44]

Conversation in the Cathedral may be the most explicit example among the boom novels of a Jamesonian "national allegory"—that is, a text where "the story of the private individual destiny is always an allegory of the embattled situation of the public third-world culture and society"

("Third World Literature" 320). In this novel, Vargas Llosa links the progressive personal and political frustrations of its protagonist, the once politically involved student turned corrupt journalist Santiago Zavala, with the history of Peru. But the answer Beltrán seeks by watching movies and by letting his memories spurt like highly pressurized Coke is, at least in principle, individual. While both Beltrán and Chile are "fucked up," to continue using the Vargas Llosian phrase, the solution to this abject situation for the protagonist and narrator of *The Movies of My Life* is personal: coming to terms with his own biography and acting on this new insight.[45] In *Conversation in the Cathedral*, on the other hand, it is clear that only a profound political transformation would permit individuals like Zavala to change their personal trajectory. But in a narrative decision that probably prefigures his later turn to the right, Vargas Llosa systematically discounts all conceivable agents of political change.

NEOLIBERAL NARRATIVES AND THE BORDER

A consequence of the constant presence of North American mass culture in Chilean life is that it becomes possible to see the country as a "border area," or "borderlands," to use Gloria Anzaldúa's term, even if the concepts are much more commonly used to describe the U.S. Southwest.[46] As mentioned above, Poblete has noted that one of the characteristics of McOndo texts is "indiscriminate cultural hybridization." This is, of course, a trait characteristic of borderlands. After all, as Anzaldúa points out in *Borderlands/La Frontera* about the ideal inhabitant of the borderland, the new mestiza: "The new mestiza copes by developing a tolerance for contradictions, a tolerance for ambiguity . . . She learns to juggle cultures" (79). In fact, throughout the novel Beltrán is Chilean without ever completely ceasing to be North American; or, in other words, Fuguet's protagonist exemplifies the fluidity of identity.[47]

The novel refers explicitly to the concept of the border, linking it with "the California" visited by the adult Beltrán. As mentioned above, the novel supposedly borrows its title from a book by the fictional "border" film director Martínez Romero. Lindsay claims that Martínez Romero's films capture "the energy of the border ['toda la energía fronteriza']" (49 [48]) ; while the latter states, in an interview supposedly aired on KCRW, the Angeleno public-radio: "My next film, called *Borderline*, is about a kid named Diego who works in a Borders Books in El Cajon, California. It's a comedy along the lines of Kevin Smith . . . My idea is to show that the border isn't just a place of suffering, but also a place where people live and even have sex" (158).[48] We have already seen that Lindsay and Martínez Romero present an optimistic vision of the border, as the location of "energy," and as the setting of a comedy à la Kevin Smith. However, Martínez Romero's words do not deny the existence of suffering as a characteristic of the border; just a decision to concentrate on its life-affirming possibilities.

Anzaldúa's description of the borderlands is different, even if she concludes *Borderlands/La Frontera* by depicting it as a potentially utopian space where all cultural and gender tensions will be resolved. Anzaldúa argues that a "borderland is a vague and undetermined place created by the emotional residue of an unnatural boundary. It is in a constant state of transition. The prohibited and forbidden are its inhabitants" (3); and "Do not enter, trespassers will be raped, maimed, strangled, gassed, shot. The only 'legitimate' inhabitants are those in power, the whites, and those who align themselves with whites" (3–4). The tension and constant strife described in the first pages of *Borderlands: La Frontera,* as characteristic of areas where cultures, nationalities, genders, and races come into contact, are absent from *The Movies of My Life.* (Although if one takes Beltrán's and his family's uprooting first to the United States and then their return to Chile as representing border experiences, it is possible to see Fuguet's portrayal as much more complex.)[49]

It is tempting to see in these divergent portrayals of the borderlands a reflection of the class and political differences between the iconic Chicano theorist and visionary and the Chilean novelist. Thus Anzaldúa's writings can be seen as expressing the experiences of what Pohl calls "migration of poverty ['migración de pobreza']" (Pohl "*Se habla español"* 264).[50] Even if Anzaldúa was not an immediate descendant of migrants—her family had lived in the Rio Grande valley before the North American annexation—she spent her childhood in poverty, doing the kind of work today frequently available to illegal immigrants: "My sister, mother and I cleaned, weighed and packaged eggs" (9). As she points out throughout *Borderlands/La Frontera,* the radical, anti-establishment nature of her thought is associated with the point of view of those excluded by white, heterosexual, and patriarchal United States (as well as Mexico). But Fuguet—and Beltrán—could be seen as exemplifying a cosmopolitan intellectual or professional capable of developing "strategies for success in a bilingual and competitive environment ['estrategias de éxito profesional en un espacio bilingüe y competitivo']" (Pohl 262).

The novel represents the migration of poverty through the character of Ambrosio Peña, a Salvadoran taxi driver Beltrán hires in Los Angeles. (Beltrán spends time there watching movies in a motel and writing about his life.) Ambrosio materially exemplifies hybridity. He wears "a García Márquez-esque guayabera, and hiking boots ['una guayabera tipo García Márquez y unos zapatos de petate']" (153[151]). His clothes thus combine the tropical garment par excellence—the guayabera—and truly

North American gear—hiking boots. This description also echoes Fuguet's critical writing, such as "Presentación" and "I Am Not a Magic Realist." If one assumes the guayabera as a marker of the local, maybe even of what is generally taken to be intrinsically Latin American, Fuguet is again connecting Magical Realism with folkloric stereotypes. (He may also be making fun of the fact that García Márquez seems to be fond of the guayabera, even wearing one to the Nobel Prize ceremony.)

Nevertheless, the overall impression given by Ambrosio is more McOndo than Macondo. Not only does he wear hiking boots, truly non-folkloric footwear, but also he is fully adapted to life in Los Angeles. He is, after all, a taxi driver, so by definition knows his way around. Moreover, this knowledge of Los Angeles, which is a sign of his adaptation to the new society, is even more noteworthy due to the fact that the novel describes the city as having "no center, no downtown" and being "so big that you can't help but get lost" (154).[51] Jameson has pointed out that one of the key traits of the new postmodern urban space is that "people are unable to map (in their minds) either their own positions or the urban totality in which they find themselves" ("Postmodernism" 229). Thus Ambrosio, despite his continued links with El Salvador, his homeland, is also at home in what from Fuguet's description can only be described as a postmodern—that is centerless and unmappable—metropolis.

But if Ambrosio is shown as comfortable in the postmodern borderlands, he is also at ease in the economic system that props it up. He is not only a taxi driver but also a small businessman: He owns three taxis and believes in capitalism (153). Furthermore, in what is almost a text case example of entrepreneurship, he has discovered a niche need. Ambrosio and his taxi drivers "pick up illegal immigrants at the airport and take them wherever they need to go; if they don't know, then they help them figure it out" (153).[52] In part, his business acumen can be seen as the result of living in Los Angeles which, in contrast with El Salvador, is seen as promoting the basic Protestant ethical values associated with capitalism: "Everyone in El Salvador is a thief, but here Salvadorans are hard workers and completely devoted to repaying what they owe. It just goes to prove that it's the environment that's bad and not the people" (153–54).[53]

The Movies of My Life is not the first text in which Fuguet has described the border as linked to capitalism. In another of his manifesto essays, "Magical Neoliberalism" (2001), Fuguet associates the border with the implementation of neoliberal reforms:

> The market reforms all over Latin America had to reform us as well. How could they not? If the point of liberalization was to open the doors, a

cultural and social flood had to pour in. And it did. Add to this mix advances in communications (cybercafes in slums, cellphones on cramped city buses), and you had a clean canvas on which to paint and new stories to tell. Yes, the economy grew (for a while), but creativity did even more so. Latin America stopped looking to Europe and Cuba for recognition, and while it perhaps looked toward Miami a bit more than necessary, the continent stumbled on its own new identity. For all this change and turmoil did not erase our sense of ourselves but made us confront who we were and admit that, in many senses, we were not that original. Perhaps that was our strength—to be young, mestizo hybrids speaking and writing in a language like Spanish that has always been open to foreign influences. (71)

Thus, for Fuguet, capitalism is not only consistent with but actually a precondition for the development of the "border." In fact, the implementation of radical free-market policies has converted Latin America itself into a type of borderland. It is, therefore, not surprising that Ambrosio's entrepreneurial gifts are fully compatible with his cultural hybridity.

If Ambrosio is a mestizo hybrid, though not that young, he does not exemplify the personal progressive political evolution that, according to Anzaldúa, ultimately characterizes the borderlands and its inhabitants. Despite the violence implicit in the borderlands, Anzaldúa argues that it creates the conditions that will lead to progressive change by promoting the break down of dualisms: "A massive uprooting of dualistic thinking in the individual and collective consciousness is the beginning of a long struggle, but one that could, in our best hopes, bring us to the end of rape, of violence, of war" (80). Ambrosio, however, has not experienced this breakdown of "dualistic thinking" and, it would seem, is in no danger of ever doing so. Ambrosio not only believes in capitalism but also "has a U.S. flag and photos of George W. Bush stuck to his visor" (83).[54] Ambrosio's hybridity is thus compatible with an extremely conservative "North Americanization" and also with a lasting concern with El Salvador and incoming immigrants.

But Ambrosio is not only a capitalist or a Republican, he is also a fascist or, at least, a fascist sympathizer, as the following exchange with Beltrán makes clear:

> "*Chileno o argentino?*" [*sic*]
> "*Chileno.*"
> "Like Don Francisco."
> "And Pinochet."
> "Two great men. You must be proud."
> "Neruda was Chilean too."
> "And a Communist, like Archbishop Romero." (154)[55]

Ambrosio is here shown to use right-wing political and media criteria in his evaluation of greatness. If Don Francisco is "great," it is because he is an extremely well-known media personality among U.S. Latinos. Pinochet's murderous policies are precisely the reason why Ambrosio admires him. Ambrosio implicitly validates the execution of Archbishop Romero, the most notorious of the murders committed by the right-wing Arena party during that country's civil war. One can safely assume that Ambrosio when he lived in El Salvador was at best an Arena sympathizer.

Creating Support for the Dictatorship
What gives this exchange—as well as Beltrán's refusal to continue contradicting Ambrosio—extra significance is the fact that the novel is condemnatory of the Pinochet dictatorship. Moreover, Fuguet is unusually perceptive in describing the ideological reasons behind middle class support for the brutal regime and how the latter was able to construct not only acquiescence but also enthusiasm for its policies. We have already seen how *The Movies of My Life* links the cynical manipulation of the idea of family (and of family values) with the creation of support for the dictatorship. But, distortions within family relations are also seen as creating a fertile ground for political violence. Thus "Grandma Guillermina," also known as "Mina," transforms her hatred toward her husband into support for counterrevolution and fascism: "Mina took advantage of Allende's triumph to bring to the surface decades of anger and resentment toward my grandfather, toward his family and towards the world in general" (117).[56] And: "When the right wing women took to the street to demand Allende's resignation, Mina felt that the Revolution had come. Nobody, it seemed had explained to her that actually the opposite was true" (117).[57] In the novel, the dictatorship is presented as tapping into a reservoir of personal gender and social resentment.

The novel provides more insight into the regime's techniques of public manipulation. For instance, it recounts the designation of the isolated and frequently put-upon young Beltrán as a classroom monitor for Operación Deyse, the government's public safety program. His "job was to watch over the 'safe and smooth evacuation from the classroom to an open patio'" (221). Then Beltrán adds: "Years later, I came to understand that that's the way a dictator can exert his power everywhere: he recruits the weak and the isolated and gives them power and responsibility" (221).[58]

The issue of the disappeared is also handled with subtlety. The novel introduces Tyrone Acosta Acosta, an adopted relative, who is described as a leftist, "a student and disciple of Ariel Dorfman ['alumno y discípulo de Ariel Dorfman']," a friend or boyfriend of one of Allende's daughters, a dandy and a gourmet whose goal was "to fight the cultural battle ['dar la batalla cultural']" (122 [121]). After he is disappeared, the young Beltrán, his sister Manuela, and their fanatically anticommunist grandmother Mina watch Franco Zeffirelli's *Brother Sun, Sister Moon* (1972). (Mina "claimed that the movie was Communist propaganda" [184]).[59] When Manuela mentions that "Saint Francis looked a bit like Tyrone Acosta Acosta with his beard and long hair," Beltrán asks, "if we could go visit Tyrone ['si lo íbamos a ver']" (184 [182]). (The children do not know he has been disappeared.) Their grandmother answers: "That boy was so smart, and yet he was stupid as well. I warned him not to get mixed up in any trouble, but he didn't pay any attention to me" (184).[60]

Guillermina places on Tyrone the responsibility for his own disappearance. For the Chilean right, the disappeared, rather than being victims of the brutality of the illegal military regime, have brought on themselves by their own actions just retribution. Guillermina's statement is experienced by the reader as particularly outrageous given that the novel has in a characteristically laconic manner already described Tyrone's disappearance: "Tyrone spent his last day correcting the proofs for the popular edition of *Cataclismo en Valdivia* [a book written by Teodoro, Guillermina's husband]" (123).[61] Despite the topsy-turvy logic that blames the victim, this (false) reasoning is in practice successful in that it justifies forgetting the disappeared. Thus according to the novel, after Guillermina's explanation of Tyrone's disappearance: "No family member ever spoke of him again. It was almost as if Tyrone Acosta Acosta had never existed" (184).[62] For the Chilean conservative middle class represented not without contradictions by Beltrán's family, the disappeared are ultimately responsible for their fates and, therefore, unworthy of mourning.

Fuguet is also aware of the role played by the United States in the Chilean coup. The novel briefly introduces Mike Tanner, "a gringo" Beltrán's father "had met on the plane ['un gringo que había conocido en el avión']" (199 [197]). Beltrán then laconically notes: "A year later, my father found out that the tall, kind gringo . . . was called Mike Tanner and that he'd just been arrested for setting off a car bomb in the Washington suburb of Bethesda, Maryland" (199).[63] Mike Tanner is thus the fictionalized version of Michael Townley, who placed a bomb in the car of Orlando Letelier, the former Chilean ambassador to the United States during Allende's government. But the exact relationship between Tanner and Pinochet's—or for that matter, Nixon's—government is never explained.

CALIFORNIA DREAMING

Despite this awareness of the role played by the United States in the Chilean coup, the United States is depicted as a kind of utopia. The supple investigation into the links between political events and social structures and beliefs that characterize Beltrán's memories of his Chilean youth is missing from the description of the United States. Earlier in this chapter we have seen how Beltrán compares an Encino "colonized by Frank Capra and Jimmy Stewart" favorably to a Chile conquered "by a group of stinking, resentful Spaniards who escaped their native land to kill Indians and rob them of their riches" (86). Beltrán thus forgets the fact that before Capra's and Stewart's benevolent "colonization"—as he calls what was only urban development—there was a real conquest: first by "resentful" Spaniards robbing land from the Indians, and then by equally morally suspect North Americans taking it from Mexicans.

A similar comparison between Encino and Chile, though this time dealing with contemporary politics rather than "colonial" history, is established later in the novel. Thus according to Beltrán: "In Encino, everyone hated Nixon and called him a liar and a cheat; in Chile, however, everyone seemed to love Pinochet and think of him as their savior" (182).[64] This passage illustrates the key limitation of the novel's political analysis. Beltrán seems unable to see beyond his immediate social circle. Many North Americans supported Nixon, even if he was hated by the (according to the novel) mostly Jewish and liberal inhabitants of Encino. Likewise, the novel ignores poorer or left-wing Chileans, who surely did not have a positive opinion of the dictator. Given Fuguet's astute description of the manner in which the fascist dictatorship gained consent among the middle class, this omission of significant sectors of the population only points out the limits of the world represented in the novel. And the absence of any representation of the manner in which the Nixon administration achieved consensus—he was reelected president and only lost significant support shortly before he resigned—reinforces the idyllic representation of the United States. The description of the United States as unblemished is surprising given the central role played by the Nixon administration in prodding and propping up the Pinochet regime. In *The Movies of My Life,* Nixon, and his support for Pinochet, is an unexplained and unexplainable fact. U.S. politics is presented as having no connection to North American society.

Conclusion: The End of Latin America?

The Movies of My Life can be seen, as Vargas Llosa notes, as "a bridge between the United States and Latin America" (back cover), in that it incorporates North American mass culture at every level of the narrative, including its basic semantic structure. The difficulty that Fuguet raises from and for a hypothetical Latin American position is that the term Latin America was adopted as a signifier for a group resistance to North American political and cultural imperialism. His writings, however, embrace rather than resist the culture of the United States.

This implicit anti–North Americanism, historically motivated by the actions of the United States, has characterized much of the region's literature. In the introduction to the anthology of short stories *Se habla español,* Paz Soldán and Fuguet write about José Donoso's negative portrayal of U.S. life in his novels, which they see as representative of that found in Latin American literature: "In order to justify his cruel characterization of the North American world, Donoso points out that it is about exercising 'our right to invade them and colonize them . . . and ignore them—and, why not?, avenge ourselves—like they invade, take over, and colonize us'" (18).[65] The problem with this symbolic revenge is that, at least according to Paz Soldán and Fuguet, it has generally led to substandard literature. Thus they ask, and try to answer with their story anthology, "Can one imagine the USA in its own terms?" (18).[66]

Despite (Paz Soldán's and) Fuguet's opposition to "combat a negative stereotype with another stereotype ['combatir un estereotipo de manera negativa con otro estereotipo']" (18), *The Movies of My Life* fails in that it is unable to maintain an equal subtlety in its description of social interactions in Chile and the United States. The result is that *The Movies of My Life* ultimately reverses the pattern Fuguet and Paz identify in earlier Latin American literature set in the United States. According to the editors of *Se habla español,* earlier writers such as Donoso and Fuentes[67] are only able to write unflattering caricatures of life in the United States. But Fuguet's representation of the United States as a land without a negative past or present—Encino was conquered by the beloved Jimmy Stewart and Frank Capra, and the Nixon administration is devoid of a social base—can be seen as the mirror image of these earlier texts.

There is no denying that Fuguet's work, in particular, *The Movies of My Life,* by incorporating the globalized North American culture as a key semantic element, implies a move beyond the binary opposition between the United States and Latin America. In a similar manner, the incorporation of the Latino experience in the United States in the narrative can also be seen as making the opposition much less strong since, at least to a degree, "One cannot conceive of Latin America without including the United States. And one cannot conceive of the United States without thinking about Latin America" (Paz Soldán and Fuguet 19).[68] Fuguet clearly describes a world commonality, and maybe even community, emerging from a globalized North American mass and commercial culture.

Rather than implying the disappearance of Latin America as an identifiable cultural space, *The Movies of My Life* can be interpreted as another example of Canclinian glocalization. Fuguet, like Caetano Veloso and other key contemporary cultural producers articulates "information, beliefs, and rituals deriving from the local, the national, and the international" (*Consumidores y ciudadanos* 86).[69] One of the consequences of this articulation of cultural elements belonging to what have, until recently, seemed clearly differentiated fields is the resemantization of what has been understood as Latin America. To continue with the Canclinian vocabulary, in *The Movies of My Life,* Fuguet attempts to reterritorialize Latin America by practicing "a radical restructuring of the links between the traditional and the modern, the popular and high culture, the local and the foreign" (*Culturas híbridas* 223). Thus, Fuguet's work, despite its contradictions, can be seen as an example of a Latin America—or, at least, a differentiated regional space—beyond Latin America as it was previously understood.

Epilogue: Latin America beyond Latin America?

Introduction

As *The Movies of My Life* illustrates, conventional notions of Latin America have been shaken by the social and cultural dynamics of the last decades. If Latin America was defined in opposition to the United States, globalization has led to the omnipresence of North American culture. Moreover, migration from the region to the North has created, to a greater or lesser degree throughout the region, what Román de la Campa has called split states:

> More than half the Latin American nations now have in the United States permanent diasporas, whose dollar remittances constitute a leading item in their former nation's economies [*sic*]. A split state implies a permanently severed entity, a loss in many respects; but, perhaps it could also suggest a postnational symptom that has many possibilities and applies to more than just states whose paths to modernity came under stress or failed to materialize altogether. (376)

Given the fluidity of location and an ever-growing cultural rate of change, notions of identity as linked exclusively to a specific geography and history have often become untenable. National and regional territorializations are undermined by the fact that they are acknowledged as temporary rather than as permanent. As the Chicano poet Francis X Alarcón once said, "Every Mexican is a potential Chicano." And something similar could be said about the inhabitants of most other Latin American countries.

However, it must be noted that this "splitting" of Latin America is itself a consequence of the evolving structural inequality between centers and peripheries, no matter how proliferating both may be, that constitutes globalized capitalism. In turn, the world economic system can be seen as the development rather than as the negation of international colonial economic structures. Thus, if the hegemonic position achieved by U.S. mass culture in Latin America originates in the unequal strength of their respective culture industries, the migration of, mainly though not exclusively, untrained labor from Latin America to the United States is also a response to this economic differential.

It is, however, also obvious that North American culture has been impacted by immigration. Latin American communities have modified the food eaten, as we all know, (Mexican) salsa is the favored condiment in the United States; entertainment, Shakira, Ricky Martin, Salma Hayek, and Jennifer López are household names; and even language, as Spanish words enter the mainstream. With characteristic eloquence, the Mexican American commentator Richard Rodriguez writes:

> Mexicans have slipped America a darker beer, a cuisine of *tú*... Mexicans have forced Southwestern Americans to speak Spanish whenever they want their eggs fried or their roses pruned. Mexicans have overwhelmed the Church—eleven o'clock masses in most Valley towns are Spanish masses. By force of numbers, Mexicans have taken over grammar-school classrooms. The Southwest is besotted with the culture of *tú*. (72)

And one can add that, with obvious differences, other Latin American migrations have had similar impacts throughout regions beside the Southwest. Furthermore, in the years since Rodriguez wrote *Days of Obligation* (1992), the text from where the quotation cited above comes, Mexican migration has expanded into all regions of the United States. Given this breakdown of real-life and imaginary boundaries between these two regions, it is impossible to speak about Latin America without including the United States and vice versa.

However, in Rodriguez's quotation, the blurring of cultural borders does not eradicate all differences. International neocolonial structures are implicit in Latin American immigration to the United States, but despite the significant impact of migrants on North American society and culture, class structures remain unchanged. The assimilation of the culture of *tú*—Rodriguez's term for the emphasis on the private and familial sphere that he finds characteristic of Mexico—by the "Southwestern Americans" is predicated precisely on the need to reproduce under new conditions their class hegemony. It is because they need to have their eggs fried and roses pruned that they are described as learning a very basic Spanish. For the migrants, on the other hand, the incorporation of cultural and linguistic North American traits is based on their need to survive, that is, to get work that permits them to cover their basic needs and those of their families. (Obviously, the situation of the professional migrants is different, but so is their number.) If, as Burkhard Pohl has pointed out, there is a migration of the poor and one of professionals, there is also a hybridity of the poor and of the rich.

Developmentalism, Neoliberalism, and Inequality

This unequal relationship between both regions has existed since the independence of Latin America and underlies regional identity constructions, from Bolívar's *América,* through Martí's *Nuestra América,* to Latin America. In fact, migration from Latin America to the United States dates back to the eighteenth century (de la Campa 377). However, it is also true that the economic developments in the region during the 1970s and 1980s—the breakdown of developmentalist policies and expectations, and the implementation of neoliberal economic policies, which was its consequence—have led to a great increase in the number of people forced to migrate.

The hegemony of neoliberal economic policy originated in the crisis of the developmentalist state beginning in the late 1970s as extreme bureaucratic expansion and careless fiscal policies led to hyperinflation. In fact, neoliberalism has found public justification in its success in controlling rising prices. Thus, according to Reinhardt and Savastano, "In Latin America and the Caribbean, the average rate of inflation dropped from 233 percent a year in 1990–94 to 7 percent in 2000–02" (20). Given this success, neoliberal policies were embraced throughout the region and permitted otherwise unsavory politicians, such as Alberto Fujimori and Carlos Saúl Menem, not only to gain power but also to be reelected. However, "the reduction and control of inflation is the only systematic success neoliberalization can claim" (Harvey 156). In fact, neoliberalism created mass unemployment, as the opening of internal markets to foreign competition destroyed the less efficient economic units in industry and agriculture, and led to a lowering of wages and income. Moreover, the implementation of neoliberal policies has frequently involved dismantling most of the protections achieved by workers and peasants after decades of political struggle.

The case of Mexico, of particular relevance in an examination of Latin American immigration to the United States, is far from unique in its general details. As David Harvey points out, the approval of NAFTA

(North American Free Trade Agreement) implied serious modifications in the legal structure of the country. The 1917 Constitution

> protected the legal rights of indigenous peoples and enshrined those rights in the *ejido* system that allowed land to be collectively held and used. In 1991 the Salinas government passed a reform law that both permitted and encouraged privatization of the *ejido* lands, opening them up to foreign ownership. Since the *ejido* provided the basis of collective security among indigenous groups, the government was, in effect, divesting itself of its responsibilities to maintain that security. The subsequent lowering of import barriers delivered yet another blow, as cheap imports from the efficient, but also highly subsidized agribusinesses in the United States drove down the price of corn and other products to the point where only the most efficient and affluent Mexican farmers could compete. Close to starvation, many peasants were forced off the land, only to augment the pool of unemployed in already overcrowded cities. (101)

In response to this crisis, Mexican immigration to the United States grew exponentially during the 1990s, in particular given that similar measures were taken in other sectors of the economy. And in Mexico, the informal economy, including drugs and, more generally, criminality, also flourished.

Neoliberalism, by definition, attempts to limit state intervention in the economy, as well as the protection of any social group no matter how underprivileged, being instead concerned with "liberating individual entrepreneurial freedoms and skills within an institutional framework characterized by strong private property rights, free markets, and free trade" (Harvey 2). Thus the weakening of constraints on the exploitation of labor or nature is central to the establishment of neoliberalism. Not surprisingly, the replacement of stable with temporary and lower paying jobs, and environmental degradation have gone hand in hand with the implementation of radical free-market policies.

The continuous state of emergency faced by the region from the 1970s to the present—first that of developmentalism in the late 1970s and 1980s, then the crisis promoted by neoliberalism in the 1980s and 1990s—is one of the underlying causes for the breakdown of the book and publishing industry in the region, analyzed earlier in the study. Thus the paradoxical dual cultural subalternity of Latin America at the start of the twenty-first century as being under the simultaneous tutelage of Spain and the United States is a consequence of the collapse of developmentalism and the implementation of neoliberal reforms. As the national economic infrastructures were broken down throughout the region, Spanish and North American capital rushed in to fill the vacuum and take benefit from the comparative advantages—low wages and lack of labor and environmental protections—offered.

Civil Rights and the Breakdown of National Identity

If migration and the impact of transnational culture put into question traditional notions of Latin America, these are not the only social forces undermining earlier regional and national identities. In addition to responding to North American and European developments and, in part, reacting to the impact of neoliberalism and its dismantling of state institutions, civil rights movements have flourished in Latin America. It is, however, important to remember that organized indigenous, women, and Afro-Latin civil rights movements have a long history in the region. (Only lesbian, gay, bisexual, and transgender movements can be seen as true innovations.) For instance, in 1919, a group of Peruvian "Indians or *indigenistas* [non-Indian sympathizers] who had become integrated radically and definitely to the Andean world" founded the Central Pro-Derecho Indígena Tahuantinsuyo (Arroyo n.p.).[1] And, at least since 1876, when the Chilean suffragists campaigned for the right to vote, women have been struggling for equality. Nevertheless, it is also obvious that the African American civil rights movement in the United States during the 1960s—and its expansion to other ethnic and gender groups during that decade and the following one—has played a key role in the recent development of similar concerns throughout Latin America. These movements have achieved successes. For instance, civil unions for partners of the same gender have been approved in the cities of Buenos Aires and Mexico, as well as limited rights for long-term partners throughout Colombia.

The fight for indigenous rights exhibits the greatest potential for modifying what is understood as Latin America by the inhabitants of the region themselves. They were implicitly excluded or assimilated under the concepts of Latin America and Spanish America but never accepted in their alterity. (Even mestizaje, that is, the belief that cultural and/or racial mixture roots Latin American national identities, can be seen as covert assimilationism.) Indigenous groups have in the last couple of decades made their presence profoundly felt, in particular, but not exclusively, in Bolivia and Ecuador. In fact, at least from a "racial" perspective, two presidents elected in the twenty-first century can be considered indigenous: Peru's Alejandro Toledo, who governed from 2001 to 2006, and Bolivia's Evo Morales, elected in 2006. (Despite the former's occasional use of Quechua trappings in speeches and ceremonies, only Morales can be seen as the product of an indigenous rights movement).[2]

But, in what can only seem a paradox, this rise of group identities and struggles has not necessarily been incompatible with neoliberalism and the reorganization of state and society it promoted. Harvey argues:

> For almost everyone involved in the movement of '68, the intrusive state was the enemy and it had to be reformed. And on that, the neoliberals could easily agree... Neoliberalization required both politically and economically the construction of a neoliberal market-based populist culture of differentiated consumerism and individual libertarianism. (42)

The weakening of patriarchal and racist state ideologies is thus not necessarily opposed to the free-market ideologies that privilege the individual over the collectivity. Thus the rise of a culture of civil rights—insofar as it does not contradict the free market—is compatible with neoliberalism. In fact, the writings of Vargas Llosa, the noted novelist who since the late 1970s has also become a vocal proponent of neoliberal policies, can serve as an example of the congruence of what could be called multicultural empowerment and the free market.

Neoliberal Multiculturalism
In one of his best-known articles, "The Culture of Liberty" (2000), Vargas Llosa criticizes the notion of collective identity:

> The concept of identity, when not employed on an exclusively individual scale is inherently reductionist and dehumanizing, a collectivist and ideological abstraction of all that is original and creative in the human being, of all that has not been imposed by inheritance, geography, or social pressure. Rather, true identity springs from the capacity of human beings to resist these influences and counter them with free acts of their own invention. (68)[3]

For Vargas Llosa, this breakdown of rigid identities is caused by modernization and globalization, the latter being for him a consequence of the former, and both intrinsically connected to the free market. In "The Culture of Liberty," maybe inconsistently, this breakdown of group identity seems limited to nationality—"the notion of collective identity is an 'ideological fiction' and the foundation of nationalism" (68).[4] According to Vargas Llosa, "Thanks to the weakening of the nation state, we are seeing forgotten, marginalized, and silent local cultures reemerging and displaying dynamic signs of life in the great concert of this globalized planet" (71).[5] Thus, for the Peruvian writer, Latin America is as much Hispanic, as indigenous, as African (69–70). However, in this essay, his prime example of this Renaissance of local cultures permitted by modernization, or to be more exact, the free market and globalization, is Spain (70–71).⁶

Vargas Llosa was more explicit about the possibilities for a similar rebirth of indigenous cultures in Latin America in his "Questions of Conquest and Culture," a lecture given in London in 1993. After asking whether traditional cultures can "become modern and overcome oppression while conserving what are essential or at least fundamental elements of their language, beliefs and traditions," he answers, "I believe this is possible for cultures like the Quechuas of the Andean region who number in the millions and have a long history" (n.p.). Even if Vargas Llosa presents this as potentiality rather than as actuality, for him neoliberalism is not in principle incompatible with the development and arguably defense of indigenous culture and cultural rights.⁷

Given Vargas Llosa's celebration of multiculturalism, it is not surprising that he also has great sympathy for the gay civil rights movement and for immigrants in the United States and Europe. Vargas Llosa thus describes the legalization of gay marriage in Spain as "an extraordinary step forward in the file of human rights and the culture of liberty" ("El matrimonio gay" 35).⁸ And in his speech during the reception of the Irving Kristol Award, the (U.S.) neoconservative "Nobel Prize," he argues about Latin American immigrants: "Without denouncing its origins, this community is integrating with loyalty and affection into its new country and forging strong ties between the two Americas" (n.p.). Immigration is, therefore, weakening exclusive national and regional identities that Vargas Llosa decries as inimical to tolerance and what he calls the culture of liberty. Instead, the arrival of Latin Americans in the United States creates plural identities and affections, enriching what it means to be North American.

*Postcolonial Multiculturalism
and the Deconstruction of Latin America*
This celebration of the disruptive and creative potential of minority civil rights movements and groups is also present in the writings of many progressive intellectuals. Prominent among these is Walter Mignolo, arguably the most important postcolonial theorist writing about Latin America. In his *The Idea of Latin America* (2005), he provides a powerful and convincing deconstruction of the concept of Latin America. Mignolo with great theoretical insight taps into Edmundo O'Gorman's argument about the "invention of America," using it to undermine any essentialistic vision of the region. Rather than an objective representation of a geographic or cultural entity, the idea of America implies "the appropriation and integration of the continent into the Euro-Christian imaginary" (3).

The concept and name *Latin America* would just be another avatar of the process of invention, moreover, one in which the already Eurocentric core of the concept would be renewed, if not deepened: "To conceive themselves as a 'Latin' race ... Creoles in 'Latin' America had to rearticulate the colonial difference in a new format: to become the internal colonizers vis-à-vis the Indians and Blacks while living an illusion of independence from the logic of coloniality" (86).

Despite Mignolo's convincing demystification of the idea of Latin America, there is a surprising lack of concern with the historical context during which this notion was developed. The term *Latin America* was taken up by criollo intellectuals precisely during the period when U.S. imperialism in the region had become a reality. In fact, the expansion of the United States into then Mexican territory was justified by a virulent racialist rhetoric in which the celebration of putative Anglo-Saxon traits—such as democratic values—was juxtaposed against the denigration and animalization of the Mexican population. According to Reginald Horsman, "The process of dehumanizing those who were to be misused or destroyed proceeded rapidly in the United States of the 1840s. To take lands from inferior barbarians was no crime; it was simply following God's injunction to make the land fruitful" (211). And:

> The American dismissal of the Mexicans as an inferior, largely-Indian race did not pass unnoticed in Mexico. Mexican ministers in the United States warned their government that the Americans considered the Mexicans an inferior people ... Mexicans who served as diplomatic representatives in the United States were shocked at the rabid anti-Mexican attitudes and at the manner in which Mexicans were lumped together with Indians and blacks as an inferior race. (212–13)

Thus the adoption of *Latinidad* attempted to answer the racialist rhetoric in the United States by claiming a common mantle of whiteness for the region's population. Granted that Mignolo is correct in that it marked another moment in the conceptual marginalization of populations of indigenous and African background, but given the cultural moment in which Latinidad was developed, one in which racialism had unfortunately become internationally accepted as science, the adoption of this notion is understandable. What Horsman says about the intellectual climate in North America is also characteristic of the West as a whole during the second half of the nineteenth century: "It was unusual by the late 1840s to profess a belief in innate human equality and to challenge the idea that a superior race was about to shape the fates of other races for the future good of the world. To assert this meant challenging not only popular opinion, but also the opinion of most American intellectuals" (250). Moreover, Latin American claims to whiteness are not new. They were, in fact, present already in Bolívar's emphasis on being "European by right ['europeos por derecho']" (56). However, the adoption of Latinidad restructured these claims in response to this intensely racialized cultural and political climate. In fact, the few North American critics of their country's expansion into Mexico frequently justified their position in terms that remind one of the Latin American espousal of Latinidad by claiming that Mexicans were also descended from Europeans (Horsman 252, 260).

Given this negative view of "the idea of Latin America," Mignolo warmly welcomes the rise of civil and cultural rights movements that, in his opinion, problematize it: "Delinking from that concept [*Latinidad*] and building an 'after-(Latin) America' is one of the steps being taken by Indians, Afros, women of color, gays, and lesbians" (101). While Mignolo has not included Latinas and Latinos in this passage, they are central to this building of an "after-(Latin)America": "The idea of Latin America . . . is not only broken up by the massive migration of people from the South to the North but also by the critical consciousness that develops in that movement, the epistemology of the borderlands and the Mestiza consciousness" (137). It is, therefore, not surprising that according to Mignolo, "the Latino/a experience in the US parallels the emergent critical consciousness of Afro-Andean, Afro-Brazilian, Afro-Caribbean, and indigenous people throughout the Americas" (137). For Mignolo, the breakdown of this racist and patriarchal notion of Latin America is empowering the American multitude—both North and South.[9]

Right and left contrasted. It should be clear that I have not juxtaposed Vargas Llosa and Mignolo, right and left, in order to invalidate their arguments. (One assumes that for some neoliberals, the fact that ideas are held by Mignolo would automatically render them invalid; in a similar manner, for others, Vargas Llosa, the personification of neoliberalism is also necessarily wrong.) Nor am I attempting to hide their numerous differences. After all, Vargas Llosa, despite his multicultural rhetoric, has been critical of practically all real-life indigenous movements in Latin America. Thus he has attacked Evo Morales for what Vargas Llosa claims is his stress on racial antagonisms as well as Bolivian nationalism ("Asoma en la región un nuevo racismo" 1). But the core of his opposition to Morales and other indigenous movements resides in his belief that, like Hugo Chávez, they are trying to bring back developmentalist economic policies.¹⁰ Mignolo, on the contrary, is opposed to neoliberalism and celebrates "noalca" (opposition to the Free Trade of the Americas) composed of diverse social groups—feminists, Zapatistas, indigenous groups, and even the progressive governments that have risen in the region.¹¹

However, the presence of key points in common—opposition to traditional identity, celebration of cultural differences, and defense of expanding civil rights—is significant. In fact, I would argue that they serve to point out, what could be called, a common economic horizon of expectations shared not only by these but also by most other critics. This commonality is brought into focus if one notices that, curiously, both Vargas Llosa and Mignolo admire some of the same political figures: Luiz Inácio Lula da Silva, the current president of Brazil, as well as some of the other "left" leaning presidents recently elected in Latin America.

During his Irving Kristol Award speech, Vargas Llosa extolled "Lula in Brazil who, before becoming president, espoused a populist doctrine, an economic nationalism and the traditional hostility of the left towards the market, but who is now a practitioner of fiscal discipline and a promoter of foreign investment, private business and globalization, although he wrongly opposes the Free Trade Area of the Americas" (n.p.). For Vargas Llosa, Luiz Inácio Lula da Silva is an example of "a certain modernization of the left, which, without recognizing it, is admitting that the road to economic progress and social justice passes through democracy and the market, which we liberals have long preached into the void" (n.p.). In the case of Lula, as well as Tabaré Vásquez, and, with some hesitation, Néstor Kirchner, Vargas Llosa identifies a will to govern within the limits of the free market. Despite the fact that Lula, to his credit, has implemented a number of progressive policies, such as his *Fome Zero* (Zero Hunger) initiative, he has done so basically within the inherited framework of Fernando Henrique Cardoso's neoliberal policies.¹² Implicit in Vargas Llosa's praise for Lula, as in his celebration of civil rights movements, is the condition that any attempt to improve society be maintained within limits established by the free market.

For Mignolo, Lula is also an exemplary figure: "The democratic victory of Inacio Lula da Silva in Brazil adds to the radical scope of current transformations" (92). Moreover, like Vargas Llosa, Mignolo admires the manner in which Lula's policies seem to contradict those of the traditional (and not so traditional) left: "He is on his way to making obsolete any postmodern debate, in Europe, about making Lenin useful again for the future of the humanity" (93).¹³ More important for Mignolo is the way Lula's rise problematizes the notion of a "more 'Spanish' than 'Portuguese' Latin America"; his supposed disregard for the International Monetary fund and other international institutions; and his attempt to develop a G3 trade block with South Africa and India, which "will move these countries toward a proactive role in 'an-other' globalization" (93).

Despite their many differences, the case can be made that Vargas Llosa and Mignolo share a conceptual framework ultimately based on capitalism and the free market. The main difference resides in that Mignolo emphasizes the fact that "another world is possible," which in his case consists of an attack on the neocolonial divisions through which contemporary capitalism is structured, rather than a replacement of the free market or capitalism itself.[14] The question that remains is whether restructurings of global capitalism like Lula's G3 trade block, no matter how necessary, will be able to eliminate its foundational inequality. In fact, the limited success of Lula's national and international policies can only make one pessimistic about the possibility of creating a noncentralized and humane capitalism even if the quest for alternative economic and social organization continues to be indispensable.

It should be obvious that Mignolo is here presented as representative of the quandaries of contemporary radical thought. No critic, no matter how radical, has as of now presented a comprehensive alternative to free-market policies. In fact, as Vargas Llosa correctly notes, Hugo Chávez and Evo Morales have returned to developmentalist nationalism ("Asoma en la región un nuevo racismo" 1). As of now, the only alternative to the present seems to be the past.[15]

A Post–Latin American Space
In a surprisingly positive article on Isabel Allende, Alberto Fuguet argues that the best-selling Chilean author has managed in her literary career to move from being a Chilean writer—with *The House of the Spirits*—to a pan–Latin American writer—with *Eva Luna*—to a full-fledged "North American writer who writes in Spanish"—with *Paula* ("¿De qué hablamos cuando hablamos de Isabel Allende?" 78).[16] While Fuguet omits the field of Latino literature—could Allende be said to have temporarily joined that tradition with *The Infinite Plan*?—he establishes clear distinctions between these different literary spaces. However, as the case of Allende illustrates, it is possible to move from one to the other.[17]

What Fuguet's statement foregrounds is that despite immigration, globalization—of capital and culture—and the breakdown promoted by the rise of group identities and civil rights movements, the hemisphere is made up of identifiable though connected cultural spaces.

Nevertheless, how the Latin American space is constituted and what is meant by Latin America is clearly in turmoil. As we have seen, for writers like Vargas Llosa and Fuguet, the traditional opposition between Latin America and the United States has become moot due to migration and the cultural changes that have taken place in both regions. (But both seem to believe that the neocolonial structural inequality within which these cultural and other exchanges take place has somehow disappeared.) For Mignolo, on the other hand, the creation of an "after Latin America" constituted by alliances and collaborations among different anticolonial groups inside and outside the region is replacing traditional regional identities. (But he is unable to provide examples of how these collaborations would be translated into an alternative economic reality.) And for both Vargas Llosa and Mignolo, this new or (after) Latin America is seen as including previously marginalized or excluded groups, such as racial, ethnic, and sexual minorities, and, ambiguously in the case of the former, indigenous populations.

But there are alternative conceptualizations that, never having fully lost relevance, have become revitalized in recent years. Thus the influx of Spanish capital and the political activity of that country's governments have given the notion of Ibero-America and Spanish America a new relevance, as it reflects faithfully aspects of the region's cultural reality. And the discontent of large sectors in Latin America with the social effects of neoliberalism has permitted Hugo Chávez, with the support of Fidel Castro and Evo Morales, among others, to revive the anti–North American component present in Latin America, by tapping into the foundational ideas of Simón Bolívar, no matter in how modified a form.

Thus what is going to be understood in the future as Latin America, or even if the term itself will survive, is impossible to know. What we know is that we are living during a moment when ideological and political struggles, as well as changing economic, cultural, and populational realities are creating new signifiers and signifieds for the region and beyond. Nevertheless, a sense of continuity is still to be found as reterritorializations and reconceptualizations renew Latin America's location in world culture.

Notes

Introduction

1. *Webster's* provides a second dual definition of the word *criollo:* "a domestic animal of a breed or strain (as of cattle) developed in Latin America; *especially often capitalized:* any of a breed of hardy muscular ponies originally developed in Argentina." The *Oxford English Dictionary* (*OED*) defines *criollo* exclusively as "A variety of cocoa tree, Theobroma cacao, native to Central America; also, a name for high-quality cocoa or cocoa beans." However, as a kind of ghostly presence, it gives the etymology as "a. Sp. criollo native to the locality," and advises the user to see the entry for *creole,* which is presented as the English cognate and overall equivalent for the Spanish term. In fact, according to the *OED,* the first use of the word *creole,* though spelled "crollos," was in a translation of the Spanish chronicler Acosta, and the term was defined as "the Spaniard borne at the Indies." While *creole* is first defined, "In the West Indies and other parts of America, Mauritius, etc.: orig. A person born and naturalized in the country, but of European (usually Spanish or French) or of African Negro race," the *OED* notes that "now, usually, = creole white, a descendant of European settlers, born and naturalized in those colonies or regions, and more or less modified in type by the climate and surroundings." The trouble with the switch from *criollo* to *creole* proposed by the *OED* is that the definition of the former is presented as having had an unproblematic semantic evolution.
2. The following is the amended definition of the word as it will appear in the twenty-third edition of the *Diccionario de la lengua española*:

   criollo, lla. (Del port. crioulo, y este de criar). 1. adj. Dicho de un hijo y, en general, de un descendiente de padres europeos: Nacido en los antiguos territorios españoles de América y en algunas colonias europeas de dicho continente. U. t. c. s. 2. adj. Se decía de la persona de raza negra nacida en tales territorios, por oposición a la que había sido llevada de África como esclava. U. t. c. s. 3. adj. Dicho de una persona: Nacida en un país hispanoamericano, para resaltar que posee las cualidades estimadas como características de aquel país. U. t. c. s. 4. adj. Autóctono, propio, distintivo de un país hispanoamericano. 5. adj. Peculiar, propio de Hispanoamérica. 6. adj. Se dice de los idiomas que han surgido en comunidades precisadas a convivir con otras comunidades de lengua diversa y que están constituidos por elementos procedentes de ambas lenguas. Se aplica especialmente a los idiomas que han formado, sobre base española, francesa, inglesa, holandesa o portuguesa, las comunidades africanas o indígenas de ciertos territorios originariamente coloniales.

I have translated the definitions in the introduction.
3. "Un sentido que evocará valores y virtudes positivas y cuyo término contrapuesto será el de 'gringo' o 'inmigrante'" (Altamirano and Sarlo 184). José Luis Romero describes the earlier, negative connotation of criollo as "lo primitivo, lo elemental" (qtd. in Altamirano and Sarlo 183).

Throughout this book, the translations into English are mine except where an English-language source is cited.
4. In *No, Suplemento oven de Página 12,* the Argentine newspaper, Cristian Vitale writes: "The hard rock criollo owed an homage to Deep Purple, a fundamental group to explain the essence of the genre ['El hard rock criollo le debía un homenaje a Deep Purple, grupo elemental si los hay para explicar la esencia del genero']" (n.p.).
5. "Destruída la civilización inkaica por España, constituído el nuevo Estado sin el indio y contra el indio, sometida la raza aborigen a la servidumbre, la literatura peruana tenía que ser criolla, costeña, en la proporción en que dejara de ser española. No pudo por esto surgir en el Perú una literatura vigorosa. El cruzamiento del invasor con el indígena no había producido en el Perú un tipo más o menos homogéneo. A la sangre ibera y quechua se había mezclado un copioso torrente de sangre africana. Más tarde la importación de coolies debía añadir a esta mezcla un poco de sangre asiática. Por ende, no había un tipo sino diversos tipos de criollos, mestizos" (Mariátegui, *Siete ensayos* 243).
6. Mariátegui is at his best dismissive of the hegemonic racialism of the time. For instance, in *Siete ensayos,* he notes that "the racial question . . . is artificial and does not merit the attention of those who study politically the indigenous question ['la cuestión racial . . . es artificial, y no merece la atención de quienes estudian concreta y políticamente el problema indígena']" (343). On the traces of racialism in his writings, see my *Mestizo Nations* (84–92).
7. On mestizaje as a national discourse, see *Mestizo Nations: Culture, Race, and Conformity,* esp. 11–25.
8. "Sin la posicionalidad hegemónica del peninsular pero también sin la subalternidad definitiva de indios, negros y castas coloniales, el criollo elabora durante la colonia el lugar de la intermediación y la hibridez en un proceso de complejas negociaciones reales y simbólicas, en las que va inscribiendo en la categoría occidentalista de civilización los principios de una racionalidad otra, que desafía, contamina y desestabiliza la epistemología dominante" (Moraña, "La diferencia criolla" 55).
9. This binary description of colonialism is later problematized by Fanon as he describes "pitfalls of national consciousness" and the problems raised by the existence of middle, bourgeois, and intellectual classes delinked from the colonial masses. (See *The Wretched of the Earth* 148–205.)

10. At the dawn of Latin American independence, Simón Bolívar had already noted the uniqueness of the criollos and their unfortunate opposition to indigenous groups: "We are not Europeans, we are not Indians, but rather an intermediate species between the aboriginal peoples and the Spaniards. Americans by birth, Europeans by right, we find ourselves in the conflictive situation of disputing with the natives the right to the land ['No somos europeos, no somos indios, sino una especie media entre los aborígenes y los españoles. Americanos por nacimiento y europeos por derecho, nos hallamos en el conflicto de disputar a los naturales los títulos de posesión']" ("Discurso de Angostura" 56).
11. "El chino noble o burgués se siente entrañablemente chino . . . En Indo-América las circunstancias no son las mismas. La aristocracia y la burguesía criollas no se sienten solidarizadas con el pueblo por el lazo de una historia y de una cultura comunes" (Mariátegui, "Punto de vista anti-imperialista" 88).
12. The full quotation in Spanish is: "La traición de la burguesía china, la quiebra del Kuo-Min-Tang, no eran todavía conocidas en toda su magnitud. Un conocimiento capitalista, y no por razones de justicia social y doctrinaria, demostró cuan poco se podía confiar, aún en países como la China, en el sentimiento nacionalista revolucionario de la burguesía" (Mariátegui, "Punto de vista anti-imperialista" 12).
13. For a brief but lucid introduction to the indigenous literatures of Latin America, see Gordon Brotherston's "Indigenous Literatures and Cultures in Twentieth-Century Latin America." Brotherston emphasizes the continuous existence of an indigenous literary tradition from pre-Columbian times to the present, but he does not mention a single major indigenous writer working in Spanish or Portuguese. In part this is due to the fact that "collective authorship has undoubtedly been the norm in native literary production" (296). However, he mentions several indigenous-language writers. Brotherston, therefore, insinuates that differences in language, in the implied reader, and in the cultural tradition within which the act of writing is inserted are among the defining traits of what constitutes an indigenous identity.
14. While Dussel marginalizes the role of Portugal in the origins of the world system, one must remember that the Portuguese developed the plantation system, one of the key institutions of this first modernity, and played an unfortunate central role in the spread of slavery to the new world. On the Portuguese invention of the plantation system early in the 1500s in the Azores and on their role in the dissemination of slavery, see Sidney M. Greenfield's "Slavery and the Plantation in the New World" (45–49).
15. "Esos bárbaros del Nuevo Mundo e islas adyacentes . . . son tan inferiores a los españoles como los niños a los adultos, las mujeres a los varones . . . finalmente estoy por decir los monos a los hombres" (Sepúlveda 33).

   In additional to being a foundational statement of racism as a justification for colonialism, Sepúlveda's statements are proof of a genetic link between the establishment of racial hierarchy and patriarchy.

16. Edna Aizenberg's analysis of Jorge Luis Borges as a "postcolonial precursor" is an example of the links between the postcolonial texts produced in Asia and Africa and Latin American literature. As Aizenberg notes, "Borges provided a model of literary postcoloniality: an intellectual writing in a Western language, both within and without the West, who used non-Western elements, or elements at the edge of the West's table . . . to enrich literature" (*Books and Bombs in Buenos Aires* 112).

    The impact of Gabriel García Márquez's *One Hundred Years of Solitude* on the narrative of Africa and Asia is another example of the connections between the literatures of Latin America and those of the rest of the "global south."
17. Aijaz Ahmad's description of the history of India's intelligentsia is reminiscent of that of the criollo: "There was already, during the colonial period, a distinct hierarchical divide between the 'national' functions of the intelligentsia, which were carried out in English, and the regional functions, which were carried out in the indigenous languages—sometimes by the same people, but at distinct sites." After noting that Hindi has spread thanks to the electronic media and that English has become the "major language for fiction writing," Ahmad adds: "These shifts in the post-colonial period have further augmented the tendency—among the metropolitan intellectuals especially, but also in large sectors of the bourgeois intelligentsia inside India—to view the products of the English-writing intelligentsia of the cosmopolitan cities as the central documents of India's *national* literature" (76). Needless to say, the separation between an Anglophone intelligentsia and Hindi and other autochthonous-language-speaking masses can be seen as reproducing, with significant differences, the kind of cultural separation noted by Mariátegui about Latin America.
18. My interest in Moretti and, especially, Casanova is mainly heuristic, in that they help focus on the questions raised by the location of Latin American literature within world literature. However, many of their preoccupations have long been central to Latin American criticism, which, moreover, has frequently exhibited not only a greater awareness of local reality and history, but also greater rigor in its theorizations. Throughout *The Spaces of Latin American Literature,* I tap into the insights of Latin American critics—such as Antonio Cornejo Polar, Ángel Rama, or Roberto Schwarz—as well as, when useful, into those by Moretti and, in particular, by Casanova.
19. "Injértese en nuestra república el mundo; pero el tronco ha de ser el de nuestras repúblicas" (Martí 89).
20. The full sentence is: "Llegada tarde al banquete de la civilización europea, América vive saltando etapas, apresurando el paso, y corriendo de una forma u otra, sin haber dado tiempo a que madure del todo la forma precedente" (Reyes 82–83).
21. This lag of Latin American cultural production when compared with that of the central countries had already been noted in the mid-seventeenth century by Espinoza y Medrano. After acknowledging that the subject of

his writing, Luis de Góngora, had been dead for more than twenty years, he states: "It seems I come late to this task, but we criollos live very far and if interest is not involved, things from Spain take long to visit us ['Tarde parece que salgo a esta empresa. pero vivimos muy lejos los criollos y si no traen las alas del interés; perezosamente nos visitan las cosas de España']" (*Apologético* 17).
22. "Mas yo, con su licencia, tomo el *Quijote* de Cervantes, la obra maestra en clase de romances, y no veo en su acción nada raro, nada extraordinario, nada prodigioso. Todos los sucesos son demasiado vulgares y comunes" (Lizardi xiv).
23. Mario Vargas Llosa attempts to explain the prohibition of the novel in the following terms: "The Spanish Inquisitors, for instance, prohibited the publication and importation of novels in the Spanish American colonies with the argument that these absurd and nonsensical—that is, false—works could be bad for the spiritual health of the Indians ['Los inquisidores españoles, por ejemplo, prohibieron que se publicaran o importaran novelas en las colonias hispanoamericanas con el argumento de que esos libros disparatados y absurdos—es decir, mentirosos—podían ser perjudiciales para la salud espiritual de los indios']" (*La verdad de las mentiras* 15). However, Spanish authorities were not concerned with the spread of literacy among indigenous populations, so the number of Amerindians capable of reading novels was relatively small.
24. It is difficult to define the *tradición* given that, as Kristal notes, it "blurred the boundaries between history and fiction, in a dialogue with poetry and folklore" (69). However, the constant in these texts, which also frequently veer into the essayistic form, is that they are all investigations into the origins of historical, linguistic, or literary facts that for Palma constituted Latin American and Peruvian difference.
25. Kristal clearly differentiates between Latin America and the West. For instance, when he claims that "as Latin American culture moved towards modern poetry, writers in the West began to come to terms with forms developed in Latin America" (71).
26. One can ask to what degree the emphasis on the backwardness of Latin American narrative at the start of the century does not respond to what could be called a retroactive optical effect caused by our privileging of the modernist and avant-garde masterpieces over what was the literary mainstream at the time. This distortion is evident if one takes as an example what was then called the Pulitzer Prize for the Novel (1918–1947). The first, only arguably modernist, text to receive the award is Thornton Wilder's 1928 best seller, *The Bridge of San Luis Rey*. The rest of the recipients can be loosely classified as "realists"—Sinclair Lewis, Edna Ferber, Willa Cather, Edith Wharton, Booth Tarkington.
27. "Hace tiempo que entre España y nosotros existe un sentimiento de nivelación y de igualdad. Y ahora yo digo ante el tribunal de pensadores internacionales que me escucha: reconocemos el derecho a la ciudadanía universal

que ya hemos conquistado. Hemos alcanzado la mayoría de edad. Muy pronto os habituaréis a contar con nosotros" (Reyes 90).
28. The prime example of the invisibility of Palma in Euro-North American criticism is the fact that while Perry Anderson and Casanova have both singled out the importance of Darío in the history of "modernism," the specific context in which Anderson introduces the Nicaraguan poet, the coining of the term modernismo, is that of his encounter with Palma whom he does not mention (Anderson 3; Casanova "Literature as a World" 89).
29. Kristal is the author of an important analysis of nineteenth- and early twentieth-century indigenismo, where he concludes that "indigenismo is fundamentally an urban literary phenomenon: it expresses city dwellers' views on the Indian" (*The Andes Viewed from the City* 217).
30. Despite the fact that indigenismo is frequently seen as naturalist, it should be pointed out that several of the genre's classics, such as Ciro Alegría's *Los perros hambrientos* (*The Hungry Dogs*), which includes a dog's internal monologue, and the majority of José María Arguedas's texts, can be seen as exhibiting a dialogue with contemporary modernisms and avant-gardes. In fact, if one assumes, as most critics have, Clorinda Matto de Turner's *Aves sin nido* (*Torn from the Nest*) (1889) as the first major indigenista text, and José María Arguedas's *El zorro de arriba y el zorro de abajo* (*The Fox from Up Above and the Fox from Down Below*) (1971) as arguably its last important one, indigenismo can be seen as developing from a mixture of romanticism and naturalism, to a sui generis postcolonial version of postmodernism.
31. "Creo que nuestra tradición es toda la cultura occidental, y creo también que tenemos derecho a esta tradición, mayor que el que pueden tener los habitantes de una u otra nación universal . . . Creo que los argentinos, los sudamericanos en general . . . podemos manejar todos los temas europeos, manejarlos sin supersticiones, con . . . irreverencia" (Borges, "El escritor agentino y la tradición" 160–61).
32. "Um Occidente ao occidente do Occidente" (Veloso, *Verdade Tropical* 499).

Chapter 1

1. The complete Spanish title is "Carta Atenagórica, Carta de la Madre Juana Inés de la Cruz, religiosa del convento deSan Jerónimo de la ciudad de Méjico, en que hace juicio de un sermón del Mandato que predicó el Reverendísimo P. Antonio de Vieyra, de la Compañía de Jesús, en el Colegio de Lisboa."
2. The phrase "ill-fated letter" comes from the English-language version of Paz's study. Curiously, in his Spanish original, the Carta Atenagórica is simply called "una carta de más ['an unnecessary letter']" (Paz, *Sor Juana Inés de la Cruz* 511).

    Given the significant differences between the two versions of Octavio Paz's study of Sor Juana, I quote the English version in the body of this chapter.

3. Little is known about Espinoza's life. According to Tamayo Vargas, Lunarejo was born between 1619 and 1630, in the Andean region of Aymaraes and died in Cuzco in 1688 (ix). The rest of what we know about him is linked to his publications as well as to his academic and ecclesiastic activities. He was a philosophy professor and also a priest who worked in the Cathedral of Cuzco.

Criticizing the frequent representation of Lunarejo as a "pitifully poor Indian," González Echevarría argues, "Recent discoveries made by scholars bring Lunarejo closer to the figure of the 'baroque gentleman' elaborated by José Lezama Lima, which he proposes typifies the period: 'He dwells in his estate, canonry or pleasure house with a modesty that augments the amusement of the intellect. His type appears when the tumult of the Conquest and the distribution of the colonized landscape are finished'" (*Celestina's Brood* 149–50).

4. "Sor Juana Inés de la Cruz, refiriéndose a la Celestina respondió irónicamente a la supuesta superioridad del centro escribiendo, 'siempre las (comedias) de España son mejores' para luego compararlas con la Celestina mexicana que 'era mestiza/ y acabada a retazos,/ y si le faltó traza, tuvo trazos,/ y con diverso genio/ ser formó de un trapiche y de un ingenio.' Aunque reconoce Sor Juana la sofisticación de las obras importadas—'nunca son pesadas/ las cosas que por agua están pasadas,'—defiende la producción local. La combinación de trapiche e ingenio produce algo que tiene valor: el azúcar" (Franco, "Nunca son pesadas" 187).

5. "Tarde parece que salgo a esta empresa. pero vivimos muy lejos los criollos y si no traen las alas del interés; perezosamente nos visitan las cosas de España" (Espinoza, *Apologético* 17).

6. "Sátiros nos juzgan, tritones nos presumen, que brutos de alma, en vano se alientan a dementirnos máscaras de humanidad" (Espinoza, *Apologético* 17).

7. According to Paz, Sor Juana "enjoyed the protection of all the viceroys. She was confidante and friend of two vicereines, Leonor Carreto and María Luisa Manrique de Lara (271) ['Gozó sin interrupción de la protección de todos los virreyes. Fue confidente y amiga de dos virreinas: Leonor Carreto y María Luisa Manrique de Lara']" (355).

8. "La Respuesta permanece hasta hoy como el testimonio más directo de las limitaciones y desafíos que imponía sobre la jerónima su condición subalterna con respecto a los poderes peninsulares y al autoritarismo patriarcal que dirigía los espacios de la corte y el convento" (Moraña, "Barroco y transculturación" 36).

9. "La dicotomía medieval paganismo/ cristianismo tuvo en Nueva España mayor fuerza y actualidad que en la metrópoli: el catolicismo/ los otros . . . Esa dualidad era la consecuencia de una línea de división tajante: una ortodoxia. A su vez la ortodoxia requería, como la mano necesita simultáneamente la regla y la espada, una Iglesia y un Estado. También en esto España se distinguió, en el alba de la modernidad, de los otros estados europeos. En todos ellos, de una manera o de otra, se prosigue la identificación entre dos realidades que hasta la Edad Moderna habían vivido una vida independiente: el

Estado y la Nación. Pero ninguno de los Estados-naciones se identificó tan completamente como España con una religión universalista" (Paz, *Sor Juana Inés de la Cruz* 48–49).

10. Regarding the intertwining of politics and religion in the Inquisition, E. Bradford Burns writes, "The Inquisition served as much a political as a religious end in its vigilant efforts to purge and purify society in order to make it unified and loyal" (56). More recently, historians have begun emphasizing the economic role played by the Inquisition. For instance, Stanley M. Hordes points out, "Regardless of the motivation for the establishment of the Holy Office, it is clear that the Catholic Monarchs expected the institution to function as a profit-making body for the Crown. Early in its formative years, the Inquisition developed standard procedures for confiscating the estates of convicted heretics, appropriating a portion of them for its own use, and remitting the balance to the royal treasury. It is estimated that Ferdinand and Isabella derived more than ten million ducados from inquisitorial confiscations to help finance the war against the Moors at the close of the fifteenth century" (25).

11. "Éntreme religiosa, porque aunque conocía que tenía el estado cosas (de las accesorias hablo, no de las formales) muchas repugnantes a mi genio, con todo, para la total negación que tenía al matrimonio, era lo menos desproporcionado" (Sor Juana, "Respuesta" 14–16).

12. "Pareciéndome preciso, para llegar a ella, subir por los escalones de las ciencias y artes humanas, porque ¿cómo entenderá el estilo de la Reina de las Ciencias quien aún no sabe el de las ancilas?" (Sor Juana, "Respuesta" 18).

13. "Yo quisiera que estos intérpretes y expositores de San Pablo me explicaran cómo entienden aquel lugar: *Mulieres in Ecclesia taceant*. Porque o lo han de entender de lo material de los púlpitos y cátedras, o de lo formal de la universalidad de los fieles, que es la Iglesia. Si lo entienden de lo primero (que es, en mi sentir, su verdadero sentido, pues vemos que, con efecto, no se permite en la Iglesia que las mujeres lean públicamente ni prediquen), ¿por qué reprenden a las que privadamente estudian? Y si lo entienden de lo segundo... ¿cómo vemos que la Iglesia ha permitido que escriba una Gertrudis, una Teresa, una Brígida, la monja de Ágreda y otras muchas?" (Sor Juana, "Respuesta" 58).

14. "La escolástica fue cardinal en su formación. Lo que podría llamar la estructura de su pensar, es decir, no sólo las ideas sino la manera de enlazarlas y combinarlas, viene de esa filosofía" (Paz, *Sor Juana Inés de la Cruz* 330).

15. In her "Response," Sor Juana makes clear her fear of the Inquisition, "I wish no quarrel with the Holy Office, for I am ignorant, and I tremble that I may express some proposition that will cause offense or twist the true meaning of some scripture (11) ['Yo no quiero ruido con el Santo Oficio, que soy ignorante y tiemblo de decir alguna proposición malsonante o torcer la genuina inteligencia de algún lugar']" ("Respuesta" 10). Needless to say, one cannot take her affirmations of ignorance seriously.

16. "Y ¿podría profesar otra, habiéndome criado desde mi niñez y educado hasta la prefectura de la catedra primaria en el insigne seminario mayor de San Antonio del clero? Cierto es que, por gran don de Dios, nos hemos embebido con avidez de sólo la pura, auténtica, y genuina doctrina del Maestro Angélico" (Espinoza, "Prefacio" 328).

17. Regarding the university, Paz notes: "The function of the university, as a guardian of orthodoxy, was to defend the principles on which the society was based, not to question or debate them (*Sor Juana* 45) ['Guardiana de la ortodoxia, la Universidad no tenía por función examinar y discutir los principios que fundaban a la sociedad sino defenderlos']" (Paz, *Sor Juana Inés de la Cruz* 69).

18. According to González Echevarría, the modernity of Lunarejo resides in his "declaring form inseparable from content" (*Celestina's Brood* 161).

19. "Además que cuando Manuel de Faría pronunció su censura, Gongora era muerto y yo no había nacido" (Espinoza, *Apologético* 17).

20. Octavio Paz argues that Sor Juana had written the letter as part of an attack on the Jesuits with the ultimate purpose of "humiliating Aguiar y Seijas ['humillar a Aguiar y Seijas']," the archbishop of Mexico (*Sor Juana* 410; *Sor Juana Inés de la Cruz* 533). This truly baroque communicative complexity of "The Athenagoric Letter"—apparently directed at Vieira, in reality being an attack on either Nuñez de Miranda, who was a Jesuit, or Aguiar y Seijas, who was close to the order, or both—should not, however, make one forget that Sor Juana's text is a criticism of Vieira's forty-year-old sermon.

21. For these comments, I visited the valuable database of Kings College, London on seventeenth-century translations of Spanish writers into English: "A Bibliography of Spanish-English Translations 1500–1640" available at http://www.ems.kcl.ac.uk/content/proj/anglo/tldb/index.html.

22. "Sus libros . . . se colocaron en las bibliotecas de los hombres cultos de su época" (Rivers 309).

23. The information and quotations cited are from Paz's "Notes on Sources," the final section of the English version of his study on Sor Juana not found in the Spanish original.

24. "El lugar central de la biblioteca—al lado de la poesía española y los tratados de mitología—lo ocupaba la literatura latina"; and "En cambio, la poesía francesa de su tiempo—no se diga la inglesa—fue tierra incógnita para ella" (Paz, *Sor Juana Inés de la Cruz* 328).

25. "El movimiento intelectual que se inicia en el Renacimiento con la nueva ciencia y la nueva filosofía política no esta presente en esta colección de libros" (Paz, *Sor Juana Inés de la Cruz* 338).

26. "Cincuenta años antes Quevedo y Gracián lo mencionaban sin timidez" (Paz, *Sor Juana Inés de la Cruz* 333).

27. Despite his surprising mention of Erasmus and Vives among those authors "justifying" the defense of Góngora against the Portuguese critic Manuel de Faria y Souza, Lunarejo notes in the text of the *Apologético:* "Maybe

Melanchton, Erasmus, Vatablo, Escalígero, Lorenzo Valla, Luis Vives, etc., exploded in pestilential errors and maybe it was necessary that the Doctor of the Spains, San Isidoro, would tell us: *Meliores esse Grammaticos quam Haereticos* (That grammarians were better than heretics)" [Tal vez reventaron en errores pestíferos, llorénlo Melanchton, Erasmo, Vatablo, Escalígero, Laurencio Valla, Luis Vives, etcétera y tal vez fue menester que el doctor de las Españas San Isidoro nos dijese: *Meliores esse Grammaticos quam Haereticos* (Son mejores los gramáticos que los herejes)] (21).

28. According to Walter Redmond, "Espinoza belongs to a movement which has been called the Second Scholasticism: the rebirth of medieval, mainly, Thomistic philosophy occurring in Italy around 1500, and its subsequent development especially in the Iberian peninsula and its dependencies until the 19th century" (477).

29. The *Apologético* was published in Lima (1662 and 1694); Sor Juana's complete poetry was published in Madrid (volumes 1 and 3 in 1689 and 1700) and Seville (volume 2 in 1692).

30. "Uno de los ejes fundamentales de poder es la clasificación social de la población mundial sobre la idea de raza, una construcción mental que expresa la experiencia básica de la dominación colonial y que desde entonces permea las dimensiones más importantes del poder mundial, incluyendo su racionalidad específica, el eurocentrismo. Dicho eje tiene, pues, origen y carácter colonial, pero ha probado ser más duradero y estable que el colonialismo en cuya matriz fue establecido" (Quijano, "Colonialidad del poder" 201).

31. "En una sociedad estratificada en forma relativamente estática, ella constituye la única puerta—con la carrera eclesiástica, que en tanto se le asimila—para un ascenso social de las clases bajas" (Jorge Alberto Manrique 673).

32. "Pues los europeos sospechan que los estudios de los hombres del nuevo mundo son bárbaros" (Espinoza, *Apologético* 325).

33. "El Lunarejo, no obstante su sangre indígena, sobresalió sólo como gongorista, esto es una actitud característica de una literatura vieja que, agotado ya el renacimiento, llegó al barroquismo ya al culteranismo. 'El Apologetico en favor de Góngora' desde este punto de vista, está dentro de la literatura española" (Mariátegui, *Siete ensayos* 238–39).

CHAPTER 2

1. According to Anderson, "We owe the 'coinage' of 'modernism' as an aesthetic movement to a Nicaraguan poet, writing in a Guatemalan journal of a literary encounter in Peru" (3). Anderson seems unaware or, at least, gives no importance to the frequently stressed difference between Darío's modernismo, influenced by French Parnassianism and early symbolism, and the later European modernism, for which the closest Spanish American analogue would be the *vanguardia* of the 1920s and 1930s.

2. A possible earlier use of the term *modernista* as an adjective for a literary movement in the Hispanic world can be found in Catalonia. As early as

1884, the editors of the cultural journal *L'Avens,* which is also known as *L'Avenç,* used the adjective *modernista* to describe the latest trends in art, literature, and science (Orringer 138). However, the description of science as modernista may indicate lack of clarity in their use of the word. Moreover, according to Orringer, they did not use the noun *modernismo.*

3. "Flota aún sobre Lima algo del buen tiempo viejo, de la época colonial" (Darío, "Ricardo Palma" 100).
4. "En el principio de mi juventud, me había parecido un hermoso sueño irrealizable estar frente a frente con el poeta de las *Armonías*" (Darío, "Ricardo Palma" 97).
5. "Pero comprende y admira el espíritu nuevo que hoy anima a un pequeño, pero triunfante y soberbio grupo de escritores y poetas de la América española: el modernismo" (Darío, "Ricardo Palma" 97–98).
6. For a definition of the *tradición,* see note 24 of the "Introduction."
7. "Él es decidido afiliado a la corrección clásica, y respeta a la Academia" (Darío, "Ricardo Palma" 97).
8. "En la prosa reina siempre la mala tradición, ese monstruo enjendrado por las falsificaciones agridulcetes de la historia y la caricatura microscópica de la novela" (González Prada, "Discurso en el Teatro Olimpo" 27).
9. "Si un autor sale de su tiempo, ha de ser para adivinar las cosas futuras, no para desenterrar ideas i palabras muertas" (González Prada, "Conferencia en el Ateneo de Lima" 15).
10. "Uno de los más principales y eficaces agentes en la formación del sentimiento de nuestra nacionalidad" (Riva Agüero 359).
11. "Para las capas medias hacia arriba, el mundo colonial de Palma era como una infancia despreocupada y dichosa . . . Esta arcadia criolla servía a los más conservadores para denostar contra los excesos republicanos y hasta era útil para revestir proyectos sociales regresivos" (Cornejo Polar, *La formación de la tradición literaria en el Perú* 59).
12. For a summary of the critical debates around the *Tradiciones,* see Rodríguez-Arenas, esp. 405–8.

 The complete passage quoted is, "Palma fue tradicionista, pero no tradicionalista. Creo que Palma hundió la pluma en el pasado para luego blandirla en alto y reírse de él. Ninguna institución u hombre de la Colonia y aun de la República escapó a la mordedura tantas veces tan certera de la ironía, el sarcasmo y siempre el ridículo de la jocosa crítica de Palma" (qtd. in Mariátegui, *Siete ensayos* 247).
13. "Tocome pertenecer al pequeño grupo literario del Perú, después de su independencia. Nacidos bajo la sombra del pabellón de la república, cumplíanos romper con el amaneramiento de los escritores de la época del coloniaje, y nos lanzamos audazmente a la empresa" (Palma, "La bohemia de mi tiempo" 71–72).
14. I have dealt at length on the *Tradiciones* as a national text, and in particular on "El corregidor de Tinta," in *Mestizo Nations* 27–41.
15. "No hay por qué extrañarse de que, ya sacerdote, ni el rostro quisiese verles ['a las mujeres']" (Francisco Sosa qtd. in Paz, *Sor Juana Inés de la Cruz* 531).

16. "Siempre he pensado que Ricardo Palma representa para la literatura peruana (y me atrevería a decir que, en cierto modo, también para la latinoamericana) un papel muy semejante al que representó, en su momento, Mark Twain para la literatura norteamericana... Ricardo Palma y Mark Twain optaron por abandonar el salón donde se escribía como en Madrid o Londres, entrearon en la taberna... pararon la oreja ante lo que sus contemporáneos consideraban el basurero del lenguaje popular, y terminaron escribiendo como se hablaba y se debía escribir" (Bryce Echenique xvii).
17. "Palma convoca la voz más interior, más familiar, de una tía anciana cuyos cuentos encantatorios tienen el poder de la fábula" (Ortega xxi).
18. "Hablemos y escribamos en americano; es decir en lenguaje para el que creemos las voces que estimemos apropiadas a nuestra manera de ser social, a nuestras instituciones democráticas, a nuestra naturaleza física" (Palma, *Neologismos y americanismos* 12).
19. According to Palma, "I had a very Hispanophilic purpose when I began to propose the incorporation [into the dictionary] of a dozen new words of general use in America during the academic meetings I attended ['Própósito muy hispanófilo fue, pues, el que animó cuando, en las juntas académicas a las que concurrí, empecé proponiendo la admisión de una docena de vocablos de general uso en América']" (*Neologismos y americanismos*) (14). However, by the end of the congress, Palma despairs of the "anti-American spirit ['espíritu anti-americano']" of the Real Academia de la Lengua and concludes that Spanish American writers have to ignore the vocabulary and prescriptions of the Academia (16).
20. "Nosotros, los de la nueva generación, arrastrados por lo novedoso del libérrimo romanticismo, en boga a la sazón, desdeñábamos todo lo que a tirano clasicismo apestara, y nos dábamos un hartazgo de Hugo y Byron, Espronceda, García Tessara y Enrique Gil" (Palma, "La bohemia de mi tiempo" 5).
21. The passage from "Ricardo Palma" where Darío coins *modernismo* is quoted above in note 5.
22. "El fin que Rubén Darío se propuso fue prácticamente el mismo a que tendieron los últimos neoclásicos y primeros románticos de la época de la independencia: la autonomía poética de la América española como parte del proceso general de libertad continental" (Rama, *Rubén Darío y el modernismo* 5).
23. "Nuestro modernismo, si es que así puede llamarse, nos va dando un puesto aparte, independiente de la literatura castellana" (Darío, "El modernismo" 315).
24. "Testimoniando así la tardía incorporación de un siglo largo de literatura, visto desde el remate simbolista hacía el cual se dirigía" (Rama, "El poeta frente a la modernidad" 83).
25. "Las Repúblicas sudamericanas tienden a separarse cada vez más, a medida que progresan, de la nación que antes fue su metrópoli, no ya en sus instituciones que con razón han repudiado, sino también en las ideas mismas y aun en los gustos literarios" (Sarmiento 331).

26. "¡Bienaventurados los españoles! Vienen al mundo en el siglo XIX y respiran el aire del año mil" (González Prada, "Memoranda" 184).
27. "Los modernistas no querían ser franceses, querían ser modernos . . . En labios de Rubén Darío y sus amigos, modernidad y cosmopolitanismo eran términos sinónimos. No fueron anti-americanos, querían una América contemporánea de Paris y Londres" (Paz, "El caracol y la sirena" 94–95).
28. The historian E. Bradford Burns lists some of the weaknesses of the economic and cultural modernization experienced during this period: "The rising national income, gross national product, and level of technology changed the standard of living of the masses little, if at all. Their condition remained constant or declined in the nineteenth century. On the other hand, the landowners grew richer, while the middle sectors shared in the prosperity" (157).
29. "En América hemos tenido ese movimiento antes que en la España castellana, por razones clarísimas: desde luego, por nuestro inmediato comercio material y espiritual con las distintas naciones del mundo, y principalmente porque existe en la nueva generación americana un inmenso deseo de progreso y un vivo entusiasmo" (Darío, "El modernismo" 314).
30. "¡Y sobre todo, la gran afición: japonerías y chinerías . . . No sé que habría dado por hablar chino y japonés" (Darío, "La muerte de la emperatriz de la China" 81).
31. "He venido como agente de una casa californiana, importadora de sedas, lacas, marfiles y demas chinerías" (Darío, "La muerte de la emperatriz de la China" 83).
32. In addition to the exchange of goods between Chile and Asia, at the time of the writing of the story, there was a significant, if not large, Chinese presence in the Pacific region of South America. The first Chinese arrived in Chile in 1850 as indentured servants (Segall 119). In fact, according to Marcelo Segall, "A great portion of the wealth of Peru, Cuba, and, to a lesser degree, Chile in the last [nineteenth] century was the product of the enslavement of Asians" (119).
33. "Entendido como lo que realmente fue—un movimiento cuyo fundamento y meta primordial era el movimiento mismo—aún no termina: la vanguardia de 1925 y las tentativas de la poesía contemporánea están íntimamente ligadas a ese gran comienzo" (Paz, "El caracol y la sirena" 89).
34. The comparison between Palma and José Hernández, the author of *Martin Fierro,* has been made several times earlier. For instance, González Vigil argues that both Hernández and Palma achieved "the fusion of *costumbrismo* and Romanticism ['la fusión del costumbrismo y el romanticismo']" (188). And Bradford Burns argues, "With two notable exceptions Latin American culture aped European trends, particularly those set in Paris. The exceptions were Ricardo Palma, whose original 'tradiciones peruanas' . . . recreated with wit and imagination his country's past: and the Gaucho poets, foremost of whom was the Argentine José Hernández, creator of *Martín Fierro,* a true American epic" (156).

35. The persistence of the political, racial, ethnic, geographical, and class oppositions that have characterized Peruvian society and culture has recently once again come to the fore with the acrid debate between "Andean" and criollo writers that began at the "Encuentro de narradores peruanos" in Madrid, between May 23 and 27, 2005. For some key texts in this debate, which continued during much of 2005 and involved several of the best-known writers living in Peru today, see the articles published in the Peruvian newspaper *Peru21* at http://www.peru21.com/P21online/ html/ debateIndex.html.
36. See González Vigil 202.
37. A longer version of the quote in Spanish is as follows: "La gravitación del género [tradición] se torna mayor todavía si percibimos su persistencia, aunque sea parcial y tamizada, en figuras de la talla del guatemalteco Miguel Ángel Asturias . . . los argentinos Roberto J. Payró (sus famosos relatos del Pago) y M. Mujica Láinez (la reconstrucción del pasado argentino en volúmenes como *Misteriosa Buenos Aires* y *Aquí vivieron*)" (González Vigil 202).

CHAPTER 3

1. According to José Carlos González Boixo, *La Gaceta* was "one of the most important publications of the Spanish avant-garde during the years of its publication (1927–1932) ['uno de los órganos más importantes del vanguardismo español en sus años de publicación (1927–1932)']" (167).
2. The main texts in the debate have been collected in Carmen Alemany Bay's *La polémica del meridiano intelectual de Hispanoamérica (1927)*.
3. De Torre wrote regularly on the contemporary literary production of Spanish America in *La Gaceta,* which, in fact, defined itself on its title page as "ibérica-americana." (On de Torre's interest in Spanish America, see Alemany 30–31.) An example of the friendship between the two antagonists can be seen in the fact that Borges had included de Torre as one of the "co-authors" of his "Proclama," a manifesto included in the foundational one-sheet journal *Prisma*, which, on the night of November 25, 1921, he and some friends pasted on Buenos Aires walls. In reality, de Torre had not participated in the writing. (See Williamson 99–100.) After the fall of the Spanish Republic, de Torre moved to Argentina with his wife, Norah Borges, becoming professor of literature at the Universidad de Buenos Aires and concentrating on Spanish American rather than Peninsular literature. According to Alemany, in his books, "he expresses an obsession already present in the polemic editorial such as the universality of the Spanish language ['expresa una obsesión ya presente en el polémico editorial como es la universalidad de la lengua española']" (31).
4. "El mejor y el único vehículo disponible para una excursión por todas las escuelas de vanguardia" (Mariátegui, "*Literaturas europeas de vanguardia*" 118).

5. Despite their overall positive reviews, both Mariátegui and Borges had reservations about de Torre's study. For Mariátegui, as one would expect from the region's first major Marxist thinker, de Torre's main flaw was "the attempt to consider and examine literary phenomena in themselves absolutely neglecting their relationships with other historical phenomena ['el esfuerzo por considerar y examinar los fenómenos literarios en sí mismos, prescindiendo absolutamente de sus relaciones con los demás fenómenos históricos']" (117). Borges's main objection, with which Mariátegui agreed, was de Torre's "progressivism," in other words, his belief in the existence of continuous qualitative progress in literature, described by the then young Argentine writer as "that disagreeable gesture of looking at his watch all the time ['ademán molesto de sacar el reloj a cada rato']" (210). (It must be noted that Mariátegui in *Literaturas europeas de vanguardia* quotes approvingly from Borges's review.)
6. According to Alemany, while some suspected de Torre's authorship of the unsigned article, others attributed it to *La Gaceta*'s director, E. Giménez Caballero (18–19). However, both de Torre and Giménez Caballero will later in life acknowledge the former's authorship (Alemany 19).
7. "Si Madrid, Barcelona, Lisboa, Buenos Aires llegan, en efecto, a sentirse barrios de una gigante urbe de las letras, neutralizarán mutuamente sus provincialidades íntimas y vivirán y trabajarán con radio ecuménico" (Ortega y Gasset 1).
8. "Por lo demás, ya desde sus primeras páginas la revista se plantea dirigida al público hispanoamericano, con lo cual las colaboraciones y notas bibliográficas correspondientes a las obras de estos autores, desde la óptica de Revista de Occidente, comparten un espacio común. Es decir, de una u otra manera, son parte del universo de la producción en lengua española. Y de hecho, ni Borges ni Girondo son 'presentados,' cortesía que en general la revista reserva para sus colaboradores *extranjeros*" (Vásquez, "De la modernidad y sus mapas" 17).
9. As we have seen in chapter 2 "Rubén Darío Visits Ricardo Palma," the questions raised during the "Intellectual Meridian Debate," such as those regarding the relationship of the region to Spanish culture, had been central to Latin American cultural production for several decades. In fact, during the mid 1840s, an important debate on this topic took place in Santiago de Chile. Among the participants were the Chilean José Vitorino Lastarria, the Argentine exile Domingo Faustino Sarmiento, and the Venezuelan Andrés Bello. According to Efraín Kristal, this important debate "set up the terms in which discussions about the cultural emancipation of Hispanic America have been framed ever since" ("Dialogues and Polemics: Sarmiento, Lastarria, and Bello" 68). One must note that despite the presence of intellectuals from several Latin American countries, this "first great literary polemic in its [Latin American] history ['la primera gran polémica literaria de su historia']" had limited influence outside Chile (González Boixo 167).

10. "Todos los mejores valores de ayer y de hoy—históricos, artísticos, de alta significación cultural— que no sean españoles, serán autóctonos, aborígenes" (De Torre, "Madrid, meridiano intelectual de Hispanoamérica" 65).
11. I have not been able to find any information regarding *La Gaceta*'s circulation, but given its emphasis on Ibero-American literature, and the ties between its editorial staff and that of *Revista de Occidente*'s, it is safe to assume that *La Gaceta* was also concerned with participating in the Spanish American market.
12. As we will see in the "Epilogue," there were precise historico-cultural reasons that led to the adoption of this term, which are not taken into account by de Torre.
13. In his analysis of the Mexican book industry, Gabriel Zaid notes, "In 1934, of the books imported by Mexico, 55% (in pesos) were from Spain, 0.5% from Argentina. By 1939 the percentages had changed to 6% Spain and 19% from Argentina. In 1946, 7% from Spain and 61% from Argentina. From then on Spain begins to recover. In 1951, the percentages were 32% Spain and 28% Argentina ['En 1934, de los libros importados por México, el 55% (en pesos) era de España, el 0.5% de Argentina. En 1939, los porcentajes cambiaron a 6% de España y 19% de Argentina. En 1946, a 7% de España y 61% de Argentina. A partir de ahí, España empieza a recuperarse. En 1951, los porcentajes fueron 32% de España y 28% de Argentina']" (32). Moreover, not only Argentina's book exports multiplied after the Spanish civil war, but also Mexico's book industry flourished. Zaid notes that "the export of Mexican books multiplied tenfold (in pesos) between 1940 and 1951 ['La exportación de libros mexicanos se multiplicó por diez (en pesos) de 1940 a 1951']" (32).
14. The quotations in the paragraph are part of de Torre's criticism of earlier hispanoamericanismo that he contrasts with the reality of Spanish and Latin American relations: "¿De qué ha servido tamaño estruendo verbalista... si el libro español, en la mayor parte de Suramérica, no puede competir en precios con el libro francés e italiano; y si, por otra parte, la reciprocidad no existe? Esto es, que sigue dándose el caso de no ser posible encontrar en las librerías españolas, más que por azar, libros y revistas de América" ("Madrid, meridiano intelectual" 67).
15. Other Spanish Americans participants in the European avant-garde of the 1920s and 1930s are the Cuban novelist and musicologist Alejo Carpentier, the Guatemalan novelist Miguel Ángel Asturias, the Peruvian Franco and Hispanophone poet César Moro, and in the field of art, the Cuban Wilfredo Lam, the Chilean Roberto Matta, and Diego Rivera, "one of the best and most original of cubist painters" (Mulvey and Wollen 82).
16. "El nuevo paisaje urbano, la modernización de los medios de comunicación, el impacto de estos procesos sobre las costumbres son el marco y el punto de resistencia respecto del cual se articulan las respuestas producidas por los intelectuales. En el curso de muy pocos años, éstos deben procesar, incluso en su propia biografía, cambios que afectan relaciones tradicionales,

formas de hacer y difundir cultura, estilos de comportamiento, modalidades de consagración, funcionamiento de instituciones" (Sarlo, *Una modernidad periférica* 21).
17. Mariátegui writes about Chaplin's cinema: "Artistically and spiritually it exceeds Pirandello's theatre and the novels of Proust and Joyce ['Artística, espiritualmente, excede, hoy, al teatro de Pirandello y a la novela de Proust y de Joyce']" ("Esquema de una explicación de Chaplin" 70). On Mariátegui's cinephilia, see Rouillón 442–43. Borges's mention of Sternberg as an influence on his literary style is made in his "Prólogo" to his first book *Historia universal de la infamia* (5). Among the major authors who also wrote film reviews are Roberto Arlt, César Vallejo, and Alejo Carpentier.
18. Laura Mulvey and Peter Wollen have convincingly argued that the influence of Mexican art in the 1920s went far beyond the borders of Latin America: "In the 1920s after Rivera's return to Mexico, the decade of the Mexican renaissance, there was an extraordinary surge of energy in the arts, which attracted foreign visitors and admirers" (82).
19. "Desde el río Grande hasta el Estrecho de Magallanes, es muy difícil que un artista joven piense seriamente en hacer arte puro o deshumanizado" (Carpentier, "Sobre el meridiano intelectual de Nuestra América" 96).

    As should be obvious, here Carpentier is implicitly contradicting Ortega y Gasset's famous essay "The Dehumanization of Art."
20. "El movimiento de reforma confiesa la doble inspiración de la revolución rusa y la mexicana: esos ejemplos le animan a luchar por una modificación de los estatutos universitarios que elimine el todo poder de los profesores (reclutados demasiado frecuentemente dentro de cliques que son, a su vez, parte de los sectores oligárquicos) obligándolos a compartir el gobierno con los estudiantes (provenientes en parte de sectores sociales más modestos, pero sólo excepcionalmente populares)" (Halperín Donghi 298).
21. While the logical choice for the author of this essay would be Roberto Ortelli, claims of authorship have been made for Jorge Luis Borges and Carlos Mastronardi, as well. See Alemany page 13, note 1.
22. "Che meridiano: hacete a un lao, que voy a escupir" (Ortelli y Gasset 74).
23. In addition to de Torre, an older Spanish avant-gardist Rafael Cansino Assens influenced Borges. On Cansino's influence on Borges, see Aizenberg's *El tejedor del aleph* 33–37 and Williamson 75–77.
24. "Madrid no nos entiende. Una ciudad cuyas orquestas no pueden intentar un tango sin desalmarlo . . . una ciudad cuyo Irigoyen es Primo de Rivera . . . ¿de dónde va a entendernos?" (Borges, "Sobre el meridiano de una gaceta" 71).
25. While none of the other participants in the debate argued as strongly as Borges for the lack of common cultural traits between the former colonies and their once metropolis, as we will see in the following chapter, this idea would become central to his development as a writer and essayist.
26. "La hora no es propicia para que Madrid solicite su reconocimiento como metrópoli espiritual de Hispanoamérica . . . Para nuestros pueblos

en crecimiento no representa siquiera el fenómeno capitalista . . . Bajo la dictadura de Primo de Rivera es inconcebiblemente oportuno invitarnos a reconocer la autoridad suprema de Madrid. El 'meridiano intelectual de Hispanoamérica' no puede estar a merced de una dictadura reaccionaria. En la ciudad que aspire a coordinarnos y dirigirnos intelectualmente necesitamos encontrar, si no espíritu revolucionario, al menos tradición liberal" (Mariátegui, "La batalla de *Martín Fierro*" 113).

27. As anyone who has read Casanova's *World Republic of Letters* will notice, Borges, Mariátegui, and de Torre, have in their discussion outlined many of the basic premises that the French critic develops in her work. The notion of a meridian, its link with political liberalism, and its role in literary space are all proposed during the debate. In fact, the case can be made that the Spanish American participants in the meridian debate are less bound to the Eurocentric idealization of international cultural networks that characterizes *The World Republic of Letters*. Casanova does not seem aware of this precedent. See Casanova 25–34.

28. "Buenos Aires, más conectada con los demás centros de Sudamérica, reúne más condiciones materiales de Metrópolis. Es ya un gran mercado literario. Un 'meridiano intelectual,' en gran parte, no es otra cosa" (Mariátegui, "La batalla de *Martín Fierro*" 113).

29. "Desde un punto de vista de libreros, los escritores de *La Gaceta Literaria* estaban en lo cierto cuando declaraban a Madrid meridiano literario de Hispanoamérica" (Mariátegui, "La batalla del libro" 118).

30. "Guillermo de Torre se sintió ofendido por la labor ejercida y por los nuevos rumbos que había tomado la literatura al otro lado del Atlántico" (Alemany 26).

"Además de un problema de nacionalismo latente en el editorial 'Madrid meridiano intelectual de Hispanoamérica' está en juego la paternidad de la vanguardia" (27).

CHAPTER 4

1. Critics, such as Rodríguez Monegal; Fishburn and Hughes; Balderston, Gallo, and Helft; and Shumway, have pointed to Eliot's influence on Borges without offering further analyses. As far as I am aware, Edna Aizenberg's "Borges, Postcolonial Precursor," a chapter in *Books and Bombs in Buenos Aires*, is the only essay analyzing Borges's theoretical debt to Eliot that enabled him to become a precursor to postcolonial authors such as Anton Shammas, Salman Rushdie, Tahar Ben Jelloun, and Sergio Chefjec.

In *El factor Borges,* Alan Pauls describes Borges's writings as "taking vampirization to its ultimate consequences until when drunk with someone else's blood, they betray their species and produce something new ['que llevan la vampirización hasta sus últimas consecuencias, hasta que, embriagados de sangre ajena, traicionan la condición de su especie y producen algo nuevo']" (107).

2. For a more detailed reading of the debate about the intellectual meridian, see chapter 3.
3. On Borges's politics, see Rodríguez Monegal's "Borges y la política" and Bell-Villada's chapter "Literature and Politics North and South" in *Borges and His Fiction* (268–85).
4. Borges develops some of the ideas found in "La eternidad y T. S. Eliot" in "A History of Eternity," an essay published in 1936, in which he pursues the idea of eternity beyond Irenaeus to Plotinus without mentioning Eliot.
5. The licenses taken by Borges in his translations of Eliot are consistent with his approach to translation in general. Efraín Kristal has shown that Borges thought of translation in terms of fidelity, not to words, but to central ideas. Thus, as translator, Borges felt free to remove words and passages that struck him as "redundant"; to excise passages that "might distract attention from another aspect Borges would prefer to highlight"; and to add "a major or minor nuance not in the original: changing a title, for instance" (*Invisible Work* 87).
6. "El sentido histórico hace escribir a un hombre, no meramente con su generación en la sangre, sino con la conciencia de que toda la literatura europea, y en ella la de su país, tiene un simultáneo existir y forma un orden que es también simultáneo . . . La aparición de una obra de arte afecta a cuantas obras de arte la precedieron. El orden ideal es modificado por la introducción de la nueva (de la efectivamente nueva) obra de arte. Ese orden es cabal antes de aparecer la obra nueva; para que ésta no lo destruya una alteración total es imprescindible, siquiera sea levísima. El pasado es modificado por el presente, el presente es dirigido por el pasado" (Borges, "La eternidad y T. S. Eliot" 50).
7. "A éste, al principio, lo pensé tan singular como el fénix de las alabanzas retóricas; a poco de frecuentarlo, creí reconocer su voz, o sus hábitos, en textos de diversas literaturas y épocas" (Borges, "Kafka y sus precursores" 145).
8. "En el vocabulario crítico, la palabra precursor es indispensable, pero habría que tratar de purificarla de toda connotación de polémica o rivalidad. El hecho es que cada escritor crea a sus precursores. Su labor modifica nuestra concepción del pasado, como ha de modificar el futuro" (Borges, "Kafka y sus precursores" 148).
9. "'Fears and Scruples' de Robert Browning profetiza la obra de Kafka, pero nuestra lectura de Kafka afina y desvía sensiblemente nuestra lectura del poema. Browning no lo leía como ahora nosotros lo leemos" (Borges, "Kafka y sus precursores" 147–48).
10. "La novela policial ha creado un tipo especial de lector . . . porque si Poe creó el relato policial, creó después el tipo de lector de ficciones policiales" (Borges, "El cuento policial" 72).
11. "El Perú, como los demás pueblos de América, gira dentro de la órbita de esta civilización, no sólo porque se trata de países políticamente independientes pero económicamente coloniales, ligados al carro del capitalismo

británico, del capitalismo americano o del capitalismo francés, sino porque europea es nuestra cultura, europeo es el tipo de nuestras instituciones" (Mariátegui, "La crisis mundial" 16).

12. "Un estuche con el daguerrotipo de un hombre inexpresivo y barbado, una vieja espada, la dicha y el coraje de ciertas músicas, el hábito de estrofas del Martín Fierro, los años, el desgano y la soledad, fomentaron ese criollismo algo voluntario, pero nunca ostentoso" (Borges, "El sur" 123).
13. There are several references to camels in the *Quran*. For instance, in Recite 5:103, it is stated, "It was not Allah who instituted (superstitions like those of) a slit-ear she-camel, or a she-camel let loose for free pasture, or idol sacrifices for twin-births in animals, or stallion-camels freed from work: It is blasphemers who invent a lie against Allah; but most of them lack wisdom." Other references to camels can be found in Recites 6:144; 7:40; 12:65; 12:72; 22:36; 56:65; 59:6; 77:33; and 88:17. (Hussein Amery brought this fact to my attention.)
14. "Mahoma, como árabe, no tenía por qué saber que los camellos eran especialmente árabes; eran para él parte de la realidad, no tenía por qué distinguirlos; en cambio, un falsario, un turista, un nacionalista árabe, lo primero que hubiera hecho es prodigar camellos, caravanas de camellos en cada página" (Borges, "El escritor argentino y la tradición" 156).
15. "Les basto el hecho de sentirse irlandeses, distintos, para innovar en la cultura inglesa. Los argentinos, los sudamericanos en general estamos en una situación análoga; podemos manejar todos los temas europeos, manejarlos in supersticiones, con una irreverencia que puede tener, y ya tiene, consequencias afortunadas" ("El escritor argentino y la tradición" 161).
16. This point has been also made by Aizenberg in *El tejedor del Aleph*. Aizenberg notes that in Borges and, more generally, in "Latin American culture," there is "a profound link with Europe intertwined with a feeling of otherness regarding the Continent and the occidental order it represents ['la profunda vinculación con Europa enlazada con una sensación de otredad frente al Continente y al orden occidental que representa']" (11–12).
17. "Yo muchas veces he prestado, a personas sin versación literaria especial obras francesas e inglesas, y estos libros han sido gustados inmediatamente, sin esfuerzo. En cambio, cuando he propuesto a mis amigos la lectura de libros españoles, he comprobado que estos libros les eran difícilmente gustables sin un aprendizaje especial" (Borges, "El escritor argentino y la tradición" 158–59).
18. Only after the Franco regime comes into power Spain loses its hegemony in the production of books.
19. "Creo que nuestra tradición es toda la cultura occidental, y creo también que tenemos derecho a esta tradición, mayor que el que pueden tener los habitantes de una u otra nación universal" (Borges, "El escritor argentino y la tradición" 160).
20. "Debemos pensar que nuestro patrimonio es el universo" (Borges, "El escritor argentino y la tradición" 162).

21. Borges once declared, "If I were asked to name the chief event in my life, I should say my father's library. In fact, sometimes I think I have never strayed outside that library" ("Autobiographical Essay" 209). As we have seen, Borges worked as a librarian. He was an assistant at the Miguel Cané Municipal Library from 1937 to 1946 and became director of the Argentine National Library in 1955, a position from which he resigned in 1973, after the return of Juan Domingo Perón to Argentina.
22. Aizenberg traces the roots of Borges's "postcolonial" literary praxis to his essays, noting that in "Kafka and His Precursors," "Borges fabricates a more provocative, postcolonial version of Eliot's majestic proposition that every writer's work modifies our conception of the past and the future. According to Borges, every writer goes further: he creates his own forerunners. And appropriately so, for at the 'periphery,' where things have as yet to cohere, one must create a genealogy, an identity, and a place" (*Books and Bombs in Buenos Aires* 109).

Chapter 5

1. Tropicalismo is also known as *tropicália* and *Tropicalism*.
2. "Todos os outros países da América consideram-se suficientemente descobertos em conjunto por Cristóvão Colombo em 1492" (Veloso, *Verdade tropical* 13).

    Given the differences between the Brazilian edition of *Verdade tropical* and the English-language *Tropical Truth*—I refer to *Tropical Truth* in the main text and provide the original Portuguese text in the notes.
3. "Como um continente independente ou uma ilha descomunal no meio do Atlântico Sul" (Veloso, *Verdade tropical* 13).
4. "Da ilha Brasil pairando eternamente a meio milímetro do chão real da América" (Veloso, *Verdade tropical* 19).
5. "O paralelo com os Estados Unidos é inevitável" (Veloso, *Verdade tropical* 14).
6. "Don't Look Black" was first published in translation in the *New York Times* as "Orpheus, Rising from Caricature," 8 Aug. 2000.

    Veloso reflects on the phrase "loneliness of Brazil," in his analysis of the reception in Brazil and abroad of the two film adaptations of Vinicius de Moraes's *Orfeu da Conceição*, Marcel Camus's *Black Orpheus* and *Orfeu* by Carlos Diegues. Writing about the contrasting reception to Camus's *Black Orpheus*, seen as a classic abroad but as an example of exoticism in Brazil, Veloso writes: "the contrast between the fascination that *Black Orpheus* generated abroad and the disdain with which Brazilians greeted it, is so significant as to ask for reflection on the loneliness of Brazil ['O contraste entre o fascínio que *Orfeu negro* exerceu no exterior e o desprezo que lhe dedicaram os brasileiros é tão gritante que convida à reflexão sobre a solidão do Brasil']" (23).
7. Veloso's omission of any significant reference to Spanish American music should be contrasted with the following statement made in 1994 shortly

after *Fina Estampa* came out: "in the town of Santa Amaro, in Bahia where I was born and lived until I was eighteen, one could hear, during the 1940s and 1950s, Cuban, Mexican, Argentine, Paraguayan, and Puerto Rican songs that influenced the development of a whole generation ['Na cidadezinha de Santo Amaro, na Bahia, onde nasci e vivi até os dezoito anos, ouviam-se, nos anos 40 e 50, canções cubanas, mexicanas, argentinas, paraguaias ou porto-riquenhas que marcaram a formação de todo uma geração']" ("Fina Estampa" 178).

8. In the case of Brazil, the post–bossa nova generation was particularly influenced by the example of Vinicius de Moraes. A respected poet and writer—he was the author of the play *Orfeu da conceição,* which was (mis)adapted into the popular French film set in Brazil *Black Orpheus*—he not only became the lyricist for some of the best-known bossa nova classics, such as "A garota de Ipanema" ("The Girl from Ipanema") but became himself a popular singer. As José Carlos Capinam, a poet who collaborated with the tropicalista Gilberto Gil, noted: "Vinicius really paved the way for lyricists. Perhaps, without bossa nova, I wouldn't have realized that poets were allowed to write song lyrics, that this didn't imply a lower level" (qtd. in Perrone, *Masters of Brazilian Song* xxiii–xxiv).

9. Many of these texts have been collected in *Alegria, Alegria* (1977) and *O mundo não e chato* (2005). A briefer but more up-to-date selection of his writings, as well as critical articles about him, can be found in the musician's webpage: www.caetanoveloso.com.br.

10. An example of this relative Brazilian musical independence can be found in the preponderance of Brazilian songs in the radio "hit parade." For instance, during the week ending August 27, 2005, the top three songs were Brazilian—"Como vai voce?" sung by Zezé di Camargo and Antònio Marcos was number one—as were six out of the top ten (http://www.hot100-brasil.com/chtsinglesb.html, accessed 29 Aug. 2005).

11. As Gerald Marzorati notes, he has "a fan base encompassing not only hundreds of thousands of Brazilians but David Byrne, Beck and much of the increasingly global music underground. He has a following, too, among the more with-it tenured types who participate in conferences devoted to postcolonial studies and such" ("Beyond the Bossa Nova" 19). This process of canonization of Caetano Veloso outside Brazil began in 1986 with his first North American release—a self-titled acoustic collection, in which he sang several of his songs as well as covers of Michael Jackson's "Billy Jean" and Cole Porter's "Get Out of Town"—and has led to him being published in the *New York Times,* featured in the *New York Times* magazine——interviewed in PBS's *The Charlie Rose Show,* profiled in PBS's *Newshour* and NPR's *All Things Considered* and *Weekend Edition,* and participate in Pedro Almodóvar's film *Talk to Her.* An interesting example of the internationalization of Veloso is that he sings the English part of the Oscar nominated song "Burn It Blue" from Julie Taymor's film *Frida,* despite the fact that Lila Downs, who sings the Spanish part, is perfectly fluent in English, having grown up partly in Minneapolis.

12. The label is HRP, which issued "Magia e Misterio," sung by Guilherme and Santiago (http://www.hot100brasil.com/ chtsinglesb.html, accessed on 29 Aug. 2005).
13. Frequently, the obvious strengths and achievements of Brazilian music are celebrated without any acknowledgment of its still peripheric status. For instance, Robert Stam in his study of Brazilian film, *Tropical Multiculturalism*, writes: "Can one imagine 'fusion' or 'disco,' for example without the Brazilian impetus? In music, Brazilian and American artists meet as equals. When Jobim collaborates with Sinatra, or João Gilberto with Stan Getz, or Milton Nascimento with Pat Metheny, or Gilberto Gil with Stevie Wonder, or Hermeto Pascoal with Miles Davis, there is no question of subordination or dependency" (362). One can contrast Stam's optimistic assessment of the relationship between Brazilian and *"central"* musicians with the following statement made by Pat Metheny and quoted by Veloso in the notes to his recording of North American songs *A Foreign Sound* (2004): "I think I dreamt I read in a Rio newspaper an interview of Pat Metheny in which he says: 'I'm sick of hearing you Brazilian journalists ask me about the effect Brazilian musicians have had on my musical development. American music has influenced me—and these Brazilian musicians you suggest defined my style—much more than Brazilian music could ever influence an American" (2). (Veloso will repeat the same story, but as fact in an interview in the *Jornal do Brasil* [4 Mar. 2004], "Os americanos estão na punta"; also available at caetanoveloso.com). While Stam is probably correct in describing the personal interaction between U.S. and Brazilian musicians, Metheny's quotation emphasizes the unequal relationship between the two musical traditions. In fact, Stam's examples may contradict his optimistic statements. While Brazilian music clearly played a role in disco and fusion, was it fundamental to the development of those musical styles? Moreover, jazz, represented by Getz or, tangentially, by Sinatra, was central to the invention of bossa nova by Jobim and Gilberto, while Brazilian music was at best a secondary influence on the North American musicians, as the Metheny/Veloso quote makes clear. In a similar way, rhythm and blues and soul were key catalysts in the evolution of Gil from a brilliant practitioner of bossa nova to one of the progenitors of tropicalismo, while Brazilian music, again, was not central to the development of Stevie Wonder, to continue with Stam's examples. A similar lacuna can be found in Dunn's celebration of a "Black Atlantic" that in his version includes Brazil. A simple perusal of Paul Gilroy's *Black Atlantic* makes it clear that the Black Atlantic is seen as clearly Anglophone—he makes no reference to Brazil or to any Latin American country. Implicit in Gilroy's argument is that only Anglophone "popular" music, in particular that rooted in rhythm and blues, is oppositional.
14. On the relations between tropicalismo and politically progressive students, see Dunn (65–68; 133–36), McGowan and Pessanha (87–89), and Veloso (*Tropical Truth* 100–10, 186–98; *Verdade tropical* 156–77, 297–308).
15. "O som típico do neo-rock'n'roll inglês" (Veloso, *Verdade tropical* 169).

In *Tropical Truth*, Veloso distinguishes the North American rock and roll of the 1950s and early 1960s, that had only a limited influence on Brazilian music from: "a second onslaught, this time via England—the entrance on the scene of the Beatles and the Rolling Stones, or what I prefer to call 'British Neo-Rock'" (20). "Da segunda investida do rock (desta vez via Inglaterra), ou seja, daquilo que prefiro sempre chamar de neo-rock'n'roll inglês, o dos Beatles e dos Rolling Stones" (*Verdade tropical* 45).

16. Veloso has made his debt to Gilberto public on numerous occasions. For instance, in *Tropical Truth*, he describes the bossa nova singer as "my supreme master ['meu mestre supremo' (18)]" (8). Regarding the early use of "universal sound" as the name for what became known as tropicalismo see Dunn 65–68; Dunn and Perrone "Chiclete com Banana" 19–20; and Campos's "Não ou não." Veloso writes about the "evolutionary line" in *Tropical Truth* 133–34, 142 and *Verdade tropical* 77, 208, 221.

17. "O desenvolvimento de um processo radical de mudança de estágio cultural que nos levou a rever o nosso gosto, o nosso acervo e—o que é mais importante—as nossas possibilidades" (Veloso, *Verdade tropical* 35).

18. "A bossa-nova (João Gilberto) levou-me a compor e cantar, a me interessar pela modernização da música brasileira" (Veloso, "Entrevista a Augusto de Campos n.p.).

19. "Das entranhas imundas (e, no entanto, saneadoras) da internacionalizante indústria do entretenimento" (Veloso, *Verdade tropical* 19).

20. "O enunciado natural de Orlando Silva e Sinatra. O tom aveludado de Dick e sua respiração. O timbre do trombone de Frank Rosolino na orquestra de Kenton. O enunciado baixinho do trio de Page Cavanaugh, de Joe Mooney, de Jonas Silva" (Castro, *Chega de saudade* 147).

    As in the case of *Verdade tropical*, the English-language version of Ruy Castro's text differs substantially from the Portuguese original. I cite the English-language version of Ruy Castro's text in the body of this book and provide the original Portuguese text in the notes.

21. One must note, however, that Silva, according to Veloso, despite being "subject to the stylistic advances introduced by Bing Crosby," "is not, in any sense, an imitator of Bing Crosby's, and his grasp of modernity establishes a freedom of invention that transcends all issues of cultural derivation" (*Tropical Truth* 166). "Mas ele [Silva] não é, em nenhuma medida, um epígono de Bing Crosby—e sua compreensão da modernidade instaura uma liberdade inventiva que transcende todas as questões de dependência cultural" (*Verdade tropical* 267). Silva is another of the major figures in Veloso's "evolutionary line" of Brazilian music.

22. "Echar mano a las aportaciones de la modernidad, revisar a la luz de ellas los contenidos culturales regionales y con unas y otras fuentes componer un híbrido que sea capaz de seguir transmitiendo la herencia recibida. Será una herencia renovada, pero que todavía pueda identificarse con su pasado" (Rama, *Transculturación narrativa* 29).

23. The traditions seen as "national" are in reality regional ones reinterpreted as national. Thus the samba, a "regional" style from Rio de Janeiro with roots

in Bahia, was elevated into a national style. However, given that the "evolutionary line" identified by Veloso includes principally Bahian names—Gilberto, like Veloso and Gil was from Bahia—the national tradition has, at least in part, also become identified with that of Bahia. For a lucid analysis of the process by which samba was turned not only into a national musical style but also into a symbol of nationality, *see* Hermano Vianna, *The Mystery of Samba: Popular Music and National Identity in Brazil*.

24. "A interpretação de João é mais introspectiva que a de Maysa, e também violentamente menos dramática . . . chega-se a ouvir—com o ouvido interior—o surdão de um bloco de rua batendo com descansada regularidade de ponta a ponta da canção. É uma aula de como o samba pode estar inteiro mesmo nas suas formas mais aparentemente descaracterizaclas; um modo de, radicalizando o refinamento, reencontrar a mão do primeiro preto batendo no couro do primeiro atabaque no nascedouro do samba. (E o arranjo de cordas é do alemão Klaus Ogerman)" (Veloso, *Verdade tropical* 40).

25. "Gal participa dessa qualidade misteriosa que habita os raros grandes cantores de samba: a capacidade de inovar, de violentar o gosto contemporâneo, lançando o samba para o futuro, com a espontaneidade de quem relembra velhas musiquinhas" (Veloso, "Domingo" 202).

The original notes are included in *O mundo não e chato* but have been omitted from the U.S. re-release of the recording (1990).

26. As befits a "pop intellectual," Veloso has theorized his musical practice. Veloso has found in Oswald de Andrade's notion of "anthropophagy" a critical framework with which to justify and understand his use of Anglo-American rock. According to Randal Johnson, "The *antropófagos* do not want to copy European culture but rather to devour it, taking advantage of its positive aspects, rejecting the negative, and creating an original national culture that would be a source of artistic expression rather than a receptacle for forms of cultural elaborated elsewhere" (49).

In *Tropical Truth,* Veloso describes the tropicalistas use of anthropophagia: "The idea of cultural cannibalism fit tropicalismo like a glove. We were 'eating' the Beatles and Jimi Hendrix. Our arguments against the nationalists defensive attitude found in this stance its most succinct and exhaustive enunciation" (136). "A idéia do canibalismo cultural servia-nos. aos tropicalistas. como uma luva. Estávamos 'comendo' os Beatles e Jimi Hendrix.Nossas argumentações contra a atitude defensiva dos nacionalistas encontravam aqui uma formulação sucinta e exaustiva" (*Verdade tropical* 247).

The trope of the cannibal proposed by de Andrade permitted the tropicalistas, in a similar way that it had the modernistas of the 1920s, to claim to being simultaneously national and international, integrated into the world republics of music and that of letters, respectively, while simultaneously tapping into the earliest traditions of Brazil. The true national tradition was not one of cultural purity but rather of appropriation and deglution. For Veloso, the evolutionary line is implicitly a genealogy of cannibals.

27. "O grande mercado era a juventude. E a música desta passara a ser o iê-iê-iê" (Castro, *Chega de saudade* 405).

Tropicalismo's preference for the new youth musical styles of the time corresponded closely to the changes taking place in Brazilian taste. Approximately one year after *Tropicália ou panis et circencis* came out, the journalist Nelson Motta published a list of what was hip and what was square. In it, he declared Sinatra, the guru of the bossa nova crowd, hopelessly square; his place in the "hip list" was taken by Bob Dylan (Dunn 24).

The *Jovem Guarda* (literally "young guard") is described by Dunn as "the homegrown rock movement," "based on British and American rock," but "also rooted in the tradition of romantic ballads going back to Brazilian *modinhas* of the nineteenth century" (7, 58).

28. "Después de su autoexamen valorativo y la selección de sus componentes válidos, se asiste a un redescubrimiento de razgos que, aunque pertenecientes al acervo tradicional no estaban vistos o no habian sido utilizados en forma sistemática, y cuyas posibilidades expresivas se evidencian en la perspectiva modernizadora" (Rama, *Transculturación narrativa* 30).

29. According to the *Diccionario Cravo Albin da Música Popular Brasileira,* the name *baião* "derives from Bahian ['deriva de baiano']." Also, "by the end of the nineteenth century it was popular in the hinterlands of the North East. It was played on concertinos throughout the countryside, always in even time measures ['Em fins do século XIX já era conhecido no interior nordestino, sendo executado em sanfonas pelo sertão, sempre em unidades de compasso par']" (n.p.). The baião is mentioned in one of the foundational bossa novas, "Bim Bom"; a song with lyrics and music by no less than João Gilberto himself.

30. The title is a macarronic Latin version of the phrase "bread and circuses" from Juvenal's "Satire 10." The correct Latin phrase is *"panem et circenses."* There are several alternative titles used for the recording, Veloso himself uses both *circencis* and *circenses* in *Tropical Truth*. I have followed the spelling on my copy of the CD.

31. Dunn writes: "By intentionally fusing these diverse elements, 'Batmacumba' suggests that products of the multinational culture industry like Batman and rock have been 'Brazilianized' and, conversely, that Afro-Brazilian religion is central to Brazilian modernity and not to [sic] a folkloric vestige of a premodern past" (105).

32. A complete version of the lyrics "written" out as a "wing" can be found in Veloso's Web page—www.caetanoveloso.com.br.

33. Caetano Veloso wrote the preface for Walter Garcia's *Bim Bom: A contradição sem conflitos de João Gilberto* (1999).

34. The concept of transculturation has rarely been applied to Brazilian topics, despite the fact Rama referred to Brazilian authors, such as, Gilberto Freyre, João Guimarães Rosa, and Marcio Souza, among others (20–32; 95–98; 80–81).

35. "El emblema mayor de la falaz armonía en la que habría concluido un proceso múltiple de mixturación" (8). And: "Todo habría quedado armonizado dentro de espacios apacibles y amenos . . . de nuestra América" (Cornejo Polar, "Mestizaje e hibridez" 8).

36. "O nacionalismo desenvolvimentista armou um imaginário social novo, que pela primeira vez se refer à nação inteira. E que aspira, tambén pela primeira vez, a certa consistência interna" (Schwarz, "Fim do século" 157).
37. "Exprime pois uma tomada de consciência dos interêsses proprios do Brasil, no âmbito das outras nações, e das massas populares, no âmbito interno do pais" (Jaguaribe 32).
38. A fuller version of the text is: "No tuvo más ambición que la de volcar en la corriente de la sabiduría y el arte del Perú criollo el caudal del arte y la sabiduría de un pueblo al que se consideraba degenerado, debilitado o 'extraño' e 'impenetrable' pero que, en realidad, no era sino lo que llega a ser un gran pueblo, oprimido" (Arguedas 256).
39. The reception of tropicalismo resembles in some aspects that of bossa nova. In the 1990s the North American musical establishment discovered tropicalismo, in the words of the *New York Times Magazine,* as merely "ingenious pop" (Marzorati "Tropicália Agora!" 1).
40. Castro's imaginative narrative of the history of bossa nova also illustrates this ambiguity present in transculturation. He writes about the Brazilian music scene in the late 1960s: "Ipanema, in Rio, was filled with other sounds: a babel of protests during song festivals, physical fights for first place and for big money prices, booing contests and cacophonous electric guitar music filling auditoriums—little music and too many arguments. Bossa nova, feeling like a fish out of water, picked up its stool and its guitar, and slipped away unnoticed.

    Fortunately it had somewhere to go: the rest of the world." (*Bossa Nova* 351).

    "Em Ipanema, os sons eram outros: uma babel de protestos, durante os festivais, brigas por primeiros lugares e por altos prêmios em dinheiro, vaias e violões voando sobre auditórios, pouca música e muita discussão. A Bossa Nova, sentindo-se fora de casa, pegou seu banquinho e seu violão, e saiu de mansinho.

    Felizmente tinha para onde ir: o mundo" (*Chega de saudade* 417).
41. The full quotation is as follows: "Na verdade, Caetano e seus companheiros passaram a se utilizar, cada vez mais, de uma metalinguagem, vale dizer, uma linguagem crítica, à base de colagens, paródias e citações, através da qual fariam, em ritmo galopante, o processo e a síntese da nossa cultura, para pôr em xeque e em choque toda a tradição musical brasileira, bossa nova inclusive, em confronto com os dados do contexto universal, revolucionado pela eletronia, pelos Beatles e pela música pop" (De Campos n.p.).
42. The lyrics of the song in Portuguese can be found in www.caetanoveloso.com.br. A rough translation is as follows:

    > You, I, we two
    > We already have a past, my love
    > A packed guitar
    > That flower
    > And other little things
    > I, you, João

Spinning on the turntable endlessly
And the dissonant world that we two
Tried to invent, tried to invent
Tried to invent, tried
Happiness, happiness
Happiness, happiness

I, you, later
Ash Wednesday in the country
And the dissonant notes were integrated
To the sound of the imbeciles
Yes, you, we two
Already have a past, my love
The bossa, the cesspool, our great pain
Like two squares
Wolf, foolish wolf
Wolf, foolish wolf

I, you, João
Spinning on the turntable endlessly
And I remain moved to remember
The time and the sound
Ah! It was so good
But no more nostalgia
The reality is that
We learned with João
For ever
To be out of tune
Be out of tune
Be out of tune
Be

No more nostalgia
No more nostalgia
No more nostalgia
No more nostalgia

43. To be exact, the title "Desafinado" is not quoted directly, but, rather, the lyric goes, "with João we learned always to be *desafinados*" ("out of tune"). The chorus then repeats "ser desafinado" ("to be out of tune"). The song refers to the singles, the original format in which Gilberto's music was issued, rather than to Gilberto's first LP, *Chega de saudade,* which includes the singles together with new songs, because the LP excludes "A felicidade."
44. "Fotografia" was first recorded in 1965, after the military coup. However, the lyrics describe a world fully compatible with that found in the earlier bossa novas, which are also referred to in "Saudosismo."
45. The full quotation is as follows: "Por outro lado, o titulo e a letra sugeriam

uma rejeição/reinvenção da saudade, essa palavra que é um lugar-comum na lírica luso-brasileira e um emblema da língua portuguesa, pois, além de ser um acidente etimológico inexplicado, cobre um campo semântico revelador de algo peculiar em nosso modo de ser" (Veloso, V*erdade tropical* 227).

46. A fuller quotation is: "'Saudosismo,' composição de 1968 . . . é uma declaração de amor e humor a João Gilberto e uma crítica à Bossa Nova institucionalizada ('e as notas dissonantes se integraram ao som dos imbecis')" (Campos n.p.).

    A similar point has recently been made by Lorraine Leu: "'Saudosismo' is . . . a song about how new relationships between existing traditions of songwriting and the changing conventions of musical creation were being worked out" (125).

47. Veloso in *Tropical Truth* narrates some of the clashes he had with the left-wing post-bossa nova musicians (175–76; *Verdade tropical* 280–82).

48. According to Veloso, "I saw in "Chega de saudade" the manifesto and the masterpiece of a movement: the mother ship" (*Tropical Truth* 146). "Eu via em 'Chega de saudade' a canção manifesto e a obra mestra do movimento: a nave-mãe" (*Verdade tropical* 226).

49. The most important study of tropicalismo as a whole, at least in English, Christopher Dunn's *Brutality Garden: Tropicalismo and the Emergence of a Brazilian Counterculture*, emphasizes, as the title indicates, the links between the movement led by Veloso and Gil and the Brazilian counterculture. Dunn even goes further. He uncovers the mutual sympathies between the tropicalistas and the Brazilian guerrillas of the 1960s. Dunn quotes Alex Polari (a member of the guerrilla movement), who claimed that "Tropicalismo and its diverse manifestations were without doubt the perfect cultural expression for that which we incipiently represented in politics" (113).

50. According to Dunn, the early period after the military coup was characterized by "relatively modest advances in literacy and infrastructure with dramatic increases in household ownership of cultural appliances such as radios and television" (45).

51. Veloso writes: "The overt experimentalism of *Sgt. Pepper's Lonely Hearts Club Band* was closer not only to what we were doing, but also to the artists I admired, whether Godard, Oswald, Augusto de Campos" (*Tropical Truth* 170). "O experimentalismo ostensivo de *Sargeant Pepper's Lonely Hearts Club Band* estava mais próximo não só do que fazíamos como dos grandes artistas que eu admirava, fossem eles Godard, Oswald, Augusto de Campos" (*Verdade tropical* 271–72).

52. Em vez de trabalharnos em conjunto no sentido de encontrar um som homogêneo que definisse o novo estilo, preferimos utilizar uma ou outra sonoridade reconhecível da música comercial, fazendo do arranjo um elemento independente que clarificasse a canção mas também se chocasse com ela" (Veloso, *Verdade tropical* 168).

    Veloso continues later in the same paragraph: "In tropicalista recordings one can find bossa nova elements dispersed among others of a different nature, but never an attempt to forge a new synthesis or even an evolution of the extraordinarily successful synthesis that bossa nova had been" (*Tropical Truth* 102). "De fato, nas gravações tropicalistas podem-se encontrar elementos da bossa nova dispostos entre outros de natureza diferente, mas nunca uma tentativa de forjar uma nova síntese ou mesmo um desenvolvimento da síntese extraordinariamente bem-sucedida que a bossa nova tinha sido" (*Verdade tropical* 168). Veloso does not deal with "Batmacumba" in his memoirs.

53. Canclini's use of the verb "to fuse" (in Spanish, fusionar) to describe hybridity in this passage may indicate, more than a certain inconsistency in his theories, the difficulty of separating one approach to cultural incorporation from the other, that is, transculturation from hybridity.

It is possible to see in this juxtaposition of apparently incongruous styles and elements that characterizes Canclinian hybridity, as exemplified in Veloso, a musical parallel to the analysis of tropicalismo proposed by Roberto Schwarz. In his classic essay "Cultura e politica, 1964–1969," Schwarz describes tropicalismo, here seen as including other arts, such as film, plastic arts, etc., as

> submitting the anachronisms... grotesque at first sight, unbelievable under later analysis, to the white light of the ultra-modern, transforming the result into an allegory of Brazil. The reserve of images and emotions characteristic of a patriarchal country, rural and urban, is exposed to the most advanced or fashionable form or technique—electronic music, Eisenteinian montage, pop colors and montage, prose à la *Finnegan's Wake*, stagings simultaneously raw and allegorical, physically attacking the audience. It's in this internal difference that the peculiar brilliance, the trade mark, of the tropicalista image is to be found.

[Na submissão de anacronismos desse tipo, grotescos à primeira vista, inevitáveis a segunda, à luz branca do ultra-moderno, transformando-se o resultado em alegoria do Brasil. A reserva de imagens e emoções próprias ao país patriarcal, rural e urbano, é exposta à forma ou tecnica mais avançada ou na moda mundial—música eletrônica, montagem eisensteiniana, côres e montagem do pop, prosa de *Finnegan's Wake*, cena ao memo tempo crua e alegórica, atacando fisicamente a platéia. É nesta diferença interna que está o brilho peculiar, a marca de registro da imagem tropicalista] (74).

54. The "invention" of the concept album, defined as "one with a thematic or framing device" (Malone 298), has been frequently credited to Sinatra: "During these years, with assistance from Riddle, Gordon Jenkins, and Billy May, among other arrangers, Sinatra originated what is generally defined as the concept album" (Davis 3).

55. "Elis soltava a voz en vibrato, como uma negona americana" (Motta 230).

56. "Cruces culturales que... incluyen una reestructuración radical de los vínculos entre lo tradicional y lo moderno, lo popular y lo culto, lo local y lo extranjero" (Canclini, *Culturas híbridas* 223).

57. "La reconversión cultural es más bien una manera de competir en la economía capitalista transnacional, adaptando tradiciones culturales, sabe-res

y prácticas a la lógica implacable del mercado, produciendo hibridez pero siempre desde la subordinación" (Kokotovic, "Hibridez e desigualdad" 297).
58. "É uma música de todas as classes, e de classe nenhuma, é uma música vulgar, é um produto para consumo geral" and "E é sob o signo de produto que a música está existindo" (Homem de Mello 199).
59. " 'Empresario-mundo' que articula en su cultura información, creencias y rituales procedentes de lo local, lo nacional y lo internacional" (García Canclini, *Consumidores y ciudadanos* 86).

Chapter 6

1. The version of Prince Felipe's statement available in the Spanish-language press is unusual in that it gives the impression of having been made by putting together isolated phrases. (There are numerous openings and closings of quotations marks that I have eliminated in the translation of the text). The actual text found in the press release is as follows: "El Príncipe Felipe invitó hoy a concebir la nueva sede del Instituto Cervantes de Beijing, primera en China, como 'un gran faro' que 'ilumina' el camino hacia una 'apasionante, rica y enorme' región del mundo como es Iberoamérica que, unida por la historia, la lengua y la cultura, en la actualidad obtiene 'impulsos importantes' en el campo de la política y la economía" ("El principe considera al Instituto Cervantes como 'gran faro' " n.p.).
2. "El Instituto Cervantes es la institución pública creada por España en 1991 para la promoción y la enseñanza de la lengua española y para la difusión de la cultura española e hispanoamericana" (Cervantes.es n.p.).
3. Out of 143 participants listed, 10 were Latin Americans (8 Spanish Americans, and 2 Brazilians). All of the information regarding "Pen World Voices" comes from the Pen American Center (http://www.pen.org/page.php/prmID/1028 n.p.).
4. All of the information regarding the organization of the Instituto Cervantes is taken from its Web page: www.cervantes.es.
5. The complete list of Spanish American representatives includes, in addition to Bryce and Mastretta, Hernando Cabarcas, the director of the Instituto Caro y Cuervo, the Colombian government sponsored school of humanities; Eulalio Ferrer Rodríguez, the Spanish-Mexican expert on advertising; Enrique Krauze, the Mexican historian and director of the well-known magazine *Letras libres;* Juan Ramón de la Fuente, the president of the National University of Mexico; and the Peruvian poet Blanca Varela.
6. The living Spanish American recipients of the Cervantes Prize are the Mexicans Sergio Pitol and Carlos Fuentes, the Peruvian-Spanish Mario Vargas Llosa, the Chileans Gonzalo Rojas and Jorge Edwards, and the Argentine Ernesto Sábato.
7. The word *encounter* misrepresents the actual events of 1492, which, at best, can be seen as the preparatory stage of the conquest.
8. The information regarding the Casa de las Américas is extracted from its

Web page (www.casamerica.es) and from Burkhard Pohl's "¿Un nuevo boom?"
9. "Casa de América es un consorcio creado en 1990 e integrado por el Ministerio de Asuntos Exteriores, a través de la Secretaría de Estado para la Cooperación Internacional y para Iberoamérica, la Comunidad de Madrid y el Ayuntamiento de Madrid" (*casamerica.es* n.p.).
10. This confluence of cultural and economic concerns is found in the "Mensaje de bienvenida de su majestad el rey" ("Welcoming Statement of His Majesty the King") to the XV Ibero-American Summit, an organization also developed during the Columbine Quintecentennial: "Spain feels profoundly connected to them [Ibero-American countries] by historical, cultural, linguistic, and human links, to which more recently has been added the decisive wager that numerous Spanish businesses are making in favor of the economic development of our sister nations ['España se siente íntimamente ligada a ellos por lazos históricos, culturales, idiomáticos y humanos, a los que más recientemente se ha venido a unir la decidida apuesta que numerosas empresas españolas están haciendo por el desarrollo económico de Naciones hermanas']" (n.p.). This political version of the concept of Ibero-America includes, in addition to Spanish America, Brazil, Portugal, and Andorra.
11. "Habría que acabar con la idea que son de un sitio o de otro. Son de la lengua española, esa es mi idea" (Cruz 322).
12. "Este nuevo discurso panhispanista, adoptado tanto desde la izquierda como desde la derecha política, abandona los rasgos imperialistas, étnicos y religiosos de la Hispanidad del ideario franquista. Los elementos característicos que lo conforman son la afirmación . . . del papel de España como mediadora de los intereses latinoamericanos hacia la UE y los EEUU" (Pohl, "¿Un nuevo boom? 275).

One must add that similar ideas had been expressed by progressive intellectuals and institutions during the 1960s and 1970s when the Franco regime experienced a profound economic liberalization. Thus the *Catalog* of Seix Barral, the publishers of Vargas Llosa and other boom authors in the 1960s and 1970s, states: "We understand that Spanish literature is any literature that is written in the varied forms of Spanish . . . We understand that that our contemporary literature is one literature and one only, even though the actual lilnguistic experience may be sited in places as distant as Santiago de Compostela (Spain), Santiago in Cuba, Santiago in Chile and Santiago del Estero (Argentina)" (qtd, in Herrero-Olaizola 19–20). Herrero Olaizola notes that this statement constitutes a "heartier pan-Hispanism" than that accepted by the Franco government, but one that was compatible with the actual economic policies of the government: "the case of Seix Barral's *Catálogo* [*Catalog*] is also a good example of the way the government's plans and those of this avant-garde publishing house became closely intermeshed under the new economic policies" (20).
13. "Acaso España tiene un plancito loco, a medio camino entre la globaliza-

ción dirigida y la invasión solapa . . . un plancito en el que cosas como el Instituto Cervantes, los viajes del príncipe Felipe y la insufrible Real Academia Española son la Niña, la Pinta y la Santa María de un expansionismo que quiere jugarse entero a la idea de que los latinoamericanos somos, en verdad, hijitos descarriados que algún día volverán al redil" (Faverón, "El faro y la reconquista" n.p.).

14. The similarities between today's Hispanophone publishing market and de Torre's proposal has already been pointed out by Jorge Fornet (1).
15. The fate of some of the best-known Spanish American book-publishing houses is illustrative of the centrality of Spanish capital. Emecé has been brought by Planeta; Editorial Losada has relocated from Argentina to Madrid; Sudamericana somewhat bucking the trend, has been bought by Random House Mondadori, a joint venture of Random House, which actually belongs to the German media conglomerate Bertelsmann and Mondadori, the major book publishers in Italy. However, Random House Mondadori's home base is in Barcelona.
16. According to Luis Hernández Navarro: "In 1999, Spain became the largest direct investor in Latin America. Spain's investment in the region went from 780 million dollars in 1990 to 100 billion Euros in 2001, of which 26.281 billion were invested in Argentina, 26.292 billion in Brazil, 9.197 billion in Mexico, and 7.816 billion in Chile. Since then the amounts invested have continued to increase ['En 1999 España se convirtió en el mayor inversor directo en América Latina. Las inversiones directas de este país en la región pasaron de 780 millones de dólares en 1990 a 100 mil millones de euros en 2001, de los cuales 26 mil 281 millones se colocaron en Argentina, 26 mil 292 millones en Brasil, 9 mil 197 millones en México y 7 mil 816 millones en Chile']" (n.p.). Hernández Navarro concludes: "The Spanish presence in South America has become complementary and, to a degree, substitutes for the tradtional hegemony of the United States. The new conquest by Iberia has come to stay ['La presencia española en América del Sur se ha vuelto complementaria, y, hasta cierto punto, substituta de la tradicional hegemonía estadounidense. La reconquista ibérica llegó para quedarse']" (n.p.). However, in recent years, Spanish investment in Latin America has decreased notoriously without fully losing its importance, especially in the cultural sector: "In 2005, the European Union absorbed 75% of Spanish foreign investment . . . France received 21.8%; the Czech Republic, 16%; the United Kingdom 10%; and Hungary, 9.5%. All of Latin America only received 15%. At the end of the '90s, Latin America absorbed about 60% of all Spanish foreign investment" ("En el 2005, la UE absorbió el 75% de la inversión española en el exterior, según datos del Registro de Inversiones Exteriores del Ministerio de Industria. Francia fue destino del 21,8%; la República Checa, del 16%; el Reino Unido, del 10%; y Hungría, del 9,5%. El conjunto de Latinoamérica solo se llevó el 15%. A finales de los 90, Latinoamérica abarcaba alrededor del 60% de la inversión multinacional española") (Sánchez n.p.). However, as the article quoted

makes clear, it was during the late 1990s and early 2000s that many of the major purchases of Latin American corporations, which frequently still remain in Spanish hands, took place.

17. In the translated text, I have fused two of Volpi's answers to the interviewer. The full exchanges are as follows:

> "–¿España vuelve a ser el centro de la cultura en nuestro idioma?
> –"El problema, más allá de dónde vivan los escritores, es que la mayor parte de las grandes editoriales en nuestro idioma están actualmente en manos de grupos españoles o internacionales. Ya no están las grandes editoriales latinoamericanas que podían competir.
> –¿Eso distorsiona la visión de nuestra cultura?
> –Bastante. Para que un escritor sea conocido en América Latina, antes debe ser decidido en España. Si no es atractivo para el público español, difícil que llegue a nuestra región." (Volpi, "Cuando nací el boom estaba allí" ns.p.).

18. For instance Noé Cárdenas writes about Roncagliolo's *Abril rojo*: "A polished thriller, *Abril Rojo,* is a novel that complies with the requirements for market success: sensationalist ingredients properly dosified and combined that generate suspense and reach a surprising conclusion that not only satisfies the expectations of a reader of commercial novels, but also looks to its adaptation into film ['Pulido thriller, *Abril rojo* es una novela enderezada a cumplir con los requisitos del mercado para ser exitosa: ingredientes sensacionalistas bien dosificados y combinados que, bajo un suspenso creciente, alcanzan una resolución inesperada que no sólo satisface los requerimientos de un lector consumidor de novelas comerciales, sino que prevé en su concepción la versión cinematográfica']" (92). Regarding Jaime Bayly, Luis Larios Vendrell, in *World Literature Today,* writes: "In 1994 Bayly published *No se lo digas a nadie*... which was extremely controversial and provided him with the keys to his following success: shock and the use of themes never before taken up by other Latin American writers. Bayly followed Mario Vargas Llosa's advice to the letter: 'Lo peor que le puede pasar a un escritor es que su primera novela pase inadvertida, lo mejor que le pueda pasar es que su primera novela produzca un escandalo descomunal.' Bayly has made sure that all his subsequent works followed that formula, although the repetitive nature of these writings reduces considerably the interest the reader might find in literary works created with the primary intention of shocking readers and defending the author's sexual inclination" (178).

19. "Ya teníamos a Donoso, en Argentina a Cortázar, en Uruguay a Tomás di Mattos y a Omar Prego, en México a Carlos Fuentes. Necesitabamos además a un gran escritor global, que era Mario Vargas Llosa y compramos toda su obra. Esto ha sido nuestra estrategia" (Cruz 320).

20. The unique position of Vargas Llosa among the boom writers is probably linked to the fact that he has, as Rita Gnutzmann notes, become a "mandarin" (72). In other words, Vargas Llosa is "a man to whom a vast audience confers

the power to legislate on issues that go from the great moral, cultural, and political questions to those most trivial ['un hombre al que una vasta audiencia confiere el poder de legislar sobre asuntos que van desde las grandes cuestiones morales, culturales y políticas hasta las más triviales']" (Vargas Llosa qtd. in Gnutzmann 72). In Spain, Vargas Llosa's position as a mandarin dates back to the 1960s. According to Mario Santana: "A simple glimpse at literary journals and debates during the 1960s and 1970s in Spain will make clear that Vargas Llosa had become a prominent presence and a model for young Spanish writers" (qtd. in Herrero-Olaizola 44). Moreover, as Herrero-Olaizola notes on the granting of Spanish citizenship to Vargas Llosa by the center-left government of Felipe González in 1993, "The Socialist government seemed to conclude that Vargas Llosa had been and would continue to be a permanent fixture on Spain's cultural scene" (44).

21. It is somewhat surprising that Vargas Llosa has not been a vocal proponent of the pan-Hispanic liberal discourse. After all, in addition to his Peruvian nationality, he is also a Spanish citizen. However, his writings, while celebrating globalization and the opening of national borders, maintain allegiance to a Latin American identity. Thus, in a recent essay, Vargas Llosa claims, that he discovered Latin America during his stay in Paris in the 1960s and that: "Since then I began to feel a Latin American, before anything else. ['Desde entonces comencé a sentirme, ante todo, un latinoamericano']" ("Dentro y fuera de América Latina" 62).

22. The full quotation is as follows: "España se encuentra en Europa. Pero no debe olvidar que se encuentra también en Hispanoamérica, 'los cachorros de la leona española,' como nos llamó el poeta Rubén Darío. ¿Podemos ser sin España? Puede España ser sin nosotros?" (Fuentes, *El espejo enterrado* 369).

23. "Definió el territorio de La Mancha diciendo que 'comienza en los Pirineos, termina en el Tajo, cruza el Atlántico, se va a América, empieza en California, sigue por México, y llega a Chile y Argentina, es un territorio vastísimo el de La Mancha'" ("La Universidad de Castilla-La Mancha nombra doctor Honoris Causa a Carlos Fuentes" n.p.).

24. "Tened cuidado. ¡Vive la América española!/ Hay mil cachorros sueltos del León Español" (Darío, "A Roosevelt" 39).

25. "Esto significa que, en el siglo que se avecina, la lengua castellana será el idioma preponderante de las tres Américas: la del Sur, la del Centro y la del Norte. La famosa pregunta de Rubén Darío—¿tantos millones hablarán inglés?—será al fin contestada: no, hablarán español" (Fuentes, "Discurso Premio Cervantes" 2).

Fuentes quotes from "Los cisnes," where the great Nicaraguan poet writes: "Will we be handed over to the fierce barbarians? / Will so many millions of men speak English? / Are there no nobles [hidalgos] or valiant knights? / Will we be silent now to cry later?" (¿Seremos entregados a los bárbaros fieros? / ¿Tantos millones de hombres hablaremos inglés? / ¿Ya no hay nobles hidalgos ni bravos caballeros? / ¿Callaremos ahora para llorar después?) (61). It is noteworthy that Darío, as a reaction to the Spanish American war and the full manifestation of U.S. desire and designs to incorporate the region developed a kind of anti-imperialist Hispanism, that, in some ways, resembles Fuentes's position. Needless to say, Fuentes is fully aware of this similarity as his quoting of Darío in key moments in his speeches and essays makes clear.

26. In his Cervantes Award speech, Fuentes speaks about his two "passports": the first Mexican and the second Hispanophone ("Discurso" 1).
27. "En todas las capitales latinoamericanas uno puede encontrar los best-sellers del momento o autores traducidos en España, pero ni hablar de autores iberoamericanos... Si uno es un escritor latinoamericano y desea estar tanto en las librerías de Quito, La Paz y San Juan hay que publicar y ojalá vivir en Barcelona. Cruzar la frontera implica atravesar el Atlántico" (Fuguet and Gómez 13).
28. "En un curioso malabarismo, la política editorial de esas empresas se vuelve a veces precapitalista y la circulación de autores se limita en la mayor parte de los casos al espacio de sus respectivos países. Por paradójico que parezca, la globalización puede actuar a favor del provincianismo" (Fornet 1).
29. "Un autor peruano no muy conocido fuera, capaz de vender tres mil ejemplares en su país, es seguro que puede vender otros cientos afuera" (Solé n.p.).
30. "Nadie sabía, en cada país, qué cosas se estaban escribiendo en otros países hispanoamericanos, sobre todo porque era tan difícil publicar y difundir una primera novela o un primer libro de cuentos. Vencer el círculo de los consagrados para conseguir que una editorial cualquiera, todas más o menos pobretonas en los países pequeños, y volcadas hacia la literatura extranjera en los países mayores, se arriezgaran a publicar un nombre desconocido, y si llegaban a hacerlo tiraran más de un par de miles de ejemplares destinados a acumular polvo en los sotanos de las editoriales sin salir del país era imposible" (Donoso, *Historia personal del boom* 26).
31. Although the novel was published posthumously in 1971, sections from the "Primer Diario" ("First Diary") in which Arguedas criticizes several of the boom writers were published in 1968, as was an essay responding to Cortázar's statements.
32. "Me asombra que a veces no se advierta hasta qué punto el eco que han podido despertar mis libros en Latinoamérica se deriva de que proponen una literatura cuya raíz nacional y regional está como potenciada por una experiencia más abierta y más compleja, y en la que cada evocación o recreación de lo originalmente mío alcanza su extrema tensión gracias a esa apertura sobre y desde un mundo que lo rebasa y en último extremo lo elige y lo perfecciona" (Cortázar 276).
33. However, Jean Franco has recently argued that at least in the case of Arguedas, "the 'loser' in this struggle for recognition by the center perhaps won in another field. Arguedas is more current than Cortázar, given that his work has provoked discussions about transculturation and heterogeneity, burning topics in a period of migration ['Pero el 'perdedor' en esta lucha por el reconocimiento del centro quizás ganó en otro campo. Es Arguedas

más actual que Cortázar, ya que su obra ha provocado discusiones sobre transculturación y heterogeneidad, temas candentes en la época de migraciones']" ("Nunca son pesadas" 187).
34. A more complete version of Arguedas' text is as follows: "Como si yo criado ente la gente de don Felipe Maywa, metido en el oqllo mismo de los indios durante algunos años de la infancia para luego volver a la esfera 'supraindia' de donde había 'descendido' entre los quechuas, dijera que mejor, mucho más esencialmente interpreto el espíritu, el apetito de don Felipe, que el propio don Felipe. ¡Falta de respeto y legítima consideración!" (14).
35. "Todos somos provincianos, don Julio (Cortázar). Provinciano de las naciones y provincianos de lo supranacional que es, también, una esfera" (Arguedas 21).
36. De todas, cupo papel central a Fabril Editora, Sudamericana, Losada, Fondo de Cultura, Seix Barral y Joaquín Mortiz" (Rama, "El Boom en perspectiva" 66).
37. One must note, however, that the Spanish book industry was the most important. As Pohl notes the 1960s were the period when the international expansion and professionalization of the book publishing industry takes place ("¿Vender el boom?" 165). Among the innovations that will affect directly the commercial aspects of the boom are the opening of a modern literary agency by Carmen Balcells, who will handle Vargas Llosa, among other important Latin American authors, mass printings and pocket books, which according to Pohl begin with the Spanish publication of *One Hundred Years of Solitude* in 1968 (165, 166).
38. On Ortega y Gasset, see chapter 3.
39. This identification of the boom with Magical Realism is not limited to the United States; it is also common in Spain, despite the media and literary importance of Vargas Llosa, a writer who has never flirted with the style. Pohl for instance notes that by 1978 "there has been a generalization of the term Magical Realism, which is used with little sense of differentiation to name (and denounce) a writing of Latin American alterity ['se ha llegado a una generalización del término realismo mágico, que se utiliza con poco sentido de diferenciación para denominar (y denunciar) una escritura de alteridad latinoamericana']" ("El post-boom en España-mercado y edición [1973–1985]" 240).
40. "Quizás una de las grandes paradojas de la globalización sea que, para muchos de nuestros escritores, el verdadero desafío ya no esté sólo en ser leído en el extranjero sino en reconquistar al lector local" (Guerrero 26).

Chapter 7

1. Some of the writers anthologized by Gómez and Fuguet—all born after 1959—are the following: Bayly (Peru), Edmundo Paz Soldán (Bolivia), Rodrigo Fresán (Argentina), and Naief Yehya (Mexico).
2. "La antología de McOndo, el manifiesto del crack, y todo cuanto ha

ocurrido recientemente con la nueva novela latinoamericana... fueron fenómenos naturales" (Padilla 137).
3. A fuller version of the text in Spanish is as follows: "Ahí hay más bien una mera reacción contra el agotamiento cansancio de que la gran literatura latinoamericana y el dudoso realismo mágico se hayan convertido, para nuestras letras, en magiquismo trágico" (Volpi et al., "Manifiesto crack" 5).
4. "Es crítico, por ejemplo, que se vea al realismo mágico como la única opción de la literatura latinoamericana" (Volpi, "Los autores del boom" n.p.).
5. The full sentence is as follows: "Contrarrestar esa idea y para tratar de entroncar nuestra literatura con la tradición más universal o cosmopolita de la literatura latinoamericana que también existía" (Volpi, "Los autores del boom" n.p.).
6. "Vender un continente rural cuando, la verdad de las cosas, es urbana... nos parece aberrante, cómodo, e inmoral" (Fuguet and Gómez 18).

   According to the United Nations: "Regarding human settlements, Latin America and the Caribbean (LAC) is the most urbanized region in the developing world, with an urbanization level rivaling that of many industrialized countries. The region's urbanization level rose from 71% in 1990 to 75% in 2000, at which time its urban population amounted to 380 million, as against 127 million rural inhabitants" (2).
7. Some critics have seen in McOndo's, as well as the Crack's, attack on Magical Realism echoes of Borges's criticisms of local color in "The Argentine Writer and Tradition." See Guerrero 25–26.
8. "Hay más cepillado de dientes y excursiones al campo (bueno, al departamento o al centro comercial) que levitaciones" (Fuguet and Gómez 19).
9. "Mientras que el Crack subraya precisamente la vuelta a los presupuestos esteticos totalizantes de la generación de los 50 y 60, los inventores de McOndo—y lo confirman los textos reunidos en la antologia susodicha, entre ellos las contribuciones de los mexicanos David Toscana, Naief Yehya y Jordi Soler—defienden una literatura voluntariamente juvenil o por lo menos abierta hacia lo cotidiano en el ambito cultural; una deliberada inscripción en los codigos culturales del mainstream internacional anglosajón" (Pohl, "Ruptura y continuidad" 60).
10. Keep in mind, however, that *One Hundred Years of Solitude* is for Vargas Llosa the very text that defined the total novel. The Peruvian author writes: "*One Hundred Years of Solitude* is a total novel, in the family of those dementially ambitious creations that compete with reality as an equal, presenting to it an image of a vitality, vastness, and complexity that is qualitatively equivalent. This totality is manifested principally in the plural nature of the novel that is, simultaneously, things that were thought to be antithetical: traditional and modern, local and universal, imaginary and realist ['*Cien años de soledad* es una novela total, en la línea de esas creaciones demencialmente ambiciosas que compiten con la realidad real de igual a igual, enfrentándole una imagen de una vitalidad, vastedad y complejidad cualitativamente equivalentes. Esta totalidad se manifiesta ante todo en la naturaleza plural de la novela, que es, simultáneamente, cosas que se creían antinómicas: tradicional

y moderna, localista y universal, imaginaria y realista']" ("*Cien años de soledad*" xxv).
11. Volpi's use of detective formulas in his novels, in particular, *In Search of Klingsor,* can be seen as establishing a link between his texts, despite their highbrow topics, and those of the McOndo group.
12. "La crítica latinoamericana nunca ha confundido al realismo mágico con el resto de nuestra literatura, y que siempre ha estado bastante claro para nosotros que se trata sólo de un modo literario, temporal como cualquiera, cuyo momento cumbre fue de hecho fugaz y queda hoy lejano" (Faverón, "Crack & McOndo" n.p.).
13. "¿Pero qué es la historia de América toda sino una crónica de lo real maravilloso?" (Carpentier, "Prólogo" 31).
14. Roberto González Echevarría, in his study of Alejo Carpentier's novels, notes the change in the theories underlying the Cuban novelist's writings from the 1950s on, from the real marvelous to that of the American baroque: "The baroque as a new metaphor, a new conceit designating that which is particularly Latin American is quite different . . . To begin with, Carpentier insists now on defining cities not the jungle or the world of nature" (*Alejo Carpentier* 224). Thus Carpentier's evolution from rural to urban in his narrative would prefigure the changes proposed by the McOndo group, only with more than thirty years of anticipation. Regardless of the results, Carpentier's complex "writing that purports to name for the first time even while conscious of naming for the second time" differs from Fuguet's much simpler and pop-tinged, though effective, writing (224).
15. "En los últimos quince años los auténticos best sellers latinoamericanos han sido casi todos escritos por notorios epígonos de García Márquez" (Guerrero 27).
16. A fuller version of Palaversich's text is: "Con este machismo virulento—evidente en la exclusión de mujeres como autoras pero sí su inclusión como personajes, sin excepción frívolos y superficiales—los mcondistas demuestran que no sólo no avanzaron con relación a sus 'padres literarios' contra los cuales se rebelan, sino que sufren un retroceso, demostrando que su pretendida (post)modernidad y coolness no afectan la relación entre los sexos opuestos" (n.p.).

    However, in a surprising gesture, Fuguet is also the author of a very positive evaluation of Allende's literary career, "¿De qué hablamos cuando hablamos de Isabel Allende?" I deal briefly with this text in the epilogue to this book.
17. "Tampoco debe dejarse de lado que en un mercado internacional saturado por realismos mágicos producidos en múltiples puntos del sur global o por sus diásporas en los países metropolitanos, parecería una buena estrategia comercial, además de una movida generacional esperable, el ofrecer un productor literario militantemente contrario al realismo mágico pero a la vez consonante con las versiones celebratorias de la hibridación cultural indiscriminada" (Poblete 295).
18. On the marketing concerns of McOndo and the Crack, see also Fornet 14.
19. "Cuando Alberto Fuguet planteó en su prólogo a McOndo su desapego, o

mejor, su despegue del universo marqueciano, no lo hizo porque éste careciera de valor, menos aún porque los autores antologados lo creyeran así, sino porque otros menos diestros que el escritor colombiano habían comenzado a caricaturizarlo creando por ello esperpentos no sólo de la literatura, sino del continente latinoamericano" (Padilla 141).

20. See Fuguet and Gomez 11–12. The major difference between the version in "Presentación" and the one in Fuguet's "I Am Not a Magical Realist" is that in the former it is presented as the common experience of "three young Latin American writers ['tres jóvenes escritores latinoamericanos']" (11), while in the latter it is exclusively Fuguet's. In the earlier version, two of the three writers are rejected and as a consequence "McOndo was created ['surgió McOndo']" (12). This leads the reader to assume that the two writers are Fuguet and Gómez, the editors of *McOndo*.

21. "*Reshaping* in Lima Barreto; *mimesis* without qualms in João do Rio; *refusal* or embarrased (but lucrative) assimilation in [Olavio] Bilac; and a perverse *displacement* of any marks of modernization in [Godofredo] Rangel—these are no more than a few of the forms assumed by the dialogue between literary technique and dissemination of new techniques in printing, reproduction, and broadcasting in turn-of the-century Brazil" (Süssekind 11).

22. According to Claudia Cabezón Doty: "In *The Death of Artemio Cruz,* Carlos Fuentes transposes the technique of investigative journalism of director Orson Welles in his movie *Citizen Kane* ['En *La muerte de Artemio Cruz* (1962), Carlos Fuentes transpone la técnica del periodismo investigativo del director Orson Welles en su película Citizen Kane']" (31n16). Moreover, Fuentes has expressed on numerous occasions his admiration for Welles's movie. In his recent *En esto creo,* he writes about "the authentic narrative, technical and visual revolution sparked by Orson Welles's *Citizen Kane* ['la autentica revolución narrativa, técnica y visual aportada por *Ciudadano Kane* de Orson Welles']" (45).

23. In an interview with the Argentine newspaper *Clarín,* Fuguet states that Puig "was the first Latin American writer with whom I could truly connect. I also like the first Vargas Llosa very much, even if he comes from an academic formation . . . *Aunt Julia and the Scriptwriter* is a book very [close to] Puig ['Fue el primer escritor latinoamericano con el que me pude conectar de verdad. También el primer Vargas Llosa me gusta mucho, aunque él viene de una formación académica . . . *La tía Julia y el escribidor* es un libro muy Puig']" ("Yo soy un gran afanador" n.p.). It must be noted that the Mexican Onda writers—José Agustín, Gustavo Sainz—had in the 1960s created a literature centered on their country's youth culture and on the mass culture—rock, films—they had embraced. Fuguet seems not to have read them.

24. The implicit criticism of popular culture in Vargas Llosa's novel has been noted, for instance, by Javier Lasarte Valcárcel: "The Vargas Llosa of *Aunt Julia and the Scriptwriter,* behind the appearance of a humoristic rapprochement, would solidify and consecrate the radical distance, the differ-

ence between the cultures of writing and scripting [escribanía] ['El Vargas Llosa *de La tía Julia y el escribidor,* tras la apariencia de un humorístico acercamiento, asentaría y consagraría la radical distancia, la diferencia de las culturas de la escritura y la escribanía']" (188–89).
25. According to Truffaut, these "Tradition of Quality" films, generally tony and politically progressive adaptations of "important" French novels, were aesthetically and morally bankrupt: "The dominant trait of psychological realism is its anti-bourgeois will. But what are Aurenche and Bost, Sigurd, Jeanson, Autant-Lara, Allegret, if not bourgeois, and what are the fifty thousand new readers, who do not fail to see each film from a novel, if not bourgeois?" ("A Certain Tendency" 234). Truffaut then asks: "What then is the value of an anti-bourgeois cinema made by the bourgeois for the bourgeois?" (234). (Jean Aurenche and Pierre Bost were an important scriptwriting team; Jacques Sigurd and Henri Jeanson were also screenwriters; Claude Autant-Lara and Yves Allégret were directors.)
26. "Un texto nada académico y vergonzosamente personal" (Fuguet, *Las películas de mi vida* 157).
27. Truffaut begins his review of Jean Vigo by detailing how he became aware of the filmmaker: "I had the pleasure of discovering Jean Vigo's films in a single Saturday afternoon session in 1946, at the Sevres-Pathé, thanks to the Ciné-club 'La Chambre Noire' organized by André Bazin" (*The Films in My Life* 23).
28. "Las películas que de verdad te llegan siempre son acerca de uno" (Fuguet, *Las películas de mi vida* 252).
29. "Todos los hijos sufrían algún mal: uno era sordo, dos padecían algún grado de retardo, tres eran diabéticos, uno era ciego, dos obesos y la mayor tenía un problema en las caderas" (Fuguet, *Las películas de mi vida* 212).
30. "Es la única película que han visto los niños" (Fuguet, *Las películas de mi vida* 213).
31. "La cinta me pareció aún más relamida de lo que la recordaba" (Fuguet, *Las películas de mi vida* 213).
32. "Era un programa 'recomendado' por los cerebros del régimen militar para apoyar a la familia 'que es el sostén y la piedra angular de este gobierno'" (Fuguet, *Las películas de mi vida* 213).
33. An earlier moment that links fascism and family values—or, maybe, presents Pinochet's regime as cynically using family values—is the section dedicated to Carol Reed's *Oliver!*. After quoting part of the lyrics of one of the movie's songs—"Consider yourself at home . . . Consider yourself part of the family" (77), Beltrán remembers his return to Chile: "The famous song 'Consider Yourself' was played ceaselessly during that year, and I was never left in peace since some old reporter had the idea to use the orchestral version as the theme song to an ultra-right-wing radio program ['La célebre canción "Consider Yourself" no dejó de sonar ese año 74 y no me dejó nunca tranquilo, pues a algún viejo reportero se le ocurrió usarla, en su versión orquestada, como la cortina del noticiario de una radio de ultraderecha']" (Fuguet, *The*

Movies of My Life 77 [*Las peliculas de mi vida* 77]). And: "Consider yourself one of us! Rang out every morning and again in the afternoon, along with Pinochet's voice ['Consider yourself part of us! (*sic*), todas las mañanas, y luego en la tarde, y la voz de Pinochet']" (78 [77]).

34. "¿Lindsay, como Lindsay Wagner?" (Fuguet, *Las películas de mi vida* 49).
35. "McQueen, como mi padre, casi no hablaba en sus filmes" (Fuguet, *Las películas de mi vida* 76).
36. "Lo pasé muy bien, fue como volver a mi infancia, cuando me devoraba las películas como si fueran M&M's" (Fuguet, *Las películas de mi vida* 59).
37. The differences between McOndo and the Crack can be brought into focus if one compares the references found in *The Movies of My Life,* invariably related to mass media, with those found in Volpi's *In Search of Klingsor.* The title of Volpi's book refers to Wagner's *Parsifal*—Klingsor is a dark magician in the opera. In fact, similar "high" cultural references are dropped throughout Volpi's text. For instance, the first sentence of the book is Hitler's supposed statement "No more light ['Basta de luz']" (*En busca de Klingsor* 11). Given its utterer, the statement is obviously significant and representative. It is also a direct inversion of Goethe's famous last words: "Light, more light," and also refers directly to the creation story. Thus Hitler is both an anti-enlightenment and a satanic figure.
38. "Pensé que tuve mucha suerte de haber vivido mis primeros años en un sitio colonizado por Frank Capra y James Stewart, y no por un grupo de españoles malolientes y resentidos que se escaparon de su tierra natal para ir a asesinar nativos y robarles su oro al otro lado del mundo" (Fuguet, *Las películas de mi vida* 87).
39. According to Roberto Ignacio Díaz, "Recent works of fiction by authors linked with the panglobal culture and affinities of the McOndo group . . . prolong this search [to represent actual spoken Spanish] by carefully depicting, as New Age *costumbristas*, the sociolects of the young in cities like Santiago de Chile and Lima" (49). And one can add that, like the nineteenth-century costumbristas, there is also in these novels, including *The Movies of My Life,* an interest in representing the most characteristic cultural experiences of, in this case, young urban dwellers. There is however an important difference between Fuguet (and by implication, other Mcondians) and the costumbristas; the latter attempted to represent cultures and, to use Raymond Williams useful term, structures of feeling that were residual, while the former are concerned with those that are arguably no longer emergent, but instead dominant.
40. "Yo trato de ser realista, y si hubiera puesto puras películas latinoamericanas en la novela, hubiera estado mintiendo. El 99 por ciento de películas que uno ve en Latinoamérica son de Estados Unidos" (Fuguet, "Estados Unidos es un país latinoamericano" n.p.).
41. "Gracias a las grandes distribuidoras, llas mismas películas se ven en diversos puntos del mundo, creando un trasfondo cultural común y un cierto 'imaginario colectivo'" (Caro Martí n.p.).

42. "Los cuentos de McOndo se centran en realidades individuales y privadas. Suponemos que ésta es una de las herencias de la fiebre privatizadora mundial" (Fuguet and Gómez 15).
43. Beltrán is reminded of Chile when watching *Soylent Green:* "1974 Santiago seemed a lot like the decrepit Manhattan of 2022 ['El Santiago de 1974 se parecía al Manhattan decrépito de 2022']" (Fuguet, *The Movies of My Life* 178 [*Las películas de mi vida* 176]).
44. "¿En qué momento se había jodido el Perú?" (Vargas Llosa, *Conversacion en La Catedral* 17).
45. In an interview with *The Barcelona Review,* Fuguet notes about *The Movies of My Life* and its potential relationship with *Conversation in the Cathedral:* "The political novel has already been written and I don't think I'll write it, even if everyone wants to write *Conversation in the Cathedral* ['La novela política ya está hecha y no creo que yo la haga, aunque todo el mundo quiere hacer *Conversación en La Catedral*']." He then adds: "I wanted to speak of Chile ['Yo quería hablar de Chile']." And claims, despite the previously mentioned difference from Vargas Llosa: "I am vargasllosian ['soy vargasllosiano']" ("Estados Unidos es un país latinoamericano" n.p.).
46. Beltrán, remembering his relatives' insistence during the beginning of the Pinochet regime that "Chile will never be like California ['Chile nunca será como California']" comments: "They were wrong, of course, but people tend to hear what they want to hear ['Estaban errados, claro, pero la gente tiende a escuchar lo que quiere escuchar']" (Fuguet, *The Movies of My Life* 188 [*Las películas de mi vida* 186]).
47. Beltrán describes his coming back to Los Angeles by stating "I was home again ['Estaba de nuevo en casa']" (Fuguet, *The Movies of My Life* 55 [*Las películas de mi vida* 55]). Also, writing about his childhood games in Encino: "I had been assigned the role of an Indian because I was a Mexican. After all, since my parents spoke Spanish, what else could I have been? ['Me habían asignado el rol de indio . . . por ser mexicano. Si mis padres hablaban español, ¿qué otra cosa podía ser?']" (113 [113]).
48. "Mi próxima cinta, que se llamará *Borderline*, es sobre un chico llamado Diego que trabaja en una librería Borders de El Cajón, California. Es una comedia fronteriza muy Kevin Smith . . . Mi meta es demostrar que en la frontera no sólo se sufre, también se vive y hasta se fornica" (Fuguet, *Las películas de mi vida* 156).
49. In the *Barcelona Review* interview, Fuguet states: "I am very interested in the subject of immigration. One gains much when one immigrates, but one also loses much. And there is a tendency to speak more about the good than the bad, especially in the United States, which is a nation of immigrants . . . It is true that many very poor people who arrive in the U.S. improve their standard of living, but they also damage their interior life, so to speak. You lose things, you lose a family . . . language, things of that sort. ['A mí el tema de la inmigración me interesa mucho. Se gana mucho al emigrar, pero también se pierde mucho. Y se tiende generalmente a

hablar más de lo bueno que de lo malo, especialmente en EE UU que es una nación de inmigrantes . . . Es verdad que mucha de la gente muy pobre que llega a EE UU mejora su estándar de vida, pero también empeora quizá su vida interior, por así decirlo. Se pierden cosas, se pierde una familia . . . El idioma, cosas por el estilo']" ("Estados Unidos es un país latinoamericano" n.p.).

50. According to Pohl in "the immigration of poverty is thematized as a dangerous movement and as a difficult process of social integration ['La migración de pobreza se tematiza como desplazamiento peligroso y como proceso de difícil integración social']" ("Se habla español" 264). Even if Pohl, unlike Anzaldúa, posits integration as the goal desired, the fact is that both present the border as the location of danger.

51. "Esta ciudad no tiene centro, es tan grandecita que te pierdes" (Fuguet, *Las películas de mi vida* 152).

52. "Recogen inmigrantes ilegales en el aeropuerto y los llevan donde necesiten; si no saben dónde ir, los ayudan" (Fuguet, *Las películas de mi vida* 151).

53. "Los salvadoreños en El Salvador son todos ladrones, pero aquí son trabajadores y se desviven por devolver lo que deben, lo que prueba que es el ambiente el malo, no la gente" (Fuguet, *Las películas de mi vida* 151–52).

54. "Tiene una bandera de los Estados Unidos y una foto de George W. Bush sonriendo pegada en su visera" (Fuguet, *Las películas de mi vida* 151).

55. In *Las películas de mi vida:*

> "—¿Chileno o argentino?
> —Chileno
> —Como Don Francisco.
> —Y Pinochet.
> —Dos grandes hombres. Debe estar orgulloso.
> —Neruda también era chileno.
> —Y comunista, como el Arzobispo Romero." (152)

I am aware that the question whether Pinochet's regime was technically fascist is open to discussion. After all, if fascist Italy and Nazi Germany were corporatist, the violence of Pinochet's regime helped usher in the first neoliberal regime in the world. My description of Chile as fascist should not be taken as a technical comment on the economic nature of the regime but, rather, as a description of how political violence was exercised and experienced during Pinochet's government.

56. "La Mina aprovechó el triunfo de Allende para sacar a flote décadas de resentimiento y odio contra mi abuelo, contra su familia y su padre, contra el mundo en general" (Fuguet, *Las películas de mi vida* 117).

57. "Cuando las mujeres momias salieron a la calle a exigir la salida de Allende, la Mina sintió que la revolución había llegado. Nadie, al parecer, le explicó que el asunto era al revés" (Fuguet, *Las películas de mi vida* 117).

58. "Mi rol era vigilar la evacuación rápida y segura desde el 'aula de clases a un patio descubierto' . . . Luego, con los años comprendí que ésa era la manera

59. "Mi abuela dijo que la película era comunista" (Fuguet, *Las películas de mi vida* 182).
60. "Tan inteligente ese chico y, a la vez, tan tonto; yo le advertí que no se metiera en problemas pero no me hizo caso" (Fuguet, *Las películas de mi vida* 182).
61. "Tyrone pasó su último día corrigiendo las pruebas de la edición popular de *Cataclismo en Valdivia*" (Fuguet, *Las películas de mi vida* 122).
62. "En la familia nunca se habló de él, casi como si Tyrone Acosta nunca hubiera existido" (Fuguet, *Las películas de mi vida* 182).
63. "Casi un año después, mi padre se enteró que ese gringo tan alto, tan buen padre, era Mike Tanner y había colocado una bomba bajo un auto en Bethesda, Maryland" (Fuguet, *Las películas de mi vida* 182).
64. "En Encino, todo el barrio odiaba a Nixon y decían que era un ladrón y un mentiroso; en Chile, parecía que todos amaban a Pinochet y consideraban que era un salvador" (Fuguet, *Las películas de mi vida* 180).

    However, Fuguet himself may not hate Nixon. In an entry (28 Feb. 2007) in his literary blog *Alberto Fuguet: Escritor/Lector* titled "El discurso de Nixon," Fuguet asks about the North American president: Perhaps it is politically correct, but maybe not [*sic*]: was Nixon worse than . . . the rest of Americans or than any other politician? ['quizas es politicamente correcto pero ni tanto fue Nixon peor q (*sic*) el resto . . . de los americanos o de cualquier politico?']" (n.p.). He also notes that: "Nixon reminds me of California. He was the president when I lived there and he reminds me of my father watching hour after hour the Watergate affair on TV ['Nixon me recuerda California, era el pdte cdo (*sic*) vivia alla']" (n.p.). After this brief introduction, he copies Nixon's "farewell speech," that Fuguet describes as "brilliant, deeply felt, intelligent, honest, and Shakespearian ['me parece brillante, sentido, inteligente, honesto y shakesperiano']" (n.p.).
65. "Para justificar su cruel caricaturización del mundo norteamericano, Donoso señala que se trata de ejercer 'nuestro derecho de invadirlos y colonizarlos . . . y de desconocerlos—¿y por qué no?, vengarnos" (Paz Soldán and Fuguet 18).
66. "¿Se puede imaginar a USA en sus proprios términos?" (Paz Soldán and Fuguet 18).

    The one exception to this Latin American inability to represent the United States is, according to Paz Soldán and Fuguet, Puig (19).
67. According to Paz Soldán and Fuguet, "Fuentes has preferred an unsubtle symbolism, the easy caricature of the gringos ['Fuentes ha preferido el poco sutil simbolismo, la facil caricatura de los gringos']" (18).
68. "No se puede hablar de Latinoamérica sin incluir a los Estados Unidos. Y no se puede concebir a los Estados Unidos sin necesariamente pensar en América Latina" (Paz Soldán and Fuguet 19).
69. Caro Martí makes a similar point in "La república invisible."

Epilogue

1. "Indios o indigenistas . . . que se habían integrado radical y definitivamente al mundo andino" (Arroyo n.p.).
2. Unlike Evo Morales, Toledo was a strict adherent to neoliberal policies.In fact, regarding the rise of indigenous movements in Latin America, Nelson Manrique has written about the "Peruvian exception" when it comes to the "process of re-ethnicization which has enveloped the continent" (239). Among the reasons he gives for this surprising lack of an indigenous movement in Peru are "the defeat of the Túpac Amaru II movement at the end of the eighteenth century"; "the absence of urban Indians, a social category which has been central in Bolivia and Ecuador for the emergence of intellectuals capable of theorizing indigenism as a political alternative"; and "the impact of political violence throughout the 1980s" (239–40).
3. "El concepto de identidad, cuando no se emplea en una escala exclusivamente individual y aspira a representar a un conglomerado, es reductor y deshumanizador, un pase mágico-ideológico de signo colectivista que abstrae todo lo que hay de original y creativo en el ser humano, aquello que no le ha sido impuesto por la herencia ni por el medio geográfico, ni por la presión social, sino que resulta de su capacidad para resistir esas influencias y contrarrestarlas con actos libres, de invención personal" (Vargas Llosa, "Las culturas y la globalización" n.p.).

    "The Culture of Liberty" is the revised, edited, and translated version of "Las culturas y la globalización," a lecture originally given in Spanish at the Inter-American Develoment Bank in 2000, and available on its Web page. It should not be confused with the similarly titled article "Cultura de la libertad" included in his 1990 collection *Contra viento y marea*. A much briefer version of the lecture was published by Vargas Llosa as one of his "Piedra de Toque" essays, 19 Apr. 2000.
4. "La noción de identidad colectiva es una ficción ideológica, cimiento del nacionalismo" (Vargas Llosa, "Las culturas y la globalización" n.p.).
5. "Gracias al debilitamiento de la rigidez que caracterizaba al Estado-nación, las olvidadas, marginadas o silenciadas culturas locales, comienzan a renacer y dar señales de una vida a veces muy dinámica, en el gran concierto de este planeta globalizado" (Vargas Llosa, "Las culturas y la globalización" n.p.).
6. One must keep in mind that Vargas Llosa, while celebrant of these cultural rebirths, insists that "we must not confuse this regional cultural rebirth . . . with the phenomenon of nationalism which poses serious threats to the culture of liberty ['no hay que confundir este renacimiento cultural regional, positivo y enriquecedor, con el fenómeno del nacionalismo, fuente de problemas y una seria amenaza para la cultura de la libertad']" ("The Culture of Liberty" 71 ['Las culturas y la globalización' n.p.]).
7. Vargas Llosa has on several other occasions expressed his belief in the ultimate incompatibility between indigenous cultures and modernity. For instance, in his "El nacimiento del Perú" (1992), he rues, "There may be no

realist manner of integrating our societies than asking Indians to pay this high price; perhaps, the ideal, in other words, the preservation of primitive cultures in América, is an utopia incompatible with another more urgent: to establish modern societies, in which social and economic differences are reduced to reasonable, humane, proportions, in which all can attain at least a life that's free and decent ['Tal vez no haya otra manera realista de integrar nuestras sociedades que pidiendo a los indios pagar ese alto precio; tal vez el ideal, es decir, la preservación de las culturas primitivas de América, es una utopía incompatible con otra meta más urgente: el establecimiento de sociedades modernas, en las que las diferencias sociales y económicas se reduzcan a proporciones razonables, humanas, en las que todos puedan alcanzar al menos una vida libre y decente']" (811).

Thus, for Vargas Llosa, the ultimate criterion for the validity of a culture is its compatibility with modernization, which, for him, is capitalism. This negative vision of indigenous cultures and populations as inconsistent with modernity and, on occasion, even the most basic human qualities is, however, characteristic of his novels, in particular *Lituma en los Andes* (*Death in the Andes*) (1993).

8. "Es un extraordinario paso adelante en el campo de los derechos humanos y la cultura de la libertad" (Vargas Llosa, "El matrimonio gay" 35).
9. One must note that pace Mignolo and Anzaldúa, statistical information does not seem to fully back their belief in the exceptionality of the Latin American migrant experience to the United States. According to the Pew Hispanic Research Center, U.S.-born children of immigrants are more likely to declare themselves white than their foreign-born parents, and the share of whiteness is higher among the grandchildren of immigrants. In addition, U.S. citizenship is associated with racial identification: "Among immigrants from the same country, those who have become U.S. citizens identify as white more often than those who are not U.S. citizens. It seems unlikely that the ability and willingness to become a U.S. citizen are somehow linked to skin color. Thus it may be that developing deeper civic bonds here can help an immigrant feel white" (Tafoya 2). And: "Immigration status and language do not play a direct role in determining economic or social outcomes for Hispanics born in this country, and their conceptions of race are primarily home grown. Among U.S.-born Latinos whiteness is clearly and consistently associated with higher social status, higher levels of civic participation and a stronger sense of acceptance" (2).

Sonya Tafoya's interpretation of these statistics brings out the absorptive power of North American society, as well as its constitutive racism, which is, in fact, what leads to this imaginary self-whitening becoming intrinsic to assimilation. Moreover, by the third generation, 57 percent of Latinos identify primarily as American (Brodie et al., *2002 National Survey of Latinos* 9). But one must acknowledge that the fact that 43 percent still identify primarily as Latino, Hispanic, or by their ancestral homeland implies a minority, though still significant, resistant to the assumption of racialized versions of North American identity.

10. In "Asoma en la región un nuevo racismo," also known as "Raza, botas y nacionalismo," Vargas Llosa compares Morales and Chávez with Juan Velasco Alvarado, whose "disastrous economic policies led Peru into a terrible crisis that affected especially the poorest sectors, workers, peasants, and marginals; the country still has not recovered completely from that catastrophe that general Velasco and his military mafia caused in Peru ['Su desastrosa política económica hundió al Perú en una crisis atroz que golpeó, sobre todo, a los sectores más humildes, obreros, campesinos y marginados, y el país todavía no se recupera del todo de aquella catástrofe que el general Velasco y su mafia castrense causaron al Perú']" (1). It must be kept in mind that Velasco was forced out of power in 1975.
11. Mignolo's *The Idea of Latin America* was published in 2005, before Evo Morales came to power. However, he briefly mentions Morales as part of an "effervescence" that is taking place in Latin America and more concretely in Bolivia as indigenous politicians have "climbed through the institutional aperture that the vice-presidency [of Aymara leader Víctor Hugo Cárdenas] opened" (91). Hugo Chávez is also briefly mentioned positively with regard to his participation in an "alliance of Atlantic countries moving toward the left" (158).
12. The *Fome Zero* program attempted to eradicate hunger among poor Brazilians by giving direct financial aid, promoting micro-credits, creating affordable popular restaurants, educating the poor about healthy eating habits, and so on.
13. Those following contemporary theoretical trends can identify the targets of Mignolo's criticism: Slavoj Zizek and Alain Badiou, among others. Despite differences, these theorists have attempted to use Lenin as an example of how radical politics can be constructed when the objective conditions that once justified revolution have disappeared. Zizek argues, "To return to Lenin aims neither at nostalgically reenacting the 'good old revolutionary times' nor at the pragmatic adjusting of the old program to 'new condition,' but at repeating, in the present, the Leninist gesture of reinventing the revolutionary project in the conditions of imperialism and colonialism, more precisely, after the politico-ideological collapse of the long era of progressivism in the catastrophe of 1914 ... What Lenin did for 1914, we should do for 1990" (195).
14. The central conceit in *The Idea of Latin America* is that the key social modification is neither political nor economic but epistemological: "The Zapatistas' theoretical revolution, Indigenous and Afro-Caribbean and Andean intellectuals, as well as Latinos/as in the US are building toward a future, toward an ideal of society not controlled by totalizing Western principles of knowledge and sovereignty of being" (140).

    What is never made clear in Mignolo's argument is why a new epistemology could not be adapted and adopted by a system, such as capitalism, that is ultimately characterized by an intrinsic dynamism and capacity for change.
15. Claudio Lomnitz has eloquently described the current impasse in radical thought and action as manifested in Latin America: "The current rise of

the Left occurs when there is no existing alternative economic system to counter capitalism. In this context, the very meaning of *left* and of *right* is difficult to pinpoint" (24).
16. "Se transformó lisa y llanamente en la primera autora norteamericana que escribe en español" (Fuguet, "¿De qué hablamos cuando hablamos de Isabel Allende?" 78).
17. The experience of Alberto Fuguet in Iowa, where, in his view, his texts were rejected for not being Latino enough, serves to emphasize the difference that, at least for now, still exists between Latino and Latin American.

WORKS CITED

Ahmad, Aijaz. *In Theory: Classes, Nations, Literatures.* London: Verso, 1994.
Aizenberg, Edna. *Books and Bombs in Buenos Aires: Borges, Gerchunoff, and Argentine-Jewish Writing.* Hanover, NH: UP of New England, 2002.
———. *El tejedor del Aleph: Biblia, Kábala y judaísmo en Borges.* Madrid: Altalena, 1986.
Alemany Bay, Carmen. "Introducción." *La polémica del meridiano intelectual de Hispanoamérica (1927): Estudio y textos.* Alicante, Spain: Universidad de Alicante, 1998. 11–61.
Altamirano, Carlos, and Beatriz Sarlo. *Ensayos argentinos: de Sarmiento a la vanguardia.* Buenos Aires: Ariel, 1997.
Anderson, Benedict. *Imagined Communities: Reflections on the Origin and Spread of Nationalism.* 2nd ed. London: Verso, 1991.
Anderson, Perry. *The Origins of Postmodernity.* London: Verso, 1998.
Anzaldúa, Gloria. *Borderlands: La Frontera: The New Mestiza.* San Francisco: Aunt Lute, 1987.
Arenal, Electa. "The Convent as Catalyst for Autonomy: Two Hispanic Nuns of the Seventeenth Century." *Women in Hispanic Literature: Icons and Fallen Idols.* Ed. Beth Miller. Berkeley: U of Ca P, 1983. 147–83.
Arguedas, José María. *El zorro de arriba y el zorro de abajo.* 1971. Ed. Eve-Marie Fell. Mexico City: Archivos, 1992.
Arroyo, Carlos. "La experiencia del Comité Central Pro-Derecho Indígena Tahuantinsuyo." *Estudios interdisciplinarios de América Latina y el Caribe* 15.1 (2004). 20 Mar. 2007 <http://www.tau.ac.il/eial/XV_1/arroyo.html>.
"Baião." *Diccionário Cravo Albin da música popular brasileira.* Instituto Cultural Cravo Albin. 2002. 28 July 2006 <http://www.dicionariompb.com.br>.
Bell-Villada, Gene. *Borges and His Fiction: A Guide to His Mind and Art.* Austin: U of Texas P, 1999.
A Bibliography of Spanish-English Translations 1500–1640. Kings College, London. Jan. 2006. 3 Mar. 2007 <http://www.ems.kcl.ac.uk/content/proj/anglo/tldb/index.html>.
Bolívar, Simón. "Discurso de Angostura." *Palabras esenciales, Simón Bolívar.* Caracas: Ministerio de Educación e Información, 2006. 51–84.
Borges, Jorge Luis. "An Autobiographical Essay." *The Aleph and Other Stories, 1933–1969.* New York: Dutton, 1970. 203–60.
———. "El Aleph." *Narraciones.* Madrid: Salvat, 1982. 59–79.

Borges, Jorge Luis. "El cuento policial." *Borges oral*. Barcelona: Bruguera, 1980. 69–88.

———. "El escritor argentino y la tradición." *Discusión*. Buenos Aires: Emecé, 1957. 151–62.

———. "El jardín de senderos que se bifurcan." *Narraciones*. Madrid: Salvat, 1982. 95–110.

———. "El sur." *Narraciones*. Madrid: Salvat, 1982. 123–32.

———. "Funes el memorioso." *Narraciones*. Madrid: Salvat, 1982. 111–22.

———. *Historia universal de la infamia*. Buenos Aires: Emecé, 1974.

———. "Kafka y sus precursores." *Otras inquisiciones*. Buenos Aires: Emecé, 1960. 145–48.

———. "La eternidad y T. S. Eliot." *Textos Recobrados 1931–1955*. Ed. Sara Luisa del Carril and Mercedes Rubio de Zocchi. Buenos Aires: Emecé, 2001. 49–52.

———. "*Literaturas europeas de vanguardia*." *Textos recobrados: 1919–1929*. Buenos Aires: Emecé, 1997. 210–11.

———. "Poema de los dones." *Twentieth-Century Latin American Poetry*. Ed. Stephen Tapscott. Austin: U of Texas P, 1996. 146–47.

———. "Poem of the Gifts." Trans. Ben Belitt. *Twentieth-Century Latin American Poetry*. Ed. Stephen Tapscott. Austin: U of Texas P, 1996. 146–47.

———. "Sobre el meridiano de una gaceta." *La polémica del meridiano intelectual de Hispanoamérica (1927): Estudio y textos*. Alicante, Spain: Universidad de Alicante, 1998. 71–72.

Brodie, Molyann, et al. *2002 National Survey of Latinos: Summary of Findings*. Washington D.C.: Pew Hispanic Center and the Henry Kaiser Family Foundation, 2002.

Brotherston, Gordon. "Indigenous Literatures and Cultures in Twentieth-Century Latin America." *Latin America Since 1930: Ideas, Culture, and Society*. Ed. Leslie Bethell. Cambridge, UK: Cambridge UP, 1995. 287–306.

Bryce Echenique, Alfredo. "Para volver a Palma." *Tradiciones peruanas: Edición crítica*. Ed. Julio Ortega. Nanterre, France: Archivos, 1993. xvii-xix.

Burns, E. Bradford. *Latin America: A Concise Interpretive History*. 6th ed. Englewood Cliffs, NJ: Prentice Hall, 1972.

Cabezón Doty, Claudia. "Latinoamérica y Europa en diálogo intermedial: Gabriel García Márquez, Hanna Schygulla y Cesare Zavattini en *Amores difíciles*." *Taller de Letras* 37 (2005): 23–50.

Cárdenas, Noé. "Thriller en los Andes." *Letras libres* (MX) June 2006: 92–93.

Caro Martí, Adelaida. "La 'república invisible' de Beltrán Soler: 'Glocalización' en la novela de Alberto Fuguet *Las películas de mi vida*." *Alpha* 23 (Dec. 2006). *Scientific Library Online*. 3 Mar. 2007 <http://www.scielo.cl/scielo.php?script=sci_arttext&pid=S0718-22012006000200016&lng=pt&nrm=iso>.

Carpentier, Alejo. "Prólogo." *El reino de este mundo. Obras escogidas*. Santiago de Chile: Andrés Bello, 1993. 9–31.

———. "Sobre el meridiano intelectual de nuestra América." *La polémica del meridiano intelectual de Hispanoamérica (1927): Estudio y textos*. Alicante, Spain: Universidad de Alicante, 1998. 95–97.

Casa de América. 4 Sept. 2006 <http://www.casadeamerica.es>.
Casanova, Pascale. "Literature as a World." *New Left Review* 31 (Jan.-Feb. 2005): 71–90.
———. *The World Republic of Letters.* Cambridge, MA: Harvard UP, 2004.
Castro, Ruy. *Bossa Nova: The Story of the Brazilian Music That Seduced the World.* Trans. Lisa Salsbury. Chicago: A Capella Books, 2000.
———. *Chega de saudade: a história e as historias da Bossa Nova.* São Paulo: Companhia das Letras, 1990.
Chang Rodríguez, Raquel. *Hidden Messages: Representation and Resistance in Andean Colonial Drama.* Lewisburg, PA: Bucknell UP, 1999.
Cornejo Polar, Antonio. *La formación de la tradición literaria en el Perú.* Lima: Centro de Estudios y Publicaciones, 1989.
———. "Mestizaje e hibridez: el riezgo de las metáforas." *Revista de crítica literaria latinoamericana* 47.1 (1998): 7–11.
Cortázar, Julio. "Acerca de la situación del intelectual latinoamericano." *Último round.* Vol. 2. Mexico City: Siglo XXI, 1989. 265–80.
"Creole." *Oxford English Dictionary Online.* 2nd ed. Oxford University Press. 1989. 7 Jan. 2007 <http://www.oed.com>.
"Criollo." *Diccionario de la lengua española de la Real Academia Española.* Preview of the 23rd ed. Real Academia Española. 7 Jan. 2007 <http://www.rae.es>.
"Criollo." *Merriam-Webster Online.* Merriam-Webster. 2007. 7 Jan. 2007 <http://www.merriam-webster.com>.
"Criollo." *Oxford English Dictionary Online.* 2nd ed. Oxford University Press. 1989. 7 Jan. 2007 <http://www.oed.com>.
Cruz, Juan. "La vocación de editar en español. Entrevista con Juan Cruz (18-II-1999)." Interview with Burkhard Pohl. *Entre el ocio y el negocio: Industria editorial y literatura.* Ed. José Manuel López de Abiada, Hans-Jörg Neuschäfer, and Augusta López Bernasocchi. Madrid: Verbum, 2001. 319–26.
Darío, Rubén. "El modernismo." *España contemporánea.* Paris: Garnier, 1901. 311–17.
———. "La muerte de la emperatriz de la China." *Azul.* Mexico City: Latino Americana, 1963. 79–87.
———. "Las albóndigas del coronel (*tradición* nicaragüense)." *Rubén Darío: Cuentos completos.* Ed. Ernesto Mejía Sánchez. Managua: Nueva Nicaragua, 1993. 85–88.
———. "Los cisnes." *Cantos de vida y esperanza.* Barcelona: F. Granada y C., 1907. 59–61.
———. "Ricardo Palma." *Crítica Literaria: Temas Americanos.* Ed. Ermilo Abreu Gómez. San Salvador, El Salvador: Ministerio de Educación Dirección General de Publicaciones, 1963. 93–101.
———. "A Roosevelt." *Cantos de vida y esperanza.* Barcelona: F. Granada y C., 1907. 37–39.
Davis, Francis. *Like Young: Jazz, Pop, Youth, and Middle Age.* New York: Da Capo, 2002.
De Andrade, Oswald. "Manifesto Antropofágo." *Revista de Antropofagia* 1 (May 1928): 3, 7.

De Campos, Augusto. "Não ao não." *CaetanoVeloso.com.br* 1971. 28 July 2006. <http://www.caetanoveloso.com.br>. Path: texto; outros autores.

De Castro, Juan E. *Mestizo Nations: Culture, Race, and Conformity in Latin American Literature.* Tucson: U of Arizona P, 2002.

De la Campa, Román. "Latin, Latino, American: Split States and Global Imaginaries." *Comparative Literature* 53.4 (2001): 373–88.

De la Cruz, Sor Juana Inés. "Response to the Most Illustrious Poetess Sor Filotea de la Cruz." Trans. Margaret Sayers Peden. *Poems, Protest, and a Dream.* Ed. Ilan Stavans. New York: Penguin, 1997. 3–75.

———. "Respuesta a Sor Filotea de la Cruz." Trans. Margaret Sayers Peden. *Poems, Protest, and a Dream.* Ed. Ilan Stavans. New York: Penguin, 1997. 2–74.

De Torre, Guillermo, et al. "Un debate apasionado. Campeonato para un meridiano intelectual." *La polémica del meridiano intelectual de Hispanoamérica (1927): Estudio y textos.* Alicante, Spain: Universidad de Alicante, 1998. 81–93.

Díaz, Roberto Ignacio. *Unhomely Rooms: Foreign Tongues and Spanish American Literature.* Lewisburg, PA: Buckness UP, 2002.

Donoso, José. *The Boom in Spanish American Literature: A Personal History.* Trans. Gregory Kolovakos. New York: Columbia UP, 1977.

———. *Historia personal del boom.* Barcelona: Seix Barral, 1983.

Dos Santos, Theotonio. "The Structure of Dependence." *The American Economic Review* 60 (May 1970): 45.

Dunn, Christopher. *Brutality Garden: Tropicália and the Emergence of Brazilian Counterculture.* Chapel Hill: U of North Carolina P, 2001.

Dunn, Christopher, and Charles Perrone. "'Chiclete com Banana': Internationalization in Brazilian Popular Music." *Brazilian Popular Music and Globalization.* Ed. Charles a Perrone and Christopher Dunn. Gainesville: U of Florida P, 2001. 1–38.

Dussell, Enrique. "Beyond Eurocentrism: The World-System and the Limits of Modernity." *The Cultures of Globalization.* Ed. Fredric Jameson and Masao Miyoshi. Durham, NC: Duke UP, 1998. 3–31.

Eliot, T. S. "Tradition and the Individual Talent." *Criticism: The Major Texts.* Ed. W. J. Bate. New York: Harcourt, 1990. 525–29.

"El principe considera al Instituto Cervantes como 'gran faro.'" *Yahoo España noticias* 14 July 2006 <http://es.news.yahoo.com/14072006/4/principe-considera-instituto-cervantes-beijing-gran-faro-ilumina-camino-hacia.html>.

Espinoza y Medrano, Juan de. *Apologético en favor de don Luis de Góngora. Apologético.* Ed. Augusto Tamayo Vargas. Caracas: Biblioteca Ayacucho, 1982. 3–109.

———. "Prefacio al lector de la lógica." *Apologético.* Ed. Augusto Tamayo Vargas. Caracas: Biblioteca Ayacucho, 1982. 323–29.

Fanon, Frantz. *The Wretched of the Earth.* Trans. Constance Farrington. New York: Grove Weidenfeld, 1963.

Faverón Patriau, Gustavo. "Crack & McOndo vs . . . ¿quién?" [Weblog entry]. *Puente Aéreo* 27 July 2006. 4 Sept. 2006 <http://puenteareo1.blogspot.com/2006/07/crack-mcondo-vs-quin.html>.

———. "El faro y la reconquista." [Weblog entry]. *Puente Aéreo* 17 July 2006.

4 Sept. 2006 <http://puenteareo1.blogspot.com/2006_07_01_puenteareo1_archive.html>.

Flores Galindo, Alberto. "Los rostros de la plebe." *Los rostros de la plebe.* Ed. Magdalena Chocano. Barcelona: Crítica, 2001. 61–102.

Fornet, Jorge. *Nuevos paradigmas en la narrativa latinoamericana.* Working Series No. 13. College Park: Latin American Studies Center, U of MD, 2005.

Franco, Jean. "Globalization and the Crisis of the Popular." *Critical Passions: Selected Essays.* Ed. Mary Louise Pratt and Kathleen Newman. Durham, NC: Duke UP, 1999. 208–20.

———. "Nunca son pesadas/las cosas que por agua están pasadas." *América Latina en la "literatura mundial."* Ed. Ignacio M. Sánchez-Prado. Pittsburgh: Instituto Internacional de Literatura Iberoamericana, 2006. 183–95.

Fuentes, Carlos. "Discurso de la ceremonia de entrega (Premio Miguel de Cervantes)." *Ministerio de cultura de España* 1987. 4 Sept. 2006 <http://www.mcu.es>. Path: Premios; Premio Cervantes; Premiados.

———. *El espejo enterrado.* Mexico City: Fondo de cultura económica, 1992.

———. *En esto creo. Diccionario de vida.* Barcelona: Planeta, 2003.

Fuguet, Alberto. "¿De qué hablamos cuando hablamos de Isabel Allende?" *Nexos: Sociedad, Ciencia, Literatura* 25 (Feb. 2002): 78.

———. "El discurso de Nixon." [Weblog entry]. *Alberto Fuguet: Escritor/Lector* 28 Feb. 2007. 1 Mar. 2007 <http://albertofuguet.blogspot.com/2007/02/el-discurso-de-nixon.html>.

———. "Estados Unidos es un país latinoamericano." Interview with Ernesto Escobar Ulloa. *The Barcelona Review* 42 (2004). 7 Mar. 2007 <http://www.barcelonareview.com/42/s_af_int.htm>.

———. "I Am Not a Magic Realist." *Salon* 11 June 1997. 8 Mar. 2007 <http://www.salon.com/june97/magical970611.html>.

———. *Las películas de mi vida.* New York: Rayo, 2003.

———. "Magical Neoliberalism." *Foreign Policy* 125 (July 2001): 66–73.

———. *The Movies of My Life.* New York: Rayo, 2003.

———. "Yo soy un gran 'afanador' de Manuel Puig." Interview with Carlos A. Maslaton. *Clarín* (29 July 2006). 13 Mar. 2007 <http://www.clarin.com/diario/2006/07/29/sociedad/s-06101.htm>.

Fuguet, Alberto, and Sergio Gómez. "Presentación al país McOndo." *McOndo.* Barcelona: Grijalbo Mondadori, 1996. 11–20.

García, Guy. *The New Mainstream: How the Multicultural Consumer Is Transforming American Business.* New York: Harper Collins, 2004.

García Canclini, Néstor. *Consumidores y ciudadanos: conflictos multiculturales de la globalización.* Mexico City: Grijalbo, 1995.

———. *Culturas híbridas: estrategias para entrar y salir de la modernidad.* Mexico City: Grijalbo, 1989.

García Lorca, Federico, and Pablo Neruda. "Discurso al Alimón sobre Rubén Darío." *Discurso al alimón.* Ed. Gilberto Bergman Padilla. Managua: Impresiones y Troqueles, 2001. 17–22.

Gil, Gilberto, and Caetano Veloso. "Bat Macumba." *Tropicália ou panis et circencis.* Rec. 1968. Universal.

———. "Entrevista a Augusto de Campos." *CaetanoVeloso.com.br* 1968. 28 July 2006 <http://www.Caetanoveloso.com.br>. Path: Texto; Entrevista.

Gnutzmann, Rita. "Mario Vargas Llosa y su obra en la prensa española." *Boom y Postboom desde el nuevo siglo: impacto y recepción*. Ed. José Manuel López de Abiada and José Morales Saravia. Madrid: Verbum, 2005. 53–73.

Gónzalez, Anibal. "Las *Tradiciones* entre la historia y el periodismo." *Tradiciones peruanas: Edición crítica*. Ed. Julio Ortega. Madrid: Archivos, 1993. 459–89.

González Boixo, José Carlos. "'El meridiano intelectual de Hispanoamérica': polémica suscitada en 1927 por *La Gaceta Literaria*." *Cuadernos Hispanoamericanos* 459 (1988): 166–71.

González Echevarría, Roberto. *Alejo Carpentier: The Pilgrim at Home*. Austin: U of Texas P, 1990.

———. *Celestina's Brood: Continuities of the Baroque in Spanish and Latin American Literature*. Durham, NC: Duke UP, 1993.

González Prada, Manuel. "Conferencia en el Ateneo de Lima." *Páginas libres/ Horas de lucha*. Caracas: Biblioteca Ayacucho, 1976. 3–21.

———. "Discurso en el Teatro Olimpo." *Páginas libres/Horas de lucha*. Caracas: Biblioteca Ayacucho, 1976. 25–33.

———. "Memoranda." *El pensamiento político de González Prada*. Ed. Bruno Podestá. Lima: Instituto Nacional de Cultura, 1973. 182–96.

González Vigil, Ricardo. *Retablo de autores peruanos*. Lima: Ediciones Arco Iris, 1990.

Gorak, Jan. *The Making of the Modern Canon: Genesis and Crisis of a Literary Idea*. London: Athlone, 1991.

Greenfield, Sidney M. "Slavery and the Plantation in the New World: The Development and Diffusion of a Social Form." *Journal of Inter-American Studies* 11.1 (1969): 44–57.

Guerrero, Gustavo. "Nueva narrativa del extremo Occidente: La encrucijada de la recepción internacional." *Letras libres* (Spain) Jan. 2007: 22–28.

Guillory, John. "Canon." *Critical Terms for Literary Study*. Ed. Frank Lentricchia and Thomas McLaughlin. Chicago: U of Chicago P, 1995. 233–49.

———. *Cultural Capital: The Problem of Literary Canon Formation*. Chicago: U of Chicago P, 1993.

Halperín Donghi, Tulio. *Historia contemporánea de América Latina*. Madrid: Alianza Editorial, 1969.

Harvey, David. *A Brief History of Neoliberalism*. London: Oxford UP, 2005.

Hernández Navarro, Luis. "La nueva conquista española: hacer la América al estilo neoliberal." *La Jornada. Masiosare* 31 Oct. 2004. 2 Jan. 2007 <http://www.jornada.unam.mx/2004/10/31/mas-hernandez.html>.

Herrero-Olaizola, Alejandro. *The Censorship Files: Latin American Writers and Franco's Spain*. Albany, NY: SUNY P, 2007.

Homem de Mello, José Eduardo. *Musica Popular Brasileira*. Sao Paulo: Melhoramentos, 1976.

Hordes, Stanley M. "The Inquisition as Economic and Political Agent: The

Campaign of the Mexican Holy Office against the Crypto-Jews in the Mid-Seventeenth Century." *The Americas* 39.1 (1982): 23–38.

Horsman, Reginald. *Race and Manifest Destiny: The Origins of American Racial Anglo-Saxonism.* Cambridge, MA: Harvard UP, 1981.

"Hot100Brasil." 29 Aug. 2005 <http://www.hot100brasil.com/chtsinglesb.html>.

Instituto Cervantes. *Quiénes somos.* 4 Sept. 2006 <http://www.cervantes.es/seg_nivel/institucion/Marcos_institucion_principal.jsp>.

Jaguaribe, Helio. *O nacionalismo na atualidade brasileira.* Rio de Janeiro: ISEB, 1958.

Jameson, Fredric. "Globalization as a Philosophical Issue." *The Cultures of Globalization.* Ed. Fredric Jameson and Masao Miyoshi. Durnham, NC: Duke UP, 1998. 54–77.

———. "Postmodernism, or the Cultural Logic of Late Capitalism." *The Jameson Reader.* Ed. Michael Hardt and Kathi Weeks. Oxford: Blackwell, 2000. 188–232.

———. "Third-World Literature in the Era of Multinational Literature." *The Jameson Reader.* Ed. Michael Hardt and Kathi Weeks. Oxford: Blackwell, 2000. 315–39.

Johnson, Randal. "Tupy or Not Tupy: Cannibalism and Nationalism in Contemporary Brazilian Literature and Culture." *Modern Latin American Fiction: A Survey.* Ed. John King. London: Faber and Faber, 1987. 41–59.

Juan Carlos I, King. "Mensaje de bienvenida de S. M. el Rey." *Cumbre-Iberoamericana.Org* 2005. 4 Sept. 2006 <http://www.cumbre-iberoamericana.org/CumbreIberoamericana/ES/informacionGeneral/xvCumbreIberoamericana/MensaRey/default.htm>.

Kerr, Lucille. *Suspended Fictions: Reading Novels by Manuel Puig.* Urbana: Illinois UP, 1987.

Kerrigan, Anthony. "Introduction." *Ficciones.* By Jorge Luis Borges. New York: Grove P, 1962. 9–11.

Klarén, Peter Flindell. *Peru: Society and Nationhood in the Andes.* New York: Oxford UP, 2000.

Klein, Naomi. *No Logo: No Space, No Choice, No Jobs.* New York: Picador, 2002.

Kokotovic, Misha. *The Colonial Divide in Peruvian Narrative: Social Conflict and Transculturation.* Brighton, UK: Sussex Academic P, 2005.

———. "Hibridez y desigualdad: García Canclini ante el neoliberalismo." *Revista de crítica literaria latinoamericana* 52 (2000): 289–300.

Kristal, Efraín. *The Andes Viewed from the City: Literary and Political Discourse on the Indian in Peru 1848–1930.* New York: Peter Lang, 1987.

———. "'Considering Coldly . . .': A Response to Franco Moretti." *New Left Review* 15 (May-June 2002): 61–74.

———. "Dialogues and Polemics: Sarmiento, Lastarria, and Bello." *Sarmiento and His Argentina.* Ed. Joseph T. Criscenti. Boulder, CO: Lynne Rienner, 1993. 61–70.

———. *Invisible Work: Borges and Translation.* Nashville, TN: Vanderbilt UP, 2002.

Larios Vendrell, Luis. "Los amigos que perdí." Review of *Los amigos que perdí*. *World Literature Today* 75.1 (2001): 178.
Larsen, Neil. *Determinations: Essays on Theory, Narrative, and Nation in the Americas*. London: Verso, 2001.
———. *Modernism and Hegemony: A Materialistic Critique of Aesthetic Agencies*. Minneapolis: U of Minnesota P, 1990.
Lasarte Valcárcel, Javier. "La letra ante la cultural de masas." Review of *Aires de Familia* by Carlos Monsiváis. *Nueva Sociedad* 170 (2000): 186–90.
"La Universidad de Castilla-La Mancha nombra doctor Honoris Causa a Carlos Fuentes." *Club Cultura.com* 4 Mar. 2005. 4 Sept. 2006 <http://www.clubcultura.com/noticias/leer.php?not_id=61>.
Leu, Lorraine. *Brazilian Popular Music: Caetano Veloso and the Regeneration of Tradition*. London: Ashgate, 2006.
Lizardi, José Joaquín Fernández de. "Apología del *Periquillo Sarniento*." *El periquillo sarniento*. Vol. 1. 4th ed. Mexico City: Galván, 1842. xii–xxii.
Lomnitz, Claudio. "Foundations of the Latin American Left." *Public Culture* 19.1 (2007): 23–27.
Lugones, Leopoldo. "De Leopoldo Lugones." *La polémica del meridiano intelectual de Hispanoamérica (1927): Estudio y textos*. Alicante, Spain: Universidad de Alicante, 1998. 145.
"Madrid, meridiano intelectual de Hispanoamérica." *La polémica del meridiano intelectual de Hispanoamérica (1927): Estudio y textos*. Alicante, Spain: Universidad de Alicante, 1998. 114–15.
Malone, Bill C. *Stars of Country Music: Uncle Dave Macon to Johnny Rodriguez*. Champaign: U of Illinois P, 1975.
Manrique, Jorge Alberto. "Del barroco a la ilustración." *Historia General de México*. Vol. 1. Ed. Daniel Cosío Villegas. Mexico City: El Colegio de México, 1976. 645–734.
Manrique, Nelson. "Modernity and Alternative Development in the Andes." Trans. Lorraine Leu. *Through the Kaleidoscope: The Experience of Modernity in Latin America*. Ed. Vivian Schelling. London: Verso, 2001. 219–47.
Mariátegui, José Carlos. "Esquema de una explicación de Chaplin." *El alma matinal y otras estaciones del hombre de hoy*. Lima: Amauta, 1981. 67–74.
———. "La batalla del libro." *Temas de nuestra América*. Lima: Amauta, 1980. 118–21.
———. "La batalla de *Martín Fierro*." *La polémica del meridiano intelectual de Hispanoamérica (1927): Estudio y textos*. Alicante, Spain: Universidad de Alicante, 1998. 112–13.
———. "La crisis mundial y el proletariado peruano." *Historia de la crisis mundial: Conferencias (años 1923 y 1924)*. Lima: Amauta, 1980. 15–25.
———. "*Literaturas europeas de vanguardia*." *El artista y la época*. Lima: Amauta, 1980. 114–19.
———. "Punto de vista anti-imperialista." *Ideología y política*. Lima: Amauta, 1981. 87–95.
———. *Siete ensayos de interpretación de la realidad peruana*. Lima: Amauta, 1981.

Martí, José. "Nuestra América." *Sus mejores páginas*. Ed. Raimundo Lazo. Mexico City: Porrúa, 1985. 87–93.
Marzorati, Gerald. "Beyond the Bossa Nova." Review of *Tropical Truth: A Story of Music and Revolution in Brazil* by Caetano Veloso. *New York Times* 29 Sept. 2002: H19.
———. "*Tropicália Agora!*" *New York Times Magazine* 15 Apr. 1999: 233–36.
McGowan, Chris, and Ricardo Pessanha. *The Brazilian Sound: Samba, Bossa Nova, and the Popular Music of Brazil*. New York: Billboard Books, 1991.
Mignolo, Walter. *The Idea of Latin America*. Malden, MA: Blackwell, 2005.
Monaghan, Jay. *Chile, Peru, and the California Gold Rush of 1849*. Berkeley: U of California P, 1973.
"Montevideo, meridiano intelectual del mundo." *La polémica del meridiano intelectual de Hispanoamérica (1927): Estudio y textos*. Alicante, Spain: Universidad de Alicante, 1998. 77.
Moraña, Mabel. "Barroco y transculturación." *Crítica impura: estudios de literatura y cultura latinoamericanas*. Madrid: Iberoamericana, 2004. 19–36.
———. "La diferencia criolla: diáspora y políticas en la lengua de la colonia." *Crítica impura: estudios de literatura y cultura latinoamericanas*. Madrid: Iberoamericana, 2004. 55–79.
Moretti, Franco. "Conjectures on World Literature." *New Left Review* 1 (2000): 54–68.
———. "More Conjectures." *New Left Review* 20 (2003): 73–81.
Motta, Nelson. *Noites tropicais: solos, improvisos e memorias musicais*. Rio de Janeiro: Editora Objetiva, 2000.
Mulvey, Laura, and Peter Wollen. "Frida Kahlo and Tina Modotti." *Visual and Other Pleasures*. By Mulvey. Bloomington: Indiana UP, 1989. 81–107.
Olivari, Nicolás. "Madrid, meridiano intelectual de América." *La polémica del meridiano intelectual de Hispanoamérica (1927): Estudio y textos*. Alicante, Spain: Universidad de Alicante, 1998. 70–71.
Orringer, Nelson. "Introduction to Hispanic Modernisms." *Bulletin of Spanish Studies* 79.2-3 (2002): 133–48.
Ortega, Julio. "Para una relectura crítica de Palma." *Tradiciones peruanas: Edición crítica*. Ed. Julio Ortega. Nanterre, France: Archivos, 1993. xxi-xxv.
Ortega y Gasset, José. "Sobre un periódico de las letras." *La Gaceta Literaria* 1 Jan. 1927: 1.
Ortelli y Gasset. "A un meridiano encontrado en una fiambrera." *La polémica del meridiano intelectual de Hispanoamérica (1927): Estudio y textos*. Alicante, Spain: Universidad de Alicante, 1998. 73–74.
Padilla, Ignacio. "*McOndo* y el *crack*: dos experiencias grupales." *Palabra de América*. Barcelona: Seix Barral, 2004. 136–47.
Palaversich, Diana. "McOndo y otros mitos." *Literaturas.com: Revista literaria independiente de los nuevos tiempos* June 2003. 25 Nov. 2006 <http://www.literaturas.com/McondoyoitrosmitosOPINIONjunio2003.htm>.
Palma, Ricardo. "Dónde y cómo el diablo perdió el poncho." *Tradiciones peruanas*. Barcelona: Oceano, 2001. 657–62.

———. "La bohemia de mi tiempo." *Recuerdos de España, precedidos por La Bohemia de mi tiempo*. Lima: La industria, 1899. 1–72.

———. *Neologismos y americanismos*. Lima: Carlos Prince, 1896.

———. "Sobre el *Quijote* en América." *Mis últimas tradiciones y cachivachería*. Barcelona: Maucci, 1906. 305–12.

———. "Tradiciones del Cuzco." *Mis últimas tradiciones y cachivachería*. Barcelona: Maucci, 1906. 470–73.

Pauls, Alan. *El factor Borges*. Buenos Aires: Anagrama, 2004.

Paz, Octavio. *Convergencias*. Barcelona: Seix Barral, 1991.

———. "El caracol y la sirena." *Los signos en rotación y otros ensayos*. Ed. Carlos Fuentes. Madrid: Alianza Editorial, 1971. 88–102.

———. *Sor Juana Inés de la Cruz o las trampas de la fe*. Barcelona: Seix Barral, 1982.

———. *Sor Juana: or, The Traps of Faith*. Cambridge, MA: Harvard UP, 1988.

Paz Soldán, Edmundo. "McOndo y después." [Weblog entry]. *Alberto Fuguet: Escritor/Lector* 1 Aug. 2006. 1 Aug 2007 <http://albertofuguet.blogspot.com/2006/08/paz-soldan-y<->mcondo-y<->el-crack.html>.

Paz Soldán, Edmundo, and Alberto Fuguet. "Prólogo." *Se habla español: Voces latinas en USA*. Ed. Alberto Fuguet and Edmundo Paz Soldán. Miami: Alfaguara, 2000. 13–22.

Pereda Valdés, Ildefonso. "Madrid, meridiano, etc." *La polémica del meridiano intelectual de Hispanoamérica (1927): Estudio y textos*. Alicante, Spain: Universidad de Alicante, 1998. 70.

Perrone, Charles A. *Masters of Contemporary Brazilian Song: MPB 1965–1985*. Austin: U of Texas P, 1989.

Poblete, Juan. "Globalización, mediación cultural y literatura nacional." *América Latina en la "literatura mundial."* Ed. Ignacio M. Sánchez-Prado. Pittsburgh: Instituto Internacional de Literatura Iberoamericana, 2006. 271–306.

Pohl, Burkhard. "El *post-boom* en España—mercado y edición (1973–1985)." *Boom y Postboom desde el nuevo siglo: impacto y recepción*. Ed. José Manuel López de Abiada and José Morales Saravia. Madrid: Verbum, 2005. 208–47.

———. "'Ruptura y continuidad.' Jorge Volpi, el crack y la herencia del 68." *Revista de crítica literaria latinoamericana* 59 (2004): 53–70.

———. "*Se habla español* (Fuguet/Paz Soldán): Estrategias literarias para entrar en la era transnacional." *Un continente en movimiento: Migraciones en América Latina*. Ed. Ingrid Wehr. Madrid: Iberoamericana, 2006. 255–67.

———. "¿Un nuevo *boom*? Editoriales españolas y literatura latinoamericana en los años 90." *Entre el ocio y el negocio: Industria editorial y literatura en la España de los 90*. Ed. José Manuel López de Abiada, Hans-Jörg Nueschäfer, and Augusta López Bernasocchi. Madrid: Verbum, 2001. 261–92.

———. "Vender el boom: El discurso de la difusión editorial." *La llegada de los bárbaros: la recepción de la narrativa hispanoamericana en España, 1960–1981*. Ed. Joaquín Marco and Jordi Gracia. Barcelona: Edhasa, 2004. 165–87.

Quijano, Aníbal. "Colonialidad del poder, eurocentrismo y América Latina." *La colonialidad del saber: eurocentrismo y ciencias sociales.* Ed. Edgardo Lander. Buenos Aires: Clacso, 2000. 201–46.

———. "Coloniality of Power, Eurocentrism, and Latin America." *Nepantla* 1.3 (2000): 533–80.

Rama, Ángel. "El 'Boom' en perspectiva." *Más allá del Boom: Literatura y mercado.* By Ángel Rama, et al. Mexico City: Marcha, 1988. 51–110.

———. "El poeta frente a la modernidad." *Literatura y clase social.* Mexico City: Folios, 1983. 78–143.

———. *Rubén Darío y el modernismo.* Caracas: Alfadil Ediciones, 1985.

———. *Transculturación narrativa en América Latina.* Mexico City: Siglo XXI, 1982.

Redmond, Walter. "Latin American Colonial Philosophy: The Logic of Espinoza Medrano." *The Americas* 30.4 (1974): 475–503.

Regina, Elis. *Ela.* Rec. 1971. Phillips, 1994.

Reinhardt, Carmen M., and Miguel A. Savastano. "The Realities of Modern Hyperinflation." *Finance and Development* June 2003: 20–23.

Reyes, Alfonso. "Notas sobre la inteligencia americana." *Obras Completas.* Vol. 9. Mexico City: Fondo de Cultura Económica, 1969. 82–90.

Riva Agüero, José de la. "La gran velada en honor de D. Ricardo Palma." *Estudios de literatura peruana del Inca Garcilaso a Eguren.* Lima: Pontificia Universidad Católica, 1961. 357–60.

Rivers, Georgina Sabat de. "Sor Juana y su 'Sueño': Antecedentes científicos en la poesía española del siglo de oro." *Estudios de literatura hispanoamericana: Sor Juana y otros poetas barrocos de la colonia.* Barcelona: PPU, 1992. 283–325.

Rodó, José Enrique. *Rubén Darío. Su personalidad literaria, su última obra.* Montevideo: Imprensa de Dornaleche y Reyes, 1899.

Rodriguez, Richard. *Days of Obligation: An Argument with My Mexican Father.* New York: Penguin, 1993.

Rodríguez-Arenas, Flor María. "Historia Editorial y Literaria." *Tradiciones peruanas: Edición crítica.* Ed. Julio Ortega. Nanterre, France: Archivos, 1993. 381–408.

Rodríguez Monegal, Emir. "Borges y la política." *Revista Iberoamericana* 43 (1977): 269–71.

———. *Jorge Luis Borges: A Literary Biography.* New York: Paragon, 1988.

Rouillón, Guillermo. *La edad revolucionaria.* Lima: Amauta, 1984. Vol. 2 of *La creación heroica de José Carlos Mariátegui.* 2 Vols. 1975–1984.

Salazar Bondy, Sebastián. *Lima la horrible.* Mexico City: Era, 1968.

Sánchez, Rosa María. "La inversión en el exterior se triplica y se vuelve europea." *El periódico Extremadura* 17 Aug. 2006. 17 May 2007 <http://www.elperiodicoextremadura.com/noticias/noticia.asp?pkid=255000>.

Sarlo, Beatriz. *Una modernidad periférica: Buenos Aires 1920–1930.* Buenos Aires: Nueva Visión, 1988.

Sarmiento, Domingo Faustino. "Investigaciones sobre el sistema colonial de los españoles." *Obras de Domingo Faustino Sarmiento.* Vol. 2. Buenos Aires: Félix Lajoune, 1885. 211–18.

"Saudade." *A Portuguese-English Dictionary.* James L. Taylor. Stanford, CA: Stanford UP, 1958.

"Saudosismo." *A Portuguese-English Dictionary.* James L. Taylor. Stanford, CA: Stanford UP, 1958.

Saul, Scott. "The Seductions of Caetano Veloso." *Raritan* 24.4 (2005): 45–69.

Schwarz, Roberto. "Cultura e política, 1964–1969." *O pai de família e outros estudos.* 2nd. ed. Rio de Janeiro: Paz e Terra, 1978. 61–92.

———. "Fim de Século." *Seqüencias Brasileiras.* Sao Paulo: Companhia das Letras, 1999. 155–62.

———. "Resolving Doubts with Roberto Schwarz." Interview with Afonso Faveró, Airton Paschoa, Francisco Mariutti, and Marcos Falleiros. Trans. Kelly Washbourne. *Cultural Critique* 49 (2001): 155–80.

Segall, Marcelo. "Esclavitud y tráfico culíes en Chile." *Journal of Inter-American Studies* 10.1 (1968): 117–33.

Sepúlveda, Juan Ginés de. *Demócrates segundo.* Ed. Ángel Losada. Madrid: Instituto Francisco de Vitoria, 1951.

Solé, Francesc. "Planeta llegó para quedarse." Interview with Enrique Planas. *El Comercio* 24 Jan. 2006. 4 Aug. 2006 <http://www.elcomercioperu.com.pe/EdicionImpresa/Html/2006-01-24/impLuces0443688.html>.

Sovik, Liv. "Globalizing Caetano Veloso: Globalization as Seen through a Brazilian Pop Prism." *Brazilian Popular Music and Globalization.* Ed. Charles A. Perrone and Christopher Dunn. Gainesville: U of Florida P, 2001. 96–105.

Stam, Robert. *Tropical Multiculturalism: A Comparative History of Race in Brazilian Cinema and Culture.* Durnham, NC: Duke UP, 1997.

Stokes, Geoffrey. "The Sixties." *Rock of Ages: The Rolling Stone History of Rock and Roll.* By Ed Ward, Geoffrey Stokes, and Ken Tucker. New York: Rolling Stone Press, 1986. 247–486.

Sussekind, Flora. *Cinematograph of Words: Literature and Modernization in Brazil.* Trans. Paulo Britto. Stanford, NJ: Stanford UP, 1997.

Tafoya, Sonya. "Shades of Belonging." *Pew Hispanic Center* 6 Dec 2004. 8 Aug. 2006 <http://www.pewhispanic.org/files/reports/35.pdf>.

Tamayo Vargas, Augusto. "Lo barroco y el lunarejo." *Apologético.* Caracas: Biblioteca Ayacucho, 1982. ix–lx.

Truffaut, François. "A Certain Tendency of the French Cinema." *Movies and Methods.* Ed. Bill Nichols. Berkeley: U of California P, 1976. 224–37.

———. *The Films in My Life.* New York: Da Capo, 1994. 23–28.

2006 Pen World Voices. 2006 Pen American Center. 2006. 4 Sept. 2006 <http://www.pen.org/page.php/prmID/1096>.

Unamuno, Miguel de. "Opinión autorizada." *La polémica del meridiano intelectual de Hispanoamérica (1927): Estudio y textos.* Alicante, Spain: Universidad de Alicante, 1998. 128.

United Nations. Commission on Sustainable Development. *Latin America and the Caribbean Regional Perspectives towards the Thirteenth Session of the United Nations Commission on Sustainable Development.* New York: United Nations, 2005.

Valera, Juan. "Carta a Rubén Darío." Darío, Rubén. *Azul*. Mexico City: Editora Latino Americana, 1963. xv-xxxv.

Vargas Llosa, Mario. "Asoma en la región un nuevo racismo: indios contra blancos." *La Nación* 20 Jan. 2006: Opinión 1.

———. "*Cien años de soledad*. Realidad total, novela total." Gabriel García Márquez. *Cien años de soledad: edición conmemorativa*. Madrid: Real Academia Española, 2007. xxv-lviii.

———. "Confessions of a Liberal." 3 Mar. 2005. 3 Mar. 2007 <http://www.aei.org/publications/pubID.22053,filter.all/pub_detail.asp>.

———. *Conversación en La Catedral*. Madrid: Punto de lectura, 2004.

———. *Conversation in the Cathedral*. New York: Harper, 2005.

———. "The Culture of Liberty." *Foreign Policy* 122 (Jan.-Feb. 2001): 66–71.

———. "Dentro y fuera de América Latina." *Letras libres* (MX) Dec. 2005: 62–66.

———. "El lunarejo en Asturias." *Contra viento y marea*. Vol. 3. Barcelona: Seix Barral, 1990. 401–7.

———. "El matrimonio gay." *La Nación* 9 July 2005: Opinión 35.

———. "El nacimiento del Perú." *Hispania* 75.4 (1992): 805–11.

———. "Las culturas y la globalización." *Bidamérica* Jan. 2001. <http://www.iadb.org/idbamerica/index.cfm?&thisid=1226&articlepreview=0&>.

———. "The Latin American Novel Today." Trans. Nick Mills. *Books Abroad* 44.1 (1970): 7–16.

———. *La verdad de las mentiras*. Madrid: Punto de Lectura, 2007.

———. "Nos mató una ideología." Interview with Héctor Aguilar Camín. *Zona libre* May 2000. 4 Sept. 2006 <http://www.geocities.com/awcampos/vista47.html>.

———. "Questions of Conquest and Culture: The Tenth Anniversary John Bonython Lecture." *Centre for Independent Studies* 9 Sept. 1993. 8 Mar. 2007 <http://www.cis.org.au/Events/JBL/JBL93%20-%20text.html>.

Vásquez, Karina. "De la modernidad y sus mapas: *Revista de Occidente* y la 'nueva generación' en la Argentina de los años veinte." *Revista Intellectus* 2.2 (2003). 1 Jan. 2007 <http://www2.uerj.br/~intellectus/textos/DE%20LA%20MODERNIDAD.%20KARINA.pdf>.

———. "Redes intelectuais hispano-americanas na Argentina de 1920." Trans. Sergio Miceli and Evania Guilhon. *Tempo Social: revista de sociologia da USP* 17.1 (2005): 55–80.

Veloso, Caetano. "Bim Bom." *O mundo não é chato*. Ed. Eucanaá Ferraz. São Paulo: Companhia das letras, 2005. 89–90.

———. Booklet. *A Foreign Sound*. Music, 2004.

———. "Domingo." *O mundo não é chato*. Ed. Eucanaá Ferraz. São Paulo: Companhia das letras, 2005. By Caetano Veloso. 202–3.

———. "Don't Look Black? O Brasil entre dois mitos: Orfeu e a democracia racial." *O mundo não é chato*. Ed. Eucanaá Ferraz. São Paulo: Companhia das letras, 2005. 23–37.

Veloso, Caetano. "Fina Estampa." *O mundo não e chato*. Ed. Eucanaá Ferraz. São Paulo: Companhia das letras, 2005. 178–82.

———. "Saudosismo." *CAETANO VELOSO E OS MUTANTES AO VIVO*. EP. Phillips, 1968.

———. "The Tropicalista Rebellion: A Conversation with Caetano Veloso." Interview with Christopher Dunn. *Transition* 70 (1996): 116–38.

———. *Tropical Truth: A Story of Music and Revolution in Brazil*. New York: Knopf, 2002.

———. *Verdade tropical*. São Paulo: Companhia das Letras, 1999.

Vianna, Hermano. *The Mystery of Samba: Popular Music and National Identity in Brazil*. Ed. and Trans. Charles Chasteen. Chappel Hill: U of North Carolina P, 1999.

Vitale, Cristian. "La selección Hard: El tributo argentino a Deep Purple." *No: Suplemento joven de Página 12*. 31 May 2001. 7 Jan. 2007 <http://www.pagina12.com.ar/2001/suple/No/01-05/01-05-30/199.HTM>.

Volpi, Jorge. "Cuando nací el boom estaba allí." Interview with Ernesto Carlín. [Weblog entry]. *Tanque de Casma* 28 July 2006. 4 Sept. 2006 <http://tanquedecasma.blogspot.com/2006/07/cuando-nac-el-boom-estaba-all.html>.

———. *En busca de Klingsor*. Barcelona: Seix Barral, 1999.

———. "Los autores del boom son clásicos vivos." Interview with Pedro Escribano. *La Republica* 2 Aug. 2006. 4 Sept. 2006 <http://www.larepublica.com.pe/./index.php?option=com_content&task=view&id=118449&Itemid=28>.

Volpi, Jorge, et al. "Manifiesto Crack." *Latin-America Institut* 1996. 23 May 2007 <http://www.lai.at/wissenschaft/lehrgang/semester/ss2005/fs/files/crack.pdf>.

Walker, Dale. *El Dorado: The California Gold Rush*. New York: Forge, 2003.

West, Cornel. "The New Cultural Politics of Difference." *Keeping Faith: Philosophy and Race in America*. New York: Routledge, 1993. 3–33.

Williamson, Edwin. *Borges: A Life*. New York: Penguin, 2004.

Zaid, Gabriel. "El libro y la cultura económica." *Letras libres* (MX) Feb. 2007: 32–33.

Zîzêk, Slavoj. "Have Michael Hardt and Antonio Negri Rewritten the Communist Manifesto for the Twenty-first Century?" *Rethinking Marxism* 13.3–4 (2001): 190–98.

Index

Agosín, Marjorie 110
Aguiar y Seijas, Francisco de 22
Agustín, José 180n23
Ahmad, Aijaz 144n17
Aizenberg, Edna 49, 52, 64, 144n16, 157n23, 158n1, 160n16, 161n22
Alarcón, Francis X. 129
Alegría, Ciro 31, 146n30
Alemany Bay, Carmen 46–47, 154n2, 154n3, 155n6, 157n21
Allégret, Yves 181n25
Allende, Isabel 109, 139, 179n16
Allende, Salvador 125
Almodóvar, Pedro 162n11
Altamirano, Carlos xii–xiii, xv
Althusser, Louis 107
Amaru, Túpac 20, 186
Anderson, Benedict xii, 59
Anderson, Perry 17, 146n28, 150n1
Anthropophagy. *See* De Andrade
Antonioni, Michelangelo xxii
Antropofagia. *See* De Andrade
Anzaldúa, Gloria 120–21, 123, 184n50, 187n9
Arenal, Electa 5, 13
Arguedas, José María 76, 78, 100–2, 146n30, 176n31, 176n33, 176n34
Arlt, Roberto 41, 157n17
Armstrong, Louis 73
Asturias, Miguel Ángel 31, 156n15
Aurenche, Jean 181n25
Autant-Lara, Claude 181n25

avant-garde xxiii, xxv, 30, 33, 34, 35, 36, 40–41, 42, 44, 46–47, 51, 95, 145n26, 154n1, 156n15

Badiou, Alain 188n13
Balcells, Carmen 177n37
Balderston, Daniel 158n1
Barth, John 49
Bayly, Jaime 96, 174n18, 177n1
Beat Boys 70
Beatles 71, 73, 74, 75, 85, 87, 88, 164n15
Beckett, Samuel xxii, xxiv
Bello, Andrés 155n9
Bell-Villada, Gene 50, 159n3
Bilac, Olavio 111
Blades, Rubén 85
Bloom, Harold 49
Bloy, Léon 55
Bolaño, Roberto 92
Bolívar, Simón 131, 137, 140, 143n10
border 120–24
borderlands, *see* border
Borges, Jorge Luis xix, xxii, xxvi, xxvii, 30, 33, 34, 36, 41, 42, 43–44, 46–47, 49–64, 95, 100, 111, 112, 144n16, 154n3, 155n5, 157n17, 157n21, 157n25, 158n27, 159n1, 159n3, 159n4, 159n5, 160n16, 161n21, 161n22, 178n7
Borges, Norah 154n3

bossa nova   70–75, 77–78, 79–83, 85, 86, 162n8, 162n52, 163n13, 164n16, 166n27, 166n29, 167n40
Bost, Pierre   181n25
Boullosa, Carmen   92, 109
Brotherston, Gordon   143n13
Browning, Robert   55, 56
Bryce Echenique, Alfredo   22, 92, 171n5
Brynner, Yul   117
Buarque de Holanda, (Francisco) Chico   67
Burns, E. Bradford   3, 42, 148n10, 153n28, 153n34
Byron, Lord George Gordon   24

Cabarcas, Hernando   171n5
Cabezón Doty, Claudia   180n22
Calleja, Diego   11, 14–15
Camões, Luis de   11
Camus, Marcel   161n6
Cannibalism. *See* De Andrade
Cansino Assens, Rafael   157n23
Capinam, José Carlos   162n8
Capra, Frank   114, 117, 126, 127
Cárdenas, Noé   174n18
Cardoso, Fernando Henrique   138
Carlos, Roberto   86
Caro Martí, Adelaida   118, 185n69
Carpentier, Alejo, xxvii   33, 42, 46, 95, 100, 108, 156n15, 157n17, 157n19, 179n14
Casa de América   93–94, 95, 172n8
Casanova, Pascale   xvi, xviii, xx–xxi, xxii, xxiii, xxiv, xxv, 8–9, 15, 18, 27, 40, 101, 144n18, 146n28, 158n27
Castro, Fidel   140
Castro, Ruy   71, 74, 164n20, 167n40
Cather, Willa   145n26
Catholicism   4–9, 11, 13, 21–22, 53
Caviedes, Juan del Valle y   23
Cervantes, Instituto. *See* Instituto Cervantes

Cervantes, Miguel de   xxii–xxiii, 10, 19
Chabrol, Claude   113
Chang Rodríguez, Raquel   14–15
Chaplin, Charles   41, 42, 157n17
Chávez, Hugo   137, 139, 140, 188n10, 188n11
Chávez Castañeda, Ricardo   105. *See also* Crack
Chefjec, Sergio   158n1
Chesterton, Gilbert Keith   62
Civil Rights Movements (Latin America)   133–34
coloniality of power   12–13
Cornejo Polar, Antonio   19, 20, 76, 144n18
Cortázar, Julio, xxii   97, 100–101, 102, 176n31, 176n33
Costa, Gal   72–73, 79, 83
Counter-Reformation   9–10
Crack (literary group)   105–11, 178n7, 179n18, 182n37
Creole. *See* criollo
criollo
  in Argentina   xii-xiii
  definition   xi–xv, 141n1
  difference   xiv–xv
  hybridity of   xiii–xiv
  location   xv–xviii, xxvi, 2-3
  in Peru   xiii
  and postcolonial world   xv–xvi, xviii, xxvi
Crosby, Bing   164n21
Cruz, Juan   94, 95, 97
cultural reconversion   88

Da Silva, Luiz Inácio   67, 138
Darío, Rubén   xix, xx, xxii, xxiv–xxv, xxvi, xxvii, 17–32, 38, 40, 98, 146n28, 150n1, 152n21, 176n25
Davis, Mike   110
De Andrade, Oswald   xxi, xxiii 42, 165n26

Index

De Campos, Augusto 68, 70, 79, 82, 164n16
De La Campa, Román 129, 131
De la Fuente, Juan Ramón 171n5
De Madariaga, Salvador 33
De Moraes, Vinicius 72, 73, 74, 81, 161n6, 162n8
De Palma, Brian 114
De Torre, Guillermo xxi, xxvii, 33–47, 51, 95, 154n3, 155n5, 155n6, 156n12, 156n14, 157n23, 158n27, 173n14
Del Valle y Caviedes, Juan 23
dependency theory 60–61
Descartes, René 12
developmentalism 77–79, 131–33, 137–38
Di Camargo, Zezé 162n10
Dias, Sérgio 83
Díaz, Roberto Ignacio 108, 182n39
Díaz Mirón, Salvador 25
Diego, Gerardo 33
Diegues, Carlos 161n6
Dixon, Mort 84
Do Rio, João 111
Donoso, José 97, 100, 127
Dorfman, Ariel 124, 125
Dos Santos, Theotonio 60
Downs, Lila 162n11
Dunn, Christopher 68, 69, 74–75, 78, 79, 87, 163n13, 163n14, 164n16, 166n27, 166n31, 169n49, 169n50
Dunsany, Lord (Edward Plunkett) 55
Duran, Dolores 86
Dussel, Enrique xvii, 143n14
Dylan, Bob 67, 74, 166n27

Eco, Umberto xxii, 49
Edwards, Jorge 171n6
Eliot, T. S. xxiii, xxvi, xxviii, 49–57, 62, 63, 158n1, 159n4, 159n5, 161n22
Erasmus, Desiderius 11, 149n27

Espinoza y Medrano, Juan xv, xix, xxvii, 1–16, 144n21, 147n3, 149n18, 150n28
Espronceda, José de 24
Esquivel, Laura 109
Estrada, Domingo 25

Fanon, Frantz xv, 142n9
Faria e Souza, Manoel de. *See* Faría y Souza
Faría y Souza, Manuel de 10, 11, 149n27
Farney, Dick 71
Faulkner, William 40
Faverón, Gustavo 94, 96, 107
Felipe, Prince 91, 94, 171n1
Ferber, Edna 145n26
Fernández de Lizardi, José Joaquín xxii, xxiii
Ferrer Rodríguez, Eulalio 171n5
Fielding, Henry xxii
Fishburn Evelyn 158n1
Flores Galindo, Alberto 20, 23, 28
Fornet, Jorge 99, 173n14, 179n18
Foucault, Michel 49
Francisco, Don (Mario Luis Kreutzberger) 123–24
Franco, Francisco 51, 160n18, 172n12
Franco, Jean 2, 78–79, 176n33
Fray Gerundio (Modesto Lafuente y Zamalloa) 25
Fresán, Rodrigo 92, 177n1
Freyre, Gilberto 166n34
Fuentes, Carlos 97–98, 102, 103, 112, 171n6, 175n25, 176n26, 180n22
Fuguet, Alberto xix, xxviii, 99, 104, 105–28, 139, 140, 177n1, 179n14, 179n16, 180n20, 180n23, 182n39, 183n45, 183n49, 185n64, 185n66, 185n67, 189n17. *See also* McOndo
Fujimori, Alberto 131

Gallo, Gastón 158n1
Garcia, Walter 166n34
García Calderón, Ventura 19
García Canclini, Néstor xxi, 84–85, 87, 88, 119, 128, 170n53. *See also* hybridity
García Lorca, Federico 30
García Márquez, Gabriel xxii, xxiv, 97, 102, 106, 107, 109, 112, 121, 122, 144n16. *See also* Magical Realism
García Tessara, Gabriel 24
Garcilaso de la Vega, Inca xv
Gautier, Judith 29
Getz, Stan 163n13
Gibbon, Edward 59
Gil, Enrique 24
Gil, Gilberto 67, 70–71, 74, 75, 89, 162n8, 163n13, 165n23, 169n49
Gilberto, João xxviii, 70–73, 76, 79–83, 84, 163n13, 164n16, 165n23, 166n29, 168n43
Gilroy, Paul 69, 163n13
Giménez Caballero, Ernesto 34, 155n6
Girondo, Oliverio 36
globalization xvii, xviii, xix, xxviii, 12, 68, 88–89, 97, 99, 103, 118, 129, 134, 135, 139, 175n21. *See also* glocalization
glocalization 88, 128
Gnutzmann, Rita 174n20
Godard, Jean Luc 113, 169n51
Goethe, Johann Wolfgang 182n37
Gómez, Sergio 99, 105–6, 109, 110, 119, 177n1, 180n20. *See also* McOndo
Gómez de la Serna, Ramón 33
Góngora, Luis de 2, 10, 11, 145n21, 149n27
Gónzalez, Felipe 175n21
Gónzalez Boixo, José Carlos 154n1, 155n9
Gónzalez Echevarría, Roberto 147n3, 149n18, 179n14

Gónzalez Prada, Manuel 19–20, 27, 31
González Viaña, Eduardo 109
González Vigil, Ricardo 31, 153n34
Gorak, Jan 54
Goulart, João 79
Goytizolo, Juan 98
Gracián, Baltazar 11
Granda, Isabel "Chabuca," 65
Greenfield, Sidney M. 143n14
Guerrero, Gustavo 103, 108, 178n7
Guilherme (Herickson Cardoso Rosa) 163n12
Guillory, John 49, 53, 63
Gutiérrez Nájera, Manuel 25

Haley, Bill 73
Halperín Donghi, Tulio 39, 43
Hammerstein, Oscar 115
Hardt, Michael 23
Harvey, David 131–33, 134
Haya de la Torre, Víctor Raúl 20
Hayek, Salma 130
Helft, Nicolás 158n1
Hendrix, Jimi 74, 75, 165n26
Hernández, José 153n34
Hernández Navarro, Luis 173n16
Herrero-Olaizola, Alejandro 172n12, 175n20
Hispanism 36–40. *See also* liberal pan-Hispanist discourse
Hispanoamérica 38, 98
Hitchcock, Alfred 114
Hitler, Adolf 182n37
Hordes, Stanley M. 148n10
Horsman, Reginald 136–37
Horton, Edward Everett 117
Hughes, Psyche 158n1
Hugo, Victor 24, 25, 27
Huidobro, Vicente 41
Huntington, Samuel 68
hybridity xi, xii, xxi, xxvi, 14, 72, 74, 75, 78, 83–85, 87, 88, 89, 90, 109, 120, 121–22, 123, 131, 170n53. *See also* transculturation

INDEX

Indigenismo xxv, 31, 58, 146n29, 146n30
Inquisition 5, 7, 148n10, 148n15
Instituto Cervantes 91–94, 171n1, 171n4
Irenaeus 53, 159n4
Irigoyen, Hipólito 44, 52

Jackson, Michael 162n11
Jaguribe, Hélio 77
Jameson, Fredric 68, 71, 77, 118, 119–20, 122
Jefferson, Thomas xii
Jelloun, Tahar Ben 158n1
Jobim, Antônio Carlos 71, 72, 73, 80, 81, 83, 86, 163n13
Jobim, Tom. *See* Jobim, Antônio Carlos
Johnson, Randal 165n26
Jovem Guarda 74, 86, 166n27
Joyce, James xxiii, 40, 62, 157n17
Juan Carlos I 92, 93, 172n10
Juana Inés de la Cruz, Sor xix, xxvi, xxvii, 1–16, 22, 147n7, 148n15, 149n20, 150n29
Juvenal 166n30

Kafka, Franz 55–57, 62
Kenton, Stan 71
Kerr, Lucille 112–113
Kerrigan, Anthony 49
Kierkegaard, Soren 55
King, John 110
Kircher, Athanasius 11
Kirchner, Néstor 138
Klarén, Peter 39
Klein, Naomi 116
Kokotovic, Misha 76, 87
Krauze, Enrique 171n5
Kristal, Efraín xxi–xxii, xxiii, xxiv–xxv, 50, 145n24, 145n25, 146n29, 155n9, 159n5
Kubitschek, Juscelino 77, 79

Lacan, Jacques 107
Lam, Wilfredo 156n15
Lamartine, Alphonse de 25
Larios Vendrell, Luis 174n18
Larra, Mariano José de 25
Larsen, Neil 58, 76
Lasarte Valcárcel, Javier 180n24
Lastarria, José Vitorino 155n9
Latin America (concept) xxviii–xxix, 38, 66, 84, 137
Leibniz, Gottfried Wilhelm 12
Lenin, Vladimir Illyich Ulianov 138, 188n13
Lennon, John 67, 86. *See also* Beatles
Leopardi, Giacomo 25
Letelier, Orlando 125
Leu, Lorraine 169n46
Levinson, Julie 110
Lewis, Sinclair 145n26
liberal pan-Hispanist discourse xxviii, 94–98, 172n12
Lima Barreto, Afonso Henriques de 111
Lindsay, Arto 84–85
Lins, Paulo 92
Lizardi, José Joaquín Fernández de. *See* Fernández de Lizardi
Locke, John 12
Lomnitz, Claudio 188n15
Lope de Vega, Félix 10
López, Jennifer 130
Loti, Pierre 29, 30
Lugones, Leopoldo xxvii, 33, 47
Lunarejo. *See* Espinoza y Medrano, Juan

Magical Realism xxii, xxiv, 97, 102, 105–11, 122, 177n39, 178n7
Manrique, Jorge Alberto 13
Manrique, Nelson 186n2
Marcos, Antônio 162n10
Mariátegui, José Carlos xiii–xvi, xviii, xxvii, 15, 20, 21, 23, 33, 34, 41, 42, 43, 44–46, 47, 58,

95, 142n6, 144n17, 155n5, 157n17, 158n27
Martí, Adelaida Caro   118, 185n69
Martí, José   xxi, 131
Martin, Ricky   88, 130
Marzorati, Gerald   162n11
Mastretta, Ángeles   92, 109, 171n5
Mastronardi, Carlos   157n21
Matta, Roberto   156n15
Matthiessen, Francis Otto   52
Matto de Turner, Clorinda   31, 146n30
Maysa (Mataraso)   72
McCartney, Paul   86. See also Beatles
McGowan, Chris   163n14
McGraw, Ali   114
McOndo (literary group)   105–11, 117, 119, 120, 122, 178n7, 179n11, 179n14, 179n18, 180n20, 182n37, 182n39
McQueen, Steve   115–16
Menem, Carlos Saúl   131
mestizaje   xiv–xv, 76, 133
Metheny, Pat   163n13
Mexican Revolution   42–43
Mignolo, Walter   xxviii, 40, 66, 135–40, 187n9, 188n11, 188n13, 188n14
Miranda, Carmen   69, 89
Mistral, Gabriela   36
Modernism   xxiii, xxv, 17–18, 102, 146n28, 150n1
modernismo   xix, xxiv, 17–18, 19, 25–30, 38, 146n28
Molina, César   92
Monaghan, Jay   29–30
Monsiváis, Carlos   92
Montaigne, Michel de   11
Morales, Evo   133, 137, 139, 140, 186n2, 188n11
Moraña, Mabel   xiv–xv, 4
Moretti, Franco   xix–xxi, xxii, xxiv, xxv, 144n18
Moro, César   156n15

Morrison, Toni   xxiv
Motta, Nelson   86, 166n27
Mujica Láinez, Manuel   31, 154n37
multiculturalism   134–37
Mulvey, Laura   156n15, 157n18
Mutantes, Os   79, 83, 84

Negri, Antonio   23
neoliberalism   xxviii–xxix, 68, 88, 90, 117, 122–23, 131–33, 134, 135, 137–39, 140
Neruda, Pablo   36, 123
Nixon, Richard   125, 126, 127, 185n64
Núñez de Miranda, Antonio   149n20

Obligado, Rafael   25
O'Gorman, Edmundo   135
Olivari, Nicolás   46
Orringer, Nelson   151n2
Ortega, Julio   23
Ortega y Gasset, José   34, 36–37, 38, 43, 102, 157n19, 177n37
Ortelli, Roberto   157n21
Ortelli y Gasset   43
Ortiz, Fernando   xxi, 71

Padilla, Ignacio   105–6, 109. See also Crack
Palaversich, Diana   109, 179n16
Palma, Ricardo   xix, xxii–xxiv, xxvi–xxvii, 17–32, 36, 145n24, 146n28, 152n19, 153n34
Palou, Pedro Ángel   105. See also Crack
Pascal, Blaise   12
Paul, Saint   6–7
Pauls, Alan   158n1
Paz, Octavio   xx, 1, 4, 7, 11, 22, 28, 30, 41, 146n2, 147n7, 149n17, 149n20
Paz Soldán, Edmundo   106, 127, 177n1, 185n66, 185n67
Pereda Valdés, Ildefonso   46

Perón, Juan Domingo   51–52, 58, 161n21
Perrone, Charles   67, 68, 162n8, 164n16
Pessanha, Ricardo   163n14
Piazolla, Astor   85
Pinochet, Augusto   114, 115, 119, 124, 125, 126, 181n33, 183n46, 184n55
Pitol, Sergio   171n6
Plotinus   159n4
Poblete, Juan   109, 119, 120
Poe, Edgar Allan   xxv, 56
Pohl, Burkhard   94, 97, 107, 121, 131, 172n8, 177n37, 177n39, 184n50
Polari, Alex   169n49
Porter, Cole   162n11
Powell, Baden   74
Presley, Elvis   73
Primo de Rivera, Miguel   44, 95
Proust, Marcel   114, 116
Puig, Manuel   112–13, 117, 180n23, 185n26

Queen, Ellery   62
Quevedo, Francisco de   10, 11
Quijano, Aníbal   12

Rabassa, Gregory   xxiv
Rama, Ángel   xxi, 26, 28, 71–73, 74, 76, 78, 102, 144n18, 166n34. See also transculturation
Redmond, Walter   150n28
Reed, Carol   181n33
Regina, Elis   86
Reinhardt, Carmen M.   131
Reverdi, Pierre   41
Reyes, Alfonso   xxi, xxiii
Riva Agüero, José de la   19
Rivera, Diego   42, 156n15
Rivette, Jacques   113
Rodgers, Richard   115
Rodó, José Enrique   26

Rodríguez, Arenas, Flor María   151n12
Rodriguez, Richard   130
Rodríguez Monegal, Emir   43, 50, 51, 158n1, 159n3
Rodríguez Zapatero, José Luis   92
Rojas, Gonzalo   171n6
Rolling Stones   74, 87, 88, 164n15
Romero, José Luis   142n3
Romero, Óscar (Archbishop)   123–24
Roncagliolo, Santiago   96, 174n18
Roosevelt, Theodore   98
Rosa, João Guimarães   166n34
Roth, Phillip   107
Rouillón, Guillermo   157n17
Rulfo, Juan   92
Rushdie, Salman xxiv   158n1

Sábato, Ernesto   171n6
Sainz, Gustavo   180n23
Salazar Bondy, Sebastián   20
Santana, Mario   175n20
Santiago (Henzo Cardoso Rosa)   163n12
Sarlo, Beatriz, xii–xiii, xv   41, 49
Sarmiento, Domingo Faustino   27, 155n9
Saul, Scott   80, 83
Savastano, Miguel A.   131
Schell, Maximilian   114
scholasticism   7–9
Schwarz, Roberto   xxi, 73, 77, 79, 82, 144n18, 170n53
Segall, Marcello   153n32
Sepúlveda, Juan Ginés de   xvii–xviii, 143n15
Shakira   88, 130
Shammas, Anton   158n1
Shumway, Nicolás   158n1
Sigurd, Jacques   181n25
Silva, Jonas   71
Silva, Orlando   71, 164n21

Sinatra, Frank   69, 71, 73, 74, 85, 163n13, 166n27, 170n54
Skármeta, Antonio   92
Skidmore, Thomas   79
Smith, Kevin   120–21
Smollett, Tobias   xxii
Solé, Francesc   99
Sousa, Márcio   166n34
Sovik, Liv   87, 88
Spivak, Gayatri   xvii
Stam, Robert   163n13
Sternberg, Josef von   42, 157n17
Stewart, James   117, 126, 127
Stokes, Geoffrey   85
Swinburne, Algernon Charles   xxv

Tafoya, Sonya   187n9
Tamayo Vargas, Augusto   147n3
Tarkington, Newton Booth   145n26
Taymor, Julie   162n11
Toledo, Alejandro   133, 186n2
Tondreau, Narciso   25
Townley, Michael   125
transculturation   xxi, 71–79, 84, 86, 89, 166n34, 167n40, 170n53, 176n33
tropicalismo   xxviii, 65–90, 161n1, 163n13, 163n14, 164n16, 165n26, 166n27, 167n39, 169n49, 170n53
Truffaut, François   113–14, 181n25, 181n27
Twain, Mark   22
Tzara, Tristan   41

ultraísmo   46, 51
Unamuno, Miguel de   xxvii, 33, 34
Updike, John   107

Valera, Juan   19, 27
Valla, Lorenzo   11, 150n27
Valle, Marcos   86
Valle, Paulo   86

Vallejo, César   xxii, xxiii, xxiv, xxv, 40–41, 157n17
vanguardia   40–41, 150n1. *See also* avant-garde; ultraísmo
Varela, Blanca   171n5
Vargas, Getúlio   79
Vargas Llosa, Mario   xxviii, 12, 97, 102, 107, 108, 112, 113, 120, 127, 134–35, 137–40, 145n23, 171n6, 172n12, 174n18, 174n19, 174n20, 175n21, 177n37, 177n39, 178n10, 180n23, 180n24, 183n45, 186n3, 186n6, 186n7, 188n10
Vásquez, Karina   36–37, 43
Vásquez, Tabaré   138
Velarde, Fernando   25
Velasco Alvarado, Juan   188n10
Veloso, Caetano   xix, xxviii, 65–90, 128, 161n6, 161n7, 162n11, 163n13, 164n15, 164n16, 164n21, 165n23, 165n26, 169n47, 169n48, 169n49, 169n51, 169n52, 170n53
Vianna, Hermano   165n23
Vieira, Antônio. *See* Vieyra, Antonio
Vieyra, Antonio   10
Vigo, Jean   181n27
Virno, Paolo   23
Vitale, Cristian   142n4
Vives, (Juan) Luis   11, 149n27
Volpi, Jorge   96, 97, 105–8, 174n17, 179n11, 182n37. *See also* Crack
Von Trapp, Maria   115

Wagner, Lindsay   115, 116
Wagner, Richard   30, 182n37
Washington, George   xii
Welles, Orson   112, 180n22
West, Cornel   50
Wharton, Edith   145n26
Whitman, Walt   xxv

Wilder, Thornton 145n26
Williams, Raymond 182n39
Williamson, Edwin 154n3, 157n23
Wollen, Peter 156n15, 157n18
Wonder, Stevie 163n13
Wood, Harry 84

Yates, Peter 114
Yehya, Naief 177n1
Yu, Han 55

Zaid, Gabriel 156n13
Zeffirelli, Franco 125
Zeno 55, 56
Zizek, Slavoj 188n13